Five Years At Sea

by James V. Lee

To Bill,

James V. Lee

ISBN: 0-9663870-7-4
ISBN: 978-0-9663870-7-0
Library of Congress Catalog Card Number: 2009900739

Published in the United States by Salado Press, LLC

Printed in Canada

P.O. Box 941006

Plano, Texas 75094-1006

All photos are the property of James V. Lee unless otherwise noted.

Contents

Acknowledgements

My small family played a vital role in the writing of this book. My travels would not have been possible without the willingness of my wife Nita to keep every-day events at home under control during my times overseas. When I decided to publish this book, she became my "sounding board" and constant source of encouragement. Living nearby, my son Kerry took over as "man of the house" in my absence to provide needed security and assistance to my wife. My daughter Gail Lee has guided me through technical problems as well as contributing her sound literary taste and creative marketing ideas.

In my quest to be absolutely correct in my use of military terminology and in my portrayal of the U. S. Navy during its countless actions—known as "evolutions,"—I asked Rear Admiral John Sigler, USN (Retired) to critique my manuscript. John was the Commanding Officer on the USS *Belknap*, the first ship to which I was assigned, and he offered extensive and invaluable corrections. To my surprise, but characteristic of John's career commitment to excellence, he voluntarily wrote the foreward for this book.

Rear Admiral Philip Cullom also added important changes in content of my manuscript. Phil was the Executive Officer aboard the USS *Mobile Bay*, the last ship to which I was assigned. He is now a two-star admiral on active duty. It was a privilege to serve with these men and an honor to call them my friends.

Many thanks go to my friend Ginnie Bivona of Atriad Press for her encouragement and professional publishing expertise, which she liberally shared with me over countless cups of coffee.

My thanks also go to my long-time friends Linda Griffith of TBC International in Salado, Texas, a graphics arts specialist, who did the tasteful cover design for the book, and her son Tim Thomas, a computer expert, who paginated the book with style and imagination.

Preface

This book is dedicated to the hundreds of sailors and marines who were members of various classes that I taught as part of the Program for Afloat College Education (PACE) during sixteen deployments on thirteen different ships of the United States Navy.

After I wrote *Nine Years In The Saddle*, I autographed the book in book stores all across the United States. The short biography in the back of the book caught the attention of readers who noted that I had traveled the world teaching college courses aboard United States Navy ships. Many began to encourage me write about those experiences that spanned five years from 1989 to 1994 on most of the oceans of the world as well as visits to nearly forty countries.

I had kept a journal of all those travels for the benefit of my wife so that she could vicariously enjoy my travels. For some time, I wrestled with the best way to present those experiences. After advice from some of my readers, I decided to simply keep the journalistic writing style. This method of presentation allows the reader to see my ongoing interaction with my students, other shipboard personnel, the mission of the various ships and my reaction to world events affecting those missions, and my experiences with people in foreign countries.

Most civilians have never heard of the PACE program, but in the 1970s, the navy introduced shipboard personnel to the opportunity to acquire undergraduate college credits from various colleges. Sailors at sea couldn't go to college, so the navy took the college to them by bringing on board qualified college instructors to teach any course requested by the ship's command. It's the responsibility of participating colleges to find the teachers wherever they may be located in the United States.

Central Texas College in Killeen, Texas, had such a contract with U. S. Navy and I was just one of many instructors from throughout the United States. My subject matter was English, which I taught at the freshman and sophomore levels. I also taught Basic English, basic math, and basic reading for sailors who more or less fell through the cracks in high school. A few eventually became naval officers. Others obtained university degrees after serving their enlistments. Some earned their G.E.D and moved on to advanced training.

Few of the ships really had adequate space to hold classes, so it was necessary to improvise. Often the spaces used for classes were either too hot or too cold and located near noise from the ship's equipment. Shipboard activities such as general quarters, flight operations, or refueling operations frequently interrupted classes. Yet these dedicated young men persevered under conditions that would dismay the typical land-based scholar. They were the sole justification for my adventure of a lifetime, and I owe them my thanks for allowing me to be a part of their lives. They were some of the best students I ever had.

James V. Lee

Foreword

"Join the Navy and See the World"

*"If you want to do great things in your world,
spend some time in ours."*

James Lee "joined" the U.S. Navy as a civilian teacher in the Navy's PACE program for five years from 1989 to 1994, and in that relatively short period of time accomplished a great deal. He saw more of the world in five years than many of us see in a twenty or even thirty-year career. He keenly observed life at sea and in the many foreign ports he visited. He has written the book that all of us who enjoyed our Navy careers wish that we had written. And—most importantly—he touched and improved the lives of hundreds of wonderful young Sailors and Marines.

My first reading of his manuscript brought back a flood of memories, some long forgotten, that reminded me not only that I immensely enjoyed my own career, but looking back, I can't imagine now trading it for any other. I was able to go places and see sights I would have never experienced in just about any other endeavor, to meet interesting people all over the world, to see firsthand history being made and to work with some of the finest men and women our great nation has to offer.

One of the things I particularly valued was seeing, time and again, both officers and enlisted people who didn't actually know how talented they were until challenged by the rigors of the Navy and particularly life at sea. Those of us who were given the opportunity and privilege to command ships, submarines or aviation squadrons were able to do so because we recognized very early on, with the help of many mentors, that we could accomplish very little by ourselves. One mantra of leadership is "to take care of your people." Different leaders do it different ways, but to me a key aspect of it meant giving the people under your command the opportunity to flourish, both in their professional and personal lives. Enter the dedicated professionals of the PACE program. Earning credits towards a college degree or even closing the gaps in an individual's secondary education, meant upward mobility, and to steal the Army slogan, to be all that you can be. The message didn't reach all of our Sailors and officers, but it did reach many and they, the Navy and our country were the better for it.

James Lee was one of the best of the number of PACE instructors with whom I worked over the years. He is a wonderful teacher and mentor, and had the right personality and attitude to deal with the challenges of teaching in a pretty harsh environment. He wasn't easy on his students; they had to earn their credits. Partly because of his skill as a teacher and partly because of living his own life to a higher standard, he was both liked and admired. From my point of view he was a terrific teammate and shipmate, who contributed greatly to our mission. I believe he would have been a superb commanding officer had he chosen that path.

Fortunately for his readers, James kept a detailed journal of his experiences and observations, and now we can vicariously share in some of his Five Years at Sea. I now work with senior officers and civilian officials from North Africa, the Middle East and South Asia. Many of their countries are not yet democracies and they are sometimes surprised by how open our American society can be. James saw his Navy experience through a particular prism and I through another, so sometimes we might interpret the same thing a bit differently—*and we can say so*, which is one of the joys of living in a vibrant democracy. For example, James suggested in one chapter that bad behavior by an officer might be due to the individual not being able to bear to see enlisted men using officers' facilities. In my experience, such behavior almost always had a more basic cause: an extremely poor self-image. The very good news for all of us is that while bad officers and stereotypical drunken Sailors do exist, they are the exception, not the rule, by a wide margin. I know that James agrees with me on this and I believe that his faith in Sailors and Marines comes through clearly in his book.

In his epilogue, James Lee hopes that his adventures have enriched his readers own lives in some way. They have done so for me, and I join James in hoping that they do so for each of his readers as well!

John Sigler
Rear Admiral, USN (Retired)
Washington, DC
April 2009

Adrift

The high school superintendent called me into his office the day before Thanksgiving of 1988. He said the private school in Houston, Texas, where I had taught for five years had run short on money and required terminating some of the teachers. And since I was one of the highest paid teachers, there would be no need for me to return to school after the Thanksgiving holidays. The termination affected me no more than a ripple on a small pond, for I was an experienced salesman and also had other employable skills.

However, I wanted to continue to teach, knowing that almost no school needs a new teacher in November. Over a period of weeks, I frequented the Texas Employment Commission to see what might be available anyway. The resultant career change thrust me into a life of travel and adventure that I could not have imagined, for eventually, my counselor scanned his computer for possible leads and finally asked, "Are you willing to travel?"

"Yes, definitely. What do you have in mind?"

"Central Texas College in Killeen, Texas, has a contract with the United States Navy to supply instructors aboard Navy ships. It's called the Program for Afloat College Education (PACE)." Handing me a slip of paper, he continued, "If you are interested, call Dan Page at this number in Norfolk, Virginia."

Returning home, I called Mr. Page, who asked, "What's your teaching field?"

"English," I replied.

"Master's degree?"

"Yes."

"We can always use English teachers, but you'll need government security clearance. Is there anything in your background that might cause a problem?"

"No, I don't think so."

He sent me a stack of forms that required quite some time to research and to complete, but shortly after he received the completed forms, he called me and said, "Pack your bags! You're going to Gaeta, Italy."

"Where?"

"Gaeta, Italy. It's about halfway between Rome and Naples, and is the home port of a guided missile cruiser called the USS *Belknap*, the flagship of the Sixth Fleet in the Mediterranean Sea."

He told me that classes aboard the ship would last about two months with another two weeks for travel to and from the ship.

At that time, my wife Nita still had about five years to go in her career with Exxon Coal and Minerals in Houston. Both of our children were adults with our son living nearby. Consequently, we didn't see any problem with my being gone for a few months at a time.

April 14, 1989, Norfolk Virginia

Dan Page with the Author at Norfolk International Airport

Arriving in Norfolk, I learned that I would be teaching two college courses on essay writing as well as remedial math and English courses. For two days I went through intensive briefing, covering such items as curriculum, forms required both by the college and the Navy, travel expenses, and the proper protocol for a civilian in a military environment. Having served in the Navy in World War II, the last detail didn't concern me. After the briefing, I took a test to verify that I had indeed absorbed all that had been thrown at me, a very important final step. For once aboard ship, I would have no one to turn to for questions or advice. But I relished the responsibility and the idea that the only thing that counted was results, a welcome departure from the myriad of distractions that face the typical high school teacher.

USS Belknap, Change of Command, June 3, 1989

USS *Belknap* CG-26

April 17, 1989

Because of a six-hour time change, the trip across the Atlantic was a short night. Prior to landing at Rome, the plane circled over the city giving the passengers an excellent view of some of Rome's ancient landmarks such as the Coliseum, Circus Maximus, Vatican, and Piazza Venetia. Upon landing, I found that Rome is a good place to stay alert. At the train station, beggars, young and old, male and female accosted me several times. Little Gypsy kids are taught to swarm around visitors and try to stick their hands into their pockets, knowing that most people will not harm a five-year-old child. Adult pickpockets also ply their trade here.

The train took me to Formia, a city situated across the bay from Gaeta, the berth of the USS *Belknap*. Another ancient landmark, the old Roman aqueduct, parallels some of the train route from Rome to Gaeta.

The sleek lines of the USS *Belknap* first came into view across the bay during a taxi ride from the railway station at Formia to Gaeta. Being a guided missile cruiser, she is known as the "Fighting Flagship" and packs the firepower to justify the name. The ship carries a crew of about 500 men plus others attached to the admiral's staff. Since many of the admiral's duties involve protocol with various NATO members, the ship carries a helicopter for his use as well as for anti-submarine warfare. The aircrew is a separate command.

Gaeta has been the homeport for the Sixth Fleet flagship since 1967. The Navy makes a point of deploying ships at strategic points around the globe. This not only cuts response time in an emergency, but also strengthens the United State's relationship with the host country.

Once aboard the ship, I shared quarters with five congenial fleet staff officers in a fairly roomy stateroom with a top bunk, desk, phone, and file cabinets.

Author's Bunk and Storage

Later, at an unofficial officers club on shore, the ship's officers and their dependents living in Gaeta warmly received me. Both the ship's captain and his executive officer seem determined to make the PACE program a success.

April 18, 1989, Gaeta, Italy

With a day to myself, I went ashore for about ten miles of a walking tour of Gaeta. The long, sandy beach on this cool April day attracted no one except a boy and girl necking in public. It seems that a lot of this goes on in public in Italy because boys and girls do not grow up going into each other's houses. It seems that if the boy goes to the girl's house that would be tantamount to engagement; if the girl goes to his house, she would be disgraced—just the first of many new customs I had to learn.

I happened to pass by Santo Paulo School as students were being dismissed about noon. Approaching a well-dressed man talking to some students, I asked, "Do you speak English?"

"Yes, I teach English in this school," he replied.

The odds of an American English teacher meeting an Italian English teacher on a first encounter in a foreign land must be astronomical! I continued, "Since the students get out of school so early, what do they do in the afternoon?"

"They're supposed to do homework, but they walk, make love, and play soccer by the sea. However, they also attend school on Saturday."

April 19, 1989, Gaeta

One of the staff officers, with whom I share a stateroom, took me ashore to see his apartment and some of the downtown points of interest. Like most of Italy, Gaeta has an interesting history, and he gave me some of the tidbits as we walked through Picallo Alley, a long narrow street through the old part of the city near the waterfront.

Picallo Alley   *WWII Damage to Picallo Alley*

Because of its mild climate, inviting beaches and proximity to the old Apian Way, Gaeta has been the playground for the rich and powerful since the days of the Roman emperors. Its population of about 23,000 triples to quadruples during the July-August tourist season. The city became part of the last territory to complete the unification of Italy under Victor Emmanuel II. An old fortress dating back to the fourteenth century sits across the street from the fleet landing. Guarding the harbor, two other old fortresses—one Spanish and one French—testify to the political turmoil through the centuries. Picallo Alley still bears evidence of the extensive damage done during World War II.

The Nazis double-mined the area by blowing up the buildings before they retreated. When workmen went in to clean up the rubble, the second mines went off, killing many people and creating a morale problem. Most of the area has been restored to its original state, using the same materials where possible, but not just to preserve history. Much of Italy lay in ruins, and the rubble provided the fastest and most economical method of rebuilding. The resultant charming atmosphere exhibits an old-world flavor of shops, apartments, and street vendors amid very narrow streets.

Back on board the ship, I checked out my teaching materials. To my dismay, some of the books had not arrived. I called Dan Page in Norfolk and explained the problem. He said that I would receive the books when the ship pulled into Sicily. In the meantime, I would just have to wing it. I knew I would have to be creative and resourceful, but so soon?

April 19, 1989, At Sea

Today we went to sea in perfect weather—sunny, cool, light breeze, and smooth water. Seeing nothing but sky and blue water for 360 degrees brought back exhilarating memories. As the day progressed, the ship did a number of maneuvers with the USS *Cunningham*, a guided missile destroyer that had been moored next to *Belknap* at Gaeta. The USS *Kalamazoo*, a Navy oiler with a few females in its crew, refueled both ships while underway.

This was my first time to observe an underway replenishment, and I was impressed with the skill and efficiency of both crews. It's

Simultaneous Uprep, Vertrep

my understanding that the Soviets never developed this type of operation. *Belknap* uses 750 gallons of fuel per hour at normal cruising speed, three times that at flank speed.

To my surprise, the Navy still uses semaphore and flashing light for sending messages between the ships. Also to my surprise, I could still read some of it after four decades.

To demonstrate a state of readiness, weapons were test fired as part of the maneuvers. The anti-missile gun, technically known as close in weapons system (CIWS), has six rotating barrels and can fire fifty rounds of 20mm shells per second from a drum of 900 shells. Controlled by radar, the CIWS, which seems to be standard equipment on all Navy combat vessels, is the last line of defense against incoming missiles. Other weapons systems can take out aircraft, ships, or submarines. In addition, the ship carries Marines armed with hand weapons to repel any potential intruders.

The crew must be starved for education. I expected to have about thirty in the PACE program. Sixty-one have signed up, and I know of others who want the course. My "classroom," a crew's lounge designed for eight people, can accommodate ten. The Navy authorized me to teach only three sections of PACE. I talked to the Executive Officer about it and proposed that we teach about half the men now and set up courses for the others at the end of this class term. He agreed and took it up with the captain who also concurred. That would keep me on board until the end of August. They may have to get another instructor for the second term. I have a lot of loose ends back in Texas, which I left with some ambivalence.

As night fell, a full moon, partly obscured by clouds, created a beautiful, enchanting scene. Reluctantly, I sacked out at a late hour.

April 21, 1989, At Sea

Dawn awoke to a chilly air, cloud cover, slight rain, but a smooth sea. The new day brought maneuvers with *Cunningham*, the USS *Roosevelt*, a carrier, an Italian frigate, and a Spanish destroyer. Two jets flew by as war games participants. As part of their training, the crew went to General Quarters (GQ). There were a few SNAFUS, but mostly everybody performed satisfactorily. During this time, the XO briefed me on some of the ship's activity, both below and above deck. To see the men dressed in battle gear both sobered and impressed me. In the event of a real battle, I think the damage control people would be least envied. They have to wear fire retardant clothing, bulky helmets, and self-contained breathing apparatuses. Any heroes in this division would mean that the ship had taken a hit.

The function of a cruiser is to attack. The first night out, the ship rigged its lights to make it appear to be a merchant ship. With its radar turned off, it came within fifty-five miles of the "enemy carrier," and according to the captain, "filled her full of holes."

Yesterday, I got the worst haircut of my life. I don't mind its being short and military style, especially since I am exposed so much to the wind. But its unevenness bothers me. The admiral's barber offered to straighten it up when he has time.

The officers' mess provides reasonably good and plentiful food. Spigots at the touch of a button dispense coffee, water, orange juice, iced tea, milk, and soft drinks twenty-four hours a day. The officers get popcorn every night about 2000. Also at about that time, the chaplain says a prayer over the 1MC. Both of these functions seem to be Navy shipboard traditions.

April 22, 1989, At Sea

It's another gorgeous night with the red rising moon lifting a curtain of alto cumulus clouds. We have been cruising off the southeast coast of Sardinia. As part of the war games, three thousand Marines hit the beach in amphibious vehicles. The ship went to General Quarters again and test-fired the 50 caliber machine guns, as well as the Phalanx Close-in Weapons System (CIWS-pronounced "sea-whiz"), a fast-reaction, Gatling gun system designed to provide a last-ditch defense against incoming missiles. You just have to hear the firing of one of those guns to appreciate the fact that it can spit out about a hundred rounds of 20mm shells in two seconds. But the colorful description of the sound by the gun crew gives a fair idea: a loud sustained fart.

The captain gave me a tour of the Combat Information Center today. Located right behind the bridge, the CIC people control the combat functions in battle. Separate consoles direct ship-to-ship missiles, ship to aircraft missiles, and ship to submarine missiles. The skipper drew an electronic box around a blip representing a ship on the radar screen then said that if he initiated the proper firing sequence for a harpoon missile, the ship would be history in four minutes. This ship can gather information anywhere in the world, including Galveston Bay, which he demonstrated. Electronic systems produce a daily satellite weather picture for the captain's use. In spite of all this sophistication, they regard this navigation equipment as back-up to a sextant, which was an ancient device when I was in the Navy. When I asked the navigator why he didn't just use GPS, he replied, "If our electronic gear gets knocked out, how can we fix the ship's position if nobody remembers how to use a sextant?" Thus my introduction to naval redundancy: A back-up exists for nearly everything.

A visiting helicopter developed an electrical problem and had to stay on our pad until fixed. In the meantime, the admiral needed to make some trips around the Sixth Fleet. No Problem. His chopper took him off the ship's bow in a sling.

My basic skills class, a remedial English course, met today. Many are young guys who have been out of high school only a year or two. I have heard many "I-wish-I-had" stories. I asked the class to write a short essay on their favorite pipe dream. Here is what one student wrote, errors included.

The Funksectional skills program in my opinion, has been a long awaited course I have wanted to see brought onboard the ship and offered to the crew. I have wanted this oppurtunity to happen in my life for many years. The dreams and hopes of myself bettering my education for self improvement and a chance to go to college has always been on my mind. Myself, my family and my Navy will all benifit from the goldne oppurtinity of finally introducing pace and funksectional skills onboard, thanks for my chance.

Any teacher that would not put forth his best effort for a guy like that is already dead.

April 23, 1989, At Sea

The weather continues to be outstanding with a glass-slick sea and clear sky. A light breeze makes a windbreaker feel good. I worked out with weights again today. Some enlisted man joined me. I appreciated his knowledge of physical fitness, but not his boring, vulgar, and incessant language. He dislikes the Navy and looks forward to becoming a civilian biker with long hair.

The captain conducted a surprise GQ drill this afternoon, and the men reacted well. The ship always sustains some simulated damage in order to give the fire control people some training. Earlier, we had gunnery practice with the five-inch gun on the fantail. Several single shots preceded two series of fifteen shots each at two-second intervals at a target nine miles away. Explosions visible to the naked eye indicated that most of the shots fell in a tight pattern right on target.

April 25, 1989, Augusta Bay, Sicily

We entered Messina Strait about 1 a.m., and I stayed up another hour to see the sights. The strait between Italy and Sicily is a passage of about two miles at its narrowest point. The lights from both shores made the area look like a fairyland. A cruise liner steamed among brilliantly lighted ferryboats and other small boats criss-crossing the channel. One ferryboat was a side-wheeler like the ones that used to ply the Mississippi River, a totally unexpected sight.

By day, Augusta Bay's huge oil refinery obstructs visibility with its haze. The town of Syracuse appears to be composed of beautiful buildings overlooking the bay. A blimp hanger rests on a hill above the city. Snow-capped Mt. Etna crowns the entire scene of anchored NATO warships too numerous to count.

April 26, 1989, At Sea

Yesterday, the admiral's aide cut my hair to correct the botched up job I received last week. I look like I just got out of boot camp.

He also repaired a broken lock on my attaché case. I asked, "How did you learn how to repair locks?" Smiling, he replied, "Well, I used to be somewhat involved with locks, and the judge told me I could either join the Navy or go to jail. So here I am."

When the admiral's helicopter flew over to *Roosevelt* today, I went along for my first chopper ride. We skimmed along at about 500 feet at seventy-five knots. Fighter planes armed with missiles crowded the flight deck of the carrier. Landing on a big carrier deck is easy. Landing on the small pad on the stern of a cruiser leaves no margin for error. After we left *Roosevelt*, the crew dropped a smoke bomb and did a simulated rescue of a swimmer.

Later, the ship's engineering officer took me on a tour of the ship's engine compartment. Each of two engines—one forward and one aft—receives steam from two 1200 psi, 950 degree boilers. The usual configuration is two boilers online and two on standby, but to make top speed requires all four boilers. There's no way I would want to work that far below deck, but I appreciate the expertise of those who do.

April 27, 1989, At Sea

We are steaming south of Greece tonight. The sea has had swells of four to six feet for the last twenty-four hours, creating white caps. The ship has very little pitch or roll except when our course is abeam of the waves. Because the ship is top heavy, it doesn't handle very well in rough weather, which usually occurs only in the winter in the Mediterranean.

The crew went to GQ again today. I used that time to get caught up on my sleep. Later, I gave one-on-one tutoring to a student until nearly 2230.

April 28, 1989, At Sea

The war games continue. We are blue; the enemy is orange. Both sides have inflicted substantial damage. One of our pilots mistakenly identified *Kalamazoo*, our tanker, as an enemy ship—three times. We sank it three times. Combatants in real wars have a history of sustaining casualties from "friendly fire," but rigorous training attempts to minimize it.

A few ships have been visible today, although most are over the horizon. I saw my first Soviet warship, which shadowed us for a long time. The command turned off the ship's electronic gathering system and resorted to flashing light for communication with ships within range.

Our course since leaving Sicily has taken us into the vicinity of the part of the Apostle Paul's voyage to Rome where he was storm-driven and finally shipwrecked on Malta. I have long wanted to explore this area and am looking forward to debarking at Izmir, Turkey.

The first class Petty Officer's Mess had bingo games and pizza on the mess deck tonight. It conflicted with my classes, but all my students showed up at all three classes. It is so refreshing to teach people who take learning seriously. A satisfying camaraderie is beginning to develop. In addition, it is just as rewarding to see the light of understanding on the face of an adult as it is on a child.

May 1, 1989, At Sea

Saturday, the dawn broke over an ocean so placid that the water reflected the clouds. Brilliant sunshine bathed a cool day that later dissipated all clouds. Some off-duty personnel flaked out in the sun.

On land, Saturday seems like Saturday, Sunday seems like Sunday, and Monday seems like Monday. At sea, one day just blends into another. One of the staff officers, who formerly served on a submarine, told me that when a sub travels submerged, the crew goes on an eighteen-hour day instead of twenty-four. Since they stand watch six hours on and twelve hours off, it makes no difference what day it is.

When I went out onto the weather deck just prior to breakfast today, the island of Rhodes materialized on our starboard beam. During the night we had entered the Aegean Sea. Soon, Patmos Island appeared on our starboard beam. The Apostle John spent his exile here while writing the book of Revelation. Searching the island with the ship's big eyes, high powered pedestal mounted binoculars on the signal bridge that allows one to see small details at long distances, I noticed a small town nestled in a pass between two mountain peaks. Otherwise, the island appeared to be uninhabited. However, a haze hung over the terrain, making it difficult to accurately survey the place.

Last night we took on fuel again from Kalamazoo, our tanker that we "sank" by mistake in the war games. The crew has really been under pressure all during Dragon Hammer '89, the name of this combined NATO naval exercise. In wartime, all refueling takes place at night, a drag for the guys who have to stand watch and then get out of the sack to do this kind of work. For days, it has been drill, drill, and more drill for them. When not involved with GQ and putting out imaginary fires, the crew stands watch and does some other kind of training. Sometimes this causes one or more of my students to miss class, but they always explain their absence. One young man was so concerned about missing class that he asked if he would be allowed to continue the course! When the ship's helicopter takes off or lands, or anyone else's chopper lands, a chief and his entire crew must suit up and stand by. Flight quarters can be called without warning at any time. Because of all the flight activity yesterday, the master chief, a dedicated student, spent the whole day on alert and held training sessions for his men during a lull. Students in a conventional learning environment back in the states have no idea how soft their lives are by comparison. The more I am around these guys, the more I'm impressed with them.

I used to read newspaper articles that would lead one to believe that the Navy recruits people too stupid or spaced-out to operate our newest technology. Rather, these men are good at what they do—very good. As for dope, everybody gets tested periodically without warning. A Captain's Mast last week sentenced four Sailors to demotions in rank and less than honorable discharges for dope possession. One of the staff officers told me that this is standard procedure in the Navy.

The enlisted personnel seem about the same as my contemporaries during my hitch in the Navy in WWII—hard working, fun-loving, somewhat amoral, and basically decent guys. The ship's officers don't differ much—just receive higher pay. I had expected the officers' mess to be the picture of decorum. Decorum mostly begins by asking the highest-ranking officer already seated, "May I join you, sir?" It ends by saying, "Please excuse me, sir" to the highest-ranking officer still at the table. Conversation includes a great deal of "navalese."

However, last Saturday evening I was invited to join the Chief of Staff and six of his officers for dinner. Decorum here was more akin to that experienced by midshipmen at the naval academy. Furthermore, there was no comparison between their food and the usual fare accorded the officers of the ship's crew. I suspect they have the chef of some famous restaurant stashed away somewhere. The Chief of Staff ranks second only to the admiral who expects him to implement his decisions for this entire naval exercise. The C.O.S. is very friendly and easy to talk to.

By mid-morning today, we traveled full speed into the wind to take up a position vacated by the USS *Platt*, a destroyer that had to pull out of position to take a sick Sailor to *Roosevelt* for emergency surgery. *Belknap* is monitoring the F-14s in the area to help keep them out of Grecian air space. If the Grecian air space were violated, there would be a protest, and nothing would happen except an exchange of diplomatic language. But there is no point in raising their hackles.

Turkish Boat at Izmir

May 2, 1989, Izmir, Turkey

The harbor at Izmir forms the shape of a giant "U." Several other towns actually make up Izmir: Bostania on the left approach, Guzelyali on the right, Konak in the middle, Hatay in the hills above the "U," and Kalsiyake just to the left of Konak. Kalsiyake is also known as Old Town that Alexander The Great completely destroyed. Remains of a castle fortress are still in evidence on the mountaintop of Hatay, which he occupied during his conquest of the Middle East. An appealing metropolis, Izmir boasts a population of about one and a half million.

The crew mounted an M-16 machine gun on the port bridge wing today. Uniformed men with automatic weapons patrol the streets here. They're an unsmiling bunch. But other people are quite friendly—some too friendly. "Hey Joes" swarm the Sailors as soon as they step ashore. They want to shine your shoes, sell you a leather jacket, sell you a rug, or take you to their "friend" who has a good deal on something. Five different people tried to shine my white Nike jogging shoes! "Hey Joe, I got white polish."

Although an interesting place to shop, I preferred to just browse the market. Some of my students tried to get me to buy a leather jacket, since they are cheaper here than elsewhere. But my need for a leather jacket back in South Texas would be quite limited. I splurged and bought a delicious sesame roll. Later, I had an excellent meal of fish and assorted vegetables and dessert that I could not identify at a cost of $11.50, including tip. Not bad for an ocean view in an exclusive restaurant.

One of the staff officers invited me to join him and some other officers at a hotel to drink some beer. I had seen it all before. We had become pretty good friends, so I said, "I can't think of anything more boring for a non-drinker than watching other people get soused."

He just laughed and replied, "You're right! If you're not going to be a part of it, there's no point in showing up."

I welcomed the change to be on land for a day and stretch my legs after two weeks at sea. Rather than ride anywhere, I walked long, far, and fast.

May 3, 1989, Izmir, Turkey

This has to be one of the most memorable days of my life. I went to the ancient city of Ephesus, or what's left of it, and discovered new emotions as I walked the same streets as did the Apostle Paul.

I stood in the same Great Theater where a silversmith named Demetrius sparked a riot because he considered Christianity a threat to his idol manufacturing business. In the third century AD, Ephesus ranked second only to Alexandra as the largest city in the world. Even its marbled ruins suggest grandeur beyond belief. The Great Theater has been sufficiently restored to hold an annual festival.

Additional decades will be required to unearth all that lies buried there. Earthquakes, mudslides, and a change in river course that silted in the bay victimized Ephesus, causing a mosquito-breeding marsh. Malaria seems to be the final factor that drove its citizens out of the city. In Paul's day, the street led straight from the Great Theater to the waterfront. Now, the ocean is at least a half-mile away.

I returned to the ship in time to shower and dress for the admiral's reception on the flight deck where an awning had been erected as protection against the sun. Various dignitaries from NATO countries came to eat, drink, and socialize with the crew and staff members of *Belknap*. I found the captain of the Italian warship Stromboli an especially interesting conversationalist. He told me quite a bit about Pompeii, which I intend to visit upon my return to Gaeta.

At Sea, May 6, 1989

We left Izmir yesterday under a cloudless sky on a smooth sea with a cool breeze. A school of dolphins played around the ship, a sign of good luck. We certainly seem to have it.

Before leaving Turkey, I spent a day at the ruins of the ancient city of Pergamon, another one of the "seven churches of Asia" mentioned by John in the book of Revelation. Unlike Ephesus, Pergamon was constructed of granite since it was indigenous to that area. However, after the Romans conquered the city, they overlaid some of the buildings with marble.

Also unlike Ephesus, it sits atop a mountain over a thermal area.

Remains of Library at Ephesus

Ephesus Amphitheater

Another View of Theater

Pergamon

View of Modern Bergama from Pergamon

It had about 40,000 permanent residents and twice that many transients who went there seeking medicinal help. Following treatment in the thermal water, patients walked through a long passageway to a large sleeping area. Enroute, priests speaking through grates spaced along the top of the passageway would practice psychosomatic medicine by whispering positive encouragement to the patients. A smaller theater that originally seated about 5,000 in the medical complex apparently augmented this technique.

Two other theaters occupied the town site. One would hold about 15,000 people.

The site where the temple of Zeus once stood is still clearly delineated. During the Ottoman Empire, the Turks allowed the building itself to be moved to East Germany. The British took the Temple of Diana at Ephesus during that same period. Modern Turks resent the loss of these structures and want to get them back. Extensive restoration continues at both sites.

In Revelation, John refers to Pergamon as the "seat of Satan." Since Zeus is the father of the gods in mythology, I wondered if John was referring to Zeus as Satan.

Smyrna, another of the "seven churches of Asia," rests beneath modern Izmir, except for about one city block. Sometime in the future, I would like to visit the other four ancient church sites. Turkey could keep a history buff busy for a lifetime.

Medical Center at Pergamon.
Theater behind columns has been restored and used for special functions.

Pergamon

Temple of Diana. Photo courtesy of Crossroads Travel, Kusadasi, Turkey

Original site of the Temple of Zeus

Visible remains of ancient Smyrna

At Sea, May 7, 1989

During the night, we left the Aegean Sea and entered the Ionian Sea, passing Albania, a communist country with a partially mined coastline. Evidently, even other communist countries don't like the Albanians.

I gave my first major test last night. Most of the students took two hours. Since we are traveling west, we gained an hour during the first class. But the second and third classes ran together, and bodies littered an area designed for eight people. It worked a hardship on some of the men who stand watch six hours on and six hours off. Before we pulled into Izmir, a GQ drill interrupted one class. Another time, flight quarters emptied a class. Once, the ship refueled during a class. When those things happen, all personnel involved must respond immediately. But still the guys hang in there and apologize when they have to miss a class. Fantastic attitude.

Dubrovnik, Yugoslavia

Dubrovnik, Yugoslavia, May 6, 1989

Dawn broke yesterday over a beautiful landfall on both sides of the ship. Rugged islands as well as rugged mainland rose abruptly from the sea. The ship tied up in Dubrovnik's small harbor rather than drop anchor offshore as we did at Izmir. Two tugs turned us around and eased us into berthing position.

This beautiful country leaves virtually no room for beaches since the land rises so sharply from the sea. Waves crash against picturesque cliffs. Roses and poppies mingle with deciduous and coniferous trees. Numerous coves add interest. One of the officers stated that if he ever decided to jump ship, he would do it here.

But Old Town caught my major interest. "Old towns" abound all over Europe, but this old high-walled city has been restored. Narrow

Interior views of the church at Old Town Dubrovnik

alleys flanked by stores and residences lead everywhere at various levels. One ancient building houses symphonies and other fine arts productions. Elaborate decorations adorn the organ of a large church.

At the stroke of noon, a cloud of pigeons descended on an open square where an old lady fed them. The entire area swarmed with tourists, including many high school students from the United States. People continually stopped our Sailors, wanting to take their pictures in their sharp dress whites. (Note: Subsequently, the war in Bosnia only two years later damaged 68% of the Old Town and completely destroyed nine buildings, but UNESCO has assisted Croatia in restoring it to the beauty that I observed in 1989.)

Dubrovnik, Yugoslavia, May 10, 1989

Yesterday, I took a boat tour of the Dubrovnik Riviera. Just off the coast from Old Town, a lovely island accommodates a building originally used as a monastery. It now houses a restaurant, but at one time, Maximillian occupied it before his ill-fated attempt to take over Mexico. The trip across the bay to Cavtac provided a good view of Napoleon's old fort that overlooks Old Town Dubrovnik. I rode the cable car to the fort the first day in port. That vantage point provided a spectacular view of the entire Dubrovnik area toward the sea and the gray inland mountains.

Everything I have seen in Yugoslavia looks picturesque, including Cavtac, known as Epidarus in the seventh century BC. However, western music right out of Texas greeted me as I stepped off the boat at Cavtac! It sometimes seems that our culture has Americanized the whole world.

One of the small islands immediately off the coast served as the first quarantine area used in Europe to prevent the spread of black plague. Established in 1337, the island confined Sailors for forty days before they could enter the mainland. Here, I visited the birthplace of Branco Radvlovic, a nationally famous artist. The house displayed some of his works. Others hang in Belgrade.

The guide for the trip to Cavtac, a young man named Gordon, spoke fluent English, having spent some time in both the United States and England. A guitarist of some national fame, he allowed me to buy him a drink and spend an hour in enlightening conversation while others in our group browsed the shops.

Returning to Old Town about 1800, I found the Sixth Fleet Stage Band setting up for a performance in the open square. Although a good performance characteristic of current American rock musicians, their music brought little response from a polite audience.

Heading back to the ship late at night, I missed a turn and ended up walking miles out of the way. I could have hopped on a bus or taken a taxi, but I just enjoyed the well-lighted scenery and cherished the exercise. I encountered several women walking alone as well as fathers with small children—even along the waterfront. I would never consider walking through such an area late at night at most American ports, but here I never sensed the slightest danger. And this is a communist country.

Site where the Virgin Mary supposedly appeared to children

Dubrovnik, Yugoslavia, May 11, 1989

A long trip yesterday took me to Medugorje. People go to this place because the Virgin Mary supposedly visited six young people about eight years ago and continues to do so daily.

My group got an audience with Ivan, one of the young visionaries. He answered many questions, but said nothing that has not already been said in countless sermons, books, and magazines. The boys and girls claimed to have seen heaven, hell, and purgatory as described in Dante's Divine Comedy. However, they claimed they had never read the book. Ivan had seen heaven, but when questioned about its appearance, replied that we would have to wait until we got there. The Catholic faithful come here by the millions and seem to accept without question the stories told to them, such as having a rosary turned into gold. Until this phenomenon started, nobody, not even in Yugoslavia, had ever heard of this little wide place in the road. Now, four-story hotels throng the area with about fifteen more under construction. No matter what happens to the visionaries, Medugorje will be an economic shot in the arm for Yugoslavia indefinitely.

While a long church service took place in a new building filled to overflowing, I decided to do some exploring by climbing a mountain supporting a huge cross overlooking the town. The trail to the top winds through a treeless terrain covered with scrub brush offering countless opportunities to turn an ankle. Even so, I met one pilgrim descending on his knees in a state of holy agony. At the top, sufficient melted wax around the cross to start a candle factory bore evidence of countless other visitors. Legend has it that before the people in the community erected the cross, hailstorms used to wipe out the local cherry crops. But after erection of the cross, the hailstorms stopped.

I don't know about the veracity of that story, but back on level ground, a little girl sold me a sack of delicious cherries.

At Sea, May 15, 1989

On Thursday, I took a tour of Herzegovina. The trip covered an extensive area of the interior of Yugoslavia, culminating in Mostar. Fertile valley land commands a premium in this mountainous region. Consequently, villages inhabit the sides of the mountains, leaving the valleys for agriculture. The land will grow just about anything, including citrus, cherries, tobacco, and wheat. The mountains contain an abundance of ancient stone fences—some to check erosion, some to create pens, and some to enclose an area for threshing grain.

At this point, part of the trip became a blur of ancient Illyrians and their strange religion, a Turkish fort, a Roman fort, and several stops to sample local wine. The tour group, which included some of my students, stopped for lunch at a restaurant in a beautiful setting on a river where the waiters and waitresses entertained their customers with dances. Their gaiety in colorful costumes seemed to be spontaneous.

At Mostar, residents in a sixteenth century Turkish home entertained us prior to visiting a Turkish mosque.

The people of Yugoslavia seem to be quite religious, being predominantly Eastern Orthodox with a smattering of Moslem. How-

Dancing waiters

Turkish Mosque

ever, the country bans no religion and has no state religion. Perhaps their religion accounts for their low crime rate. I seldom saw policemen. In my hundreds of miles of travel, I never saw a highway patrol car. Yet people move around day or night with no sense of fear. I asked a tour director about this. She shrugged and said, "It's just the people."

I never imagined that people of a country that claims to have a communist government could have this much freedom of movement. The people of the Eastern Bloc countries regard Yugoslavia as capitalistic, and the people I talked to want it to continue to move in that direction. Private citizens own sixteen percent of the agricultural land, but produces eighty percent of the total agricultural output. Anyone can start a business. A leader from each of the six provinces makes up the ruling body, and they rotate the presidency among themselves annually. The typical Yugoslav will not know the name of his president, but he will know the identity of George H. Bush.

16th Century bridge

A sixteenth century stone bridge spans the river flowing through Mostar, adding charm to that whole area. I thought it was the most interesting piece of architecture I have thus far encountered in Europe. Millions of footsteps over the centuries have worn concave depressions in the stone steps. (Note: The Bosnian War destroyed the bridge.)

This tour ended early enough for me to attend a symphony in Old Town. The Yugoslav Festival Musicians, who came from all over the country, played selections from Mozart, Beethoven, and Schumann. A sixteen-year-old cellist, stole everyone's heart with two solos, the

Music hall on right

second one being totally unaccompanied. The music hall has an open roof with excellent acoustics. I visited with people from France, Norway, and the Netherlands during this delightful evening.

Then after the concert, I went to a hotel lobby with a British couple where we drank tea and conversed until after midnight. I ended the day with a two-mile hike back to the ship.

The next day, I took another tour toward Albania, ending at Sveti Stefan, an exclusive resort by the sea. A hotel occupies an entire small peninsula, a former island. Some of the Hollywood crowd frequents this place. Here pebbles mingle with coarse sand on the beach. Water draining through the pebbles after the waves wash ashore makes an eerie sound that I have not heard since I stood on a

Beach at Sveti Stefan

Sveti Stefan

Adriatic Coast

similar beach in New Zealand years ago.

The tour covered the southern Adriatic coast with scenery as breathtaking as the northern coast. These islands number about 800, most of which are uninhabited.

We passed through the little coastal town of Risan, which was the last Illyrian settlement destroyed by the Romans in the third century BC. The Hotel there bears the name Teuta, the Illyrian queen. Before reaching Risan, we made a short stop where Gypsies swarmed the bus passengers with items for sale.

We visited another town embracing an "old town" that dates from 1667. Destroyed in 1979 by an earthquake, it's now nearly restored—walls and all—thanks to funds from UNESCO. American tax dollars end up in the strangest places.

The ship got underway about 8 a.m. yesterday after an interesting

Gypsies peddling trinkets

incident about 4 a.m. Some young woman brought her boat along-side the captain's gig tied to the ship. After setting her boat adrift, she climbed aboard, trying to claim political asylum. The ship's command had no authority to grant asylum to the lady as she wasn't in imminent danger. Our guys took her to a bus stop and didn't alert any authorities so she could stay out of trouble. Strange case.

Clearing the harbor, we encountered heavy seas for the first time since leaving Gaeta. Swells of ten feet gave us a rocking ride when we had to change course to put the waves on our beam. The fellows who spent the last night trying to drink all the booze in town had it pretty rough. Upon arising this morning, I discovered that we had just cleared the fog-shrouded Straits of Messina in a very calm sea.

Gaeta, Italy, May 16, 1989

Before coming into Gaeta yesterday, we ran at flank speed for a while, which is about thirty-two knots, or forty miles per hour. The ship's screws threw up such a huge wake that most of the crew went to the fantail just to look at it.

Upon arriving at Gaeta, women and children, whose husbands and fathers were part of the crew, created a mass evacuation from the ship since these men have apartments in town. Gaeta has a sizeable community of American families who live there for the duration of crewmen's tour of duty aboard *Belknap*.

The PACE coordinator from Naples called to say he would personally deliver my long, lost basic skills material. Teaching those classes now will take me to June 14. That being the case, I may as well stay aboard and teach another eight weeks of college English and two more four-week basic skills courses back to back.

We had a security alert drill tonight. When that happens, about a dozen men drop whatever they are doing and arm themselves with shotguns, rifles, and pistols to intercept an intruder.

Gaeta, Italy, May 20, 1989

Yesterday I went to what the crew refers to as the "armpit of Europe"—Naples, the home base of NATO. They may be right. I saw a dirty, air-fouled, and traffic-snarled city. American drivers here have adjusted to the natives' habits, who routinely use a two-lane highway as a three-lane road. They also routinely drive 80 mph in a 40-mph zone. Apparently, he who honks first has the right-of-way. I went to Naples to return the basic skills materials to the PACE coordinator since the original shipment from Norfolk arrived the day after he delivered his set!

Gaeta, Italy, May 21, 1989

The chaplain held a Protestant church service on the ship's bridge this morning. Four attended, including the chaplain. I guess most of the church-going people must have apartments in town where they spend the weekend. Later, I hiked up a hill graced by a large statue of Madonna and Child overlooking the harbor.

A large circular mausoleum containing some of the Caesar's elite, including General Munifius Plancus, crowns the summit. He commanded Caesar's army from about 67 BC to 40 BC. He defeated the Helvetian, a tribe of Gauls in Switzerland. He also defeated the Nervii, one of the most powerful Belgic tribes, and captured Vercingetorix, their chief. In addition, he founded the towns of Basil and Lyons in Switzerland. Caesar's book, Bellae Gaulika (Wars in Gaul) details these exploits.

The hill has been a fort since Roman times. The French embellished it. So did the Nazis. It appears that little has been done to preserve the place. Tunnels, storage areas, airshafts, and what not lace the entire hill.

I climbed the rather low hill right after the church service. However a series of 180-degree switchbacks made the climb rather lengthy. Large trees arched the road allowing sunlight to filter through the crisp cool air. Only the songs of countless birds and a distant church bell broke the stillness of the sunny Sunday morning. To enter such an environment immediately after worship service refreshes the soul.

Another soul-stirring experience occurs at 8 a.m. daily when everybody snaps to attention when the "Star Spangled Banner" blares over the 1MC during the hoisting of the ship's flag. Hearing the song played at an athletic event in the states seems only a perfunctory gesture for many people, but hearing our national anthem played in a foreign port stirs my emotions.

Barcelona, Spain, May 26, 1989

Learning how to function in a foreign city can take a lot of time. I put a roll of film in the shop on Monday for pick up at noon on Tuesday. I showed up at noon to a locked door. It seems that all businesses in Gaeta close from noon to 2.45 p.m. At about 3 p.m., I tried to pick up the pictures by paying with a fifty-dollar bill. The clerk wanted to give me change in lira. Since I was leaving for Spain the next day, I didn't want lira. I checked the bank two blocks away. However, they told me they only made change in the morning, referring me to a hotel several blocks away. They didn't have the money but referred me to the American Shore Detachment a few blocks away. There, the lady who changed money had just left for the day. But a man there gave me two twenties and a ten for the fifty and sent me to another hotel for the needed lira. Returning to the photo shop, I picked up my pictures at 5 p.m.

Last Wednesday the XO changed my class schedule to 8, 9, and 10 a.m. What a disaster! My 8 o'clock students had to weigh anchor. Getting underway involved the 9 o'clock students. An unannounced GQ drill shot my 10 o'clock class. During GQ, we had an abandon ship drill where everyone went to his life-raft station and checked his life jacket. I just roll with that sort of thing. Today, a civilian Leer jet simulated an incoming missile. The commanding officer took me into the CIC to watch the action on radar. At 150 miles, the radar locked on and "fired" two missiles moving at mach three. They destroyed the jet ninety miles from the ship. The jet kept coming and the five-inch gun shot it down again when it came within range. Finally, the CIWS took it out again from a few thousand yards. It made several passes at the ship, and the CIWS got it every time, indicating combat readiness.

Wednesday night we passed through the Strait of Bonifacio, the channel between Corsica and Sardina. A dark and cloudy night allowed little to see. As we approached Barcelona, we encountered ocean swells that gave the ship about a five-degree roll—just enough to rock us to sleep. We arrived today under an overcast sky with haze and anchored in the bay next to the French carrier Fuch along with twenty other NATO warships. *Belknap* the only American ship in port has the distinction of being the first U.S. Navy ship to visit Barcelona since some terrorist killed and wounded some Sailors here eighteen months ago. The presence of the Spanish king and queen require tight security. Several Spanish journalists toured the ship today. The Spaniards appear anxious to make a good impression on this flagship since it can dictate whether other U.S. Navy ships come here. The thousands of Sailors in port this weekend will have a significant economic impact on Barcelona. Consequently, they have a good incentive to keep order.

Barcelona, Spain, May 27, 1989

This has been a ceremonial day. The king and queen of Spain passed in review of all the NATO ships in the harbor. Each ship had flags flying from bow to stern. The Sailors on all the ships lined the rails in dress uniform. At the precise time, all ships cut loose with a twenty-one-gun salute. When the royalty passed by their Spanish frigate, the whole crew lifted their hats and gave a "hip, hip, hurrah." *Belknap*'s admiral also hosted a bunch of dignitaries under the awning on the flight deck. The commissioning of a new Spanish aircraft carrier in port prompted the special occasion. This afternoon, we weighed anchor and moved dockside. We have a French ship outboard and a Spanish ship inboard, which we go through in order to reach the dock. A French carrier moored behind us, and a Spanish carrier in front of us effectively locks *Belknap* in place. The French carrier has a short deck and accommodates STOLs and VTOLs.

I went ashore after dinner this evening. Two of my students and I just walked around a while and changed some dollars into pesetas. One of the most obvious sights in Barcelona that has been absent in other ports I have visited is the presence of young women in short, tight skirts. They try to be very friendly, but out of the thousands of Sailors in port, I didn't see any takers. However, the evening was young, and they may snare some of the young guys after they have had a sufficient amount of beer. One worldly-wise Sailor who has been here before said some of these people are transvestites.

Barcelona, Spain, May 29, 1989

After church service yesterday, I went ashore intending to climb a high hill overlooking the harbor. I ran into one of my roommates, an amateur geologist, who also wanted to climb the hill after exploring the face of the cliff for some interesting rocks. We picked our way through some pretty rough country but found only ordinary stones. However, the hill does have interesting strata.

Noticing a large cemetery farther around the hill, we decided to explore it. The cemetery turned out to be a bonanza of interests. Huge tombs and mausoleums extend layer after layer up the hillside. Some are at least one hundred years old. A few appear to be twice that old. I have never before seen anything like it. A Mediterranean villa could be purchased for what some of these structures cost. Farther up the hill, inexpensive crypts extend into the cliff itself. Switchback roads lead to the top, but we didn't reach the top because of a funeral in progress about half way up. I took two pictures of tombs before two motorcycle cops happened along and told me to put away my camera. Unknowingly, I had just committed a cultural faux pas—taking pictures in a Spanish cemetery. I got a shot of the general area where we happened to be at the time and another of a huge tomb with a pyramid on top about twenty feet tall. Another that appeared to be extremely old had five very ornate metal columns about fifteen feet tall. The inscription read, "A mi esposo, Vda de Mariano Regordosa." That translates into, "To my husband, widow of Mariano Regordosa." I wondered if he figured prominently in Spanish history, or whether a rich widow just wanted to express a final tribute. The tomb I was about to photograph when the cops stopped me presented an incredible sight. This huge tomb had a wall behind it with a bas-relief of a factory of some sort. In front of this wall the statue of an elderly, portly, bald-headed man clothed in a suit and tie sat in a chair. His right arm rested on a large book. The Grim Reaper stood behind the man with his hand his shoulder, a most stunning and chilling sight.

Later, I took in an event I always said I would never witness—a bullfight. I decided to see it for the same reason I saw the movie Platoon, not to be entertained but to be informed. They torture, exhaust, and bleed the pitiable animal. Then the matador goes in and does his "ballet." Two gentlemen from Belgium who sat next to me mitigated the carnage in the ring. They spoke fluent English, so we had a good visit. I left after they killed the third bull.

It was about a three-mile walk from the bullring back to the ship, and I just took in the sights of beautiful downtown Barcelona full of

Trumpeters introducing the bull

Introduction of Matadors and Picadors

Introduction of horses to remove dead bulls

The fight

Removing a dead bull

old, well-kept stone buildings averaging about seven stories high. A median wide enough to put about six cars abreast divides La Rambla, which ends at the waterfront. People, including about twenty shiploads of Sailors, just swarmed this area. A number of business activities crowd this walkway—newsstands, souvenir shops, sidewalk cafes, mime artists, sketch artists, tarot card operators, and hookers. Turning off this main thoroughfare, I occasionally came upon large plazas that allow visitors and residents of downtown Barcelona some room to move around.

Today, I took some time to smell the flowers—literally. I wound my way up a different part of the hill I explored yesterday to Jardins Mn Costa I Llobera Plantas Crasses. Walkways wind their way through dozens of different plants through this huge beautiful hillside garden. Cacti of various varieties abound, as do exotic trees and flowering plants. An anthurium measured chest high. A very large metal statue of a seated, young girl occupied a prominent place. Placed in front of her were some strange writing instruments. The inscription on the statue simply read "J. Viladomat." I don't know whether that was the name of the girl or the name of the sculptor. It would be interesting to know the girl's identity and why she occupies such a prominent position in the garden.

At the top of the hill, an old Spanish fort commands a view of the harbor. After looking over the fort's artillery pieces, I headed for the zoo. Having an air of mystery, narrow streets beckoned me off the main thoroughfare. I chose a few of them, finding them as quaint and charming as I thought they would be. Mostly, people were just minding their own business. A couple of good-looking girls tried to be very friendly. They obviously were minding their business—and so early in the day! I just gave them a nice smile and kept walking.

Some park bench-occupying derelicts, both male and female, lined the street alongside the zoo, while farther on down the way, three groups of elderly men played a game of yuego de petranca. The concept of the game is roughly the same as pitching pennies, but more sophisticated. Players roll steel balls about three inches in diameter and weighing about twenty-five ounces toward the target, a smaller ball. Six men using two of these balls played on a concrete enclosed area about forty feet by fifteen feet. Since they were such a friendly bunch, I enjoyed watching them for a while.

At the zoo, teachers chaperoned groups of little kids holding onto common ropes just as they do in the U.S. And the adults looked just as harried. I enjoyed watching the kids about as much as I did the animals, which were mostly the same as those in American zoos, except for the albino gorilla.

Albino gorilla

Barcelona impresses me as a great city, and the people have been cordial. But vandals have commonly defaced public buildings with graffiti. Communists and Nazis put much of it there. To clean it all off will require a monumental sandblasting job. Even a beautiful marble statue donated by a "sister city" in California and located on the grounds of the old fort is ruined by graffiti.

Barcelona, Spain, May 30, 1989

Today, I just decided to hit the streets and follow my instincts, which took me through a maze of narrow streets where many of the natives live. Shops of every description provided goods from hardware to butcher shops. Many people live in apartments above their shops.

I stumbled into a large quadrangle surrounded by four-story public buildings. One seemed to be a museum, so I entered. Art objects and abstract paintings filled the rooms. Models of all sorts of mechanical devices that I had never seen before especially interested me. Suddenly, I noticed a sign "Escola Massana." I was in Massana School and all these people around me were students! At about the same time I made this discovery, a distinguished-looking gentleman politely informed me that a judging of the models was about to take place and that they really didn't require my presence. Apologizing, I made a hasty withdrawal. But I have found that confidence and audacity permits one to see and do a lot of things that other people miss.

After some meandering, I spent my last Spanish pesetas on postcards and then discovered a real museum, but with no remaining time and pesetas. Heading back to the ship, I passed the same bunch of lonely girls on the same lonely corner that I had seen a few days earlier. A few looked young and very pretty. Others have been over the hill a long time. I tried to speculate as to what kind of life lay before the young ones.

At Sea, May 31, 1989

Belknap heads up a four-ship convoy cruising off the coast of Toulon, France, where an Italian drone plane provides target practice for the crews with surface to air missiles. The shoot was the real thing except explosive warheads. It isn't necessary for a missile to actually hit the target. Under battle conditions, if the missile reaches the proximity of the target, it explodes. All missiles came close enough for a kill.

Gaeta, Italy, June 4, 1989

When the ship returned to Gaeta three days ago, I went ashore to check out an old fort in a military zone on a hill overlooking the south end of Gaeta. A cove cuts into the cliff underneath the old fort. A sheer drop-off ends in massive boulders continuously smashed by the sea, covering all human noise. I sat on a wall at the base of the lichen-encrusted fort for a long time just allowing my spirit to be refreshed.

Belknap's captain has received orders to transfer to Washington as an assistant to a four-star admiral. Friday night I attended a nice outdoor restaurant for an evening of pizza, wine, and fun where some of the officers put on skits for a roast of the departing captain and the XO.

I had intended to go to Rome yesterday but decided to stay for the change-of-command ceremony. I can see Rome later. Another opportunity to witness the change of command of a Navy warship probably won't be in my future. Officers participating in the ceremony dressed in formal whites, some with swords. Festivities included a Navy band and Marine color guard. Italian dignitaries,

USS Belknap Change of Command ceremony

other civilians, and naval shore personnel also attended. After the band played the Italian anthem and the "Star-Spangled Banner," the admiral and both captains addressed the group. Later, we went to the officers club on shore for Champaign and snacks.

June 11, 1989

Yesterday, I encountered one of my students at the Navy exchange who invited me to take a drive around the immediate vicinity of Gaeta. I had already done about seven miles of beach combing at Formia, where I collected a bonanza of shells to be shipped back to Texas for a friend who collects them. I was glad to have a companion for lunch before the drive that took us toward Rome. We saw some spectacular coastline before turning inland to see some mountain ranges sprinkled with small towns and old ruins in the valleys.

At Sea, June 13, 1989

The ship left Gaeta last Friday to spend several days in training exercises and more mock warfare. On Saturday, we cruised back and forth along the south coast of Sardinia and occasionally sent five-inch shells at targets on shore. The firing did not go well. At one point the five-inch gun developed a mechanical problem and had to be repaired. Then a sailboat had to be escorted out of the firing range. Then the spotting crew ashore had to take a lunch break. It was not a good day for our new captain on his second day in command of *Belknap*.

We have since joined a sizable group of ships, including the carriers *America* and *Roosevelt*. We just cruise within a box on the chart and simulate missile firings. Carriers deploy their planes at targets. In an exercise of this type, the target vessels will sometimes set off flares or smoke bombs near their position, and the planes will actually drop their ordinance. The Mediterranean is used to simulate land areas anywhere in the world. Attack plans are carried out according to various political scenarios. This keeps the fleet sharp and combat-ready.

Two days ago, a Soviet AGI (spy ship) cruised within five hundred yards from us for quite a while. It's one of their newest information-gathering ships, and everybody on board got a picture. They probably took pictures of us too. Soviets have been known to even scoop up our garbage looking for useful information. The ship still shadows us.

New PACE classes have started. I have two sections of college English that will run for eight weeks and four basic skills classes—two back to back for four weeks. That will make about one hundred

Soviet spy ship

men who have taken the courses. Out of the last college course twenty-six completed it. The Navy people tell me that this is an exceptional ratio, which says a lot about the caliber of students. One student dropped out, and three busted the course. One boy hails from San Antonio, Texas, and never heard English spoken in his home. He knew he was in over his head from the beginning, but hung in and did his best. How he passed the placement test to get into my class is a mystery. He will be one of the new basic skills students.

At Sea, June 17, 1989

After the fleet completed its exercises in the Western Mediterranean, the battle group headed east toward Libya but stayed outside Colonel Kadahfi's so-called "line of death." But some ships routinely cruise in that area without incident.

Having completed the coordinated exercises, *Belknap* detached from the rest of the fleet to do some solo exercises. A man overboard drill sent Oscar, a dummy, over the side so the ship could come about to retrieve it. One member of the crew had hidden, so a muster of the entire crew had to be quickly completed. In the meantime, two rescue swimmers suited up preparatory to entering the water if necessary. Deck hands armed with floating lines and retrieval hooks lined the ship's bow to scoop up the dummy as the ship came around.

Today a helicopter brought a crewman from another ship in exchange for one from *Belknap*, another part of a training exercise. Since the ship's helicopter was on the flight deck, the men arrived and departed in a sling as the visiting helicopter hovered over the bow. This operation required precision flying with the ship moving at six knots and the helicopter maintaining a sideways progress of the same speed. Firefighters and medical personnel stand by during such an operation.

Until a few hours ago, the sea was smooth enough to water-ski. Whales played alongside the ship's wake. Porpoises performed crisscrossed leaps across the bow. The sea has been so smooth that the ship's wake extended all the way to the horizon. It looked as though a path had been cut through the water. I stood on the fantail a long time just looking at the sea and sky.

With the moon almost full again, the nights have been so spectacular that I have a hard time getting to bed. Since my first session of PACE classes has ended, those men have a little extra time on their hands to talk to me at night on the weather deck. Everyone has a poignant story of some sort, and it's good to know that they trust me to keep their confidence. These young men have learned more than just English composition. Barriers between them have fallen as they have come to know each other better and express their thoughts and feelings with each other through all the essays they've written. It has been a long time since my life has been blessed with the camaraderie of so many other men.

Gaeta, Italy, June 24, 1989

We pulled into Gaeta in time for the crew to enjoy most of Father's Day ashore. I just flaked out on the beach for a while. But Monday got off to a hectic start and quickly accelerated to frantic. The four-star admiral in charge of all NATO forces in Europe came to visit the ship on Thursday. Everything had to be either cleaned or painted. The extra duty, combined with daily shore leave so the men could be with their families, made a shambles of my classes. I just canceled the classes and left the ship before the admiral came on board.

It seemed like a good day to finally get to Rome, but the trains were on strike. That happens occasionally in Italy. The people who run the trains get in a snit over something and stop the trains for a few hours. Since it was a lovely cool day, I hiked the four miles to Formia in hopes of finding the hydrofoil to take me to Capri Island. Someone had given me wrong information. The hydrofoil no longer leaves from Formia. I would have to go to Naples.

Formia had one of its big market days, but with consistent luck, I arrived at the market just as the vendors were taking down their booths.

I watched the demolition from a park bench. The departing vehicles left the ground littered with fruit, vegetables, coat hangers, paper, cardboard, and other debris—all being scattered by the wind over downtown Formia, an otherwise pretty city. I asked a cop who would clean up the mess and got the usual Italian answer to an Eng-

Market Day at Formia

lish question. "No capese."

I assuaged my frustration with a delightful lunch at a restaurant having its grand opening. Then I just spent the day doing a walking tour of the area. I had already climbed Mt. Spiccata (Split Mountain), a fascinating geological oddity. Many people believe that the mountain split apart when Christ was crucified. According to Matthew 27:51, the earth at Jerusalem did indeed shake at the hour of Jesus' death. I suppose the quaking could have extended several hundred miles to Italy. Naturally, a church has been erected near the opening of the split. A stone-paved downward path about eight feet wide leads to the entrance of the crevice. Each wall on both sides of the path have seven icons depicting Christ's journey to the cross and subsequent crucifixion. According to legend, a skeptic of the story placed his hand on the inside of the mountain where the split occurred and left his "hand print" in the rock located about halfway through the narrow crevice. The "hand print" features five holes in a straight line about half the depth of bowling ball holes. Some coloration in the stone polished by countless hands vaguely resembles the outline of a hand. The far end of the crevice expands enough to house a small sanctuary, which looks out through the mountain to the sea. With the waves gently lapping at the base of the cliff below, the silent sanctuary provides a peaceful place to relax and meditate. Returning to the beach at Gaeta late in the day, I restored life to my tired legs in the cool water.

In the evening, one of my students and I went back to Formia in his car to take in a classical concert held in one of the huge churches. A magnificent orchestra featuring Brahms and Schumann played to an audience of appalling decorum. The Italians seem to be a laid-back bunch, so casual dress didn't surprise me. However, many people used the occasion to catch up on their social conversation.

People left in a middle of a selection. People arrived in the middle of a selection. Kids came and went. Kids frequently changed their seats. Parents admonished their kids throughout the performance. At the end, the audience gave the orchestra a standing ovation but got no encore.

Last Sunday, one of the staff officers invited me to his home for dinner where his mother is visiting from the United States. The next day, she drove me up the coast to Sperlonga and Teracina before turning inland to Itri on the old Apian Way. We passed various ruins and tombs as well as coastal towers formerly used by the Romans for signaling. She left me at a restaurant in Gaeta where I ate dinner with just a few other patrons. Since business was slow, the owner joined me at my table for some interesting conversation. During the meal I noticed a young couple apparently enjoying a special occasion. Leaving, they stepped out onto the sidewalk and enthusiastically embraced. So I said to the owner, "When people want to do that in the United States, they usually go to his place or her place."

Sighing he replied, "We are just as liberated as the French or you Americans, but we have the Pope, and he's a problem."

He went on to tell me that for an entrepreneur to make it in Italy, he had to be well connected politically either in Rome or at the Vatican. I don't know whether that is true, or just his opinion.

Earlier in the week, I went jogging along the waterfront late in the day. Stopping near downtown after a two-mile run, I was just relaxing and enjoying the cool air when an Italian man approached me and wanted to practice his English. We had a hard time getting it together. However, in a space of thirty minutes, I learned that he is age thirty-nine, had spent some years in the Italian merchant marine, and had made six trips to various ports in the United States. It took him several minutes to get through to me that he had been through the Strait of Gibraltar. He sounded so funny that when I finally understood, we both cracked up laughing.

Gaeta, Italy, June 23, 1989

I attended the hail and farewell party last night at the admiral's house for the Chief of Staff who has been assigned to the Pentagon. However, the word house doesn't do justice to his abode. He lives in a villa on a promontory overlooking the Mediterranean, complete with olive orchard and vineyard.

A sprawling red-tiled roof covers the three-story house and serves as a deck. Jutting out to one side about two hundred yards are the remains of an old Roman tower. The Italian Carabinieri guard the place twenty-four hours a day. When the admiral is away from his

Party at the Admiral's house

residence, a young Marine that looks like he is made out of marble becomes his second shadow.

Belknap has had to vacate its usual dock space to allow an Italian amphibious craft to moor there. The Pope visited Gaeta today for the first time in two hundred years. The whole town got in a dither about it. The town made many cosmetic improvements. Even some of the streets over which the Pope traveled have been repaved. He held mass for a crowd of fifteen to twenty thousand people in the soccer field where a makeshift platform had been constructed for him and another one for a choir. One of the ship's officers and I took our position at the back of the SRO crowd, which turned out to be fortuitous. Making his entrance in his Popemobile, a strange looking bulletproof vehicle that allows him to stand and be seen, he came within ten feet of where we were standing, catching me too surprised to get a good picture. I have no idea what the Pope said, but we enjoyed the music and festivities.

Pope's visit to Gaeta

Aboard a train bound from Paris to Milan, July 11, 1989

A short lifetime has been packed into the last two weeks. Nita flew to Paris on June 28 and then took an overnight train to meet me at Ville Franche. I had taken an overnight train to meet her. Since *Belknap* had port visits at Cannes, France, and Palma, Spain, until July 13, I decided to suspend classes so the students could enjoy their liberty ports, and I could spend some time with Nita.

The train trip from Gaeta to Ville Franche began a memorable odyssey. After a short run into Rome, I spent five hours touring some of the city's tourist attractions before boarding the train. Until I came to Europe, I never knew I had an unexpressed love of architecture. I could spend weeks in Rome just looking at the buildings. The grandeur of the coliseum must have been breathtaking before being striped of its marble. Only the knowledge of the pitiless events that took place there marred my admiration for it. I had not realized the extent of the old ruins of various sorts that still exist here.

One of the areas had been turned into a park. It seems one of the buildings had been used by the Romans for a huge sauna, a double-walled structure with enough space between them to tend to fires.

Coliseum

Inside the Coliseum

Piazza Venezia fountain

Roman forum

I got into an interesting thirty-minute discussion with a couple of Arabs from Tunis, one a student of philosophy at Damascus. They say they love Americans but don't think much of our government's international politics. To make their point, one of them assumed a stooped position, and said he didn't understand why our government keeps Arabs pressed down. We parted with warm, friendly handshakes.

The overnight train proved to be the opposite of high-roller living. I had great difficulty finding the car and cubicle where I was supposed to ride because the bunk number had been omitted from the ticket. I soon learned that the Italian conductor's indifference, aggravated by his rudeness, was a common characteristic among train personnel throughout Europe. A kind Italian lady tried to intervene with the conductor, but she couldn't get any information out of him either. A Frenchman, having observed a similar incident assured me that the train personnel were not just picking on an American, but treated everybody that way. Anyway, after it looked like I was going to be stuck on a car full of young girls going to a destination different from mine, I somehow stumbled onto the right car. The sleeping accommodations contrasted radically from the old Pullman sleepers that graced American railroads a generation ago. My quarters accommodated six fully clothed people. I shared the space with three young men and a young woman who spoke English and gave me some pointers on train travel. The noisy, rough riding train made sleep nearly impossible and stopped at every village on its route.

The next morning, the beauty of the French Riviera dispelled the discomforts of the preceding night. But the prettiest sight of all was the waiting arms of Nita at the hotel. We spent two nights there and quickly learned the value of the Eurorail passes that Nita purchased before leaving the States. The passes allowed unlimited rail travel throughout Europe. Consequently, we took in Monaco, Nice, and Cannes.

Belknap had already anchored at Cannes when we arrived. I took Nita aboard so she could see first-hand the kind of life that exists aboard a Navy cruiser. She met the admiral, the captain and his wife, as well as many of the officers and enlisted men. She and I spent some time with a few officers having drinks at a nearby sidewalk café. One of the officers insisted that Nita attend the admiral's reception that evening on the ship. I spoke up. "I have the proper attire on board, but Nita has only comfortable traveling clothes and no suitable dress for the reception."

James and Nita Lee at the Admiral's reception aboard USS Belknap, Cannes, France

One of the officers said, "Well, hell! Go buy her one!"

Nita made the fastest dress purchase of her life. It was a memorable occasion for her to be included with a bunch of French dignitaries at the reception.

After the reception, life went downhill for the next twelve hours as we took our second overnight train ride. This time we went first class—only four people in the same cubicle. The rough ride gave Nita motion sickness. Sometime during the night when we were all asleep, an Italian conductor suddenly and without warning burst into our locked compartment demanding that we fill out some forms declaring anything of value that we were bringing into Italy. A scene reminiscent out of an old World War II Gestapo movie upset Nita, and I bristled at the idea of anyone barging into the compartment that we thought was safely locked. I don't know whether the man understood all that I said, but there was no mistaking my attitude, which may explain why he never returned for the completed forms.

We arrived in Venice two-hours late, a common occurrence with Italian trains. As we stepped off the train, some man immediately approached and offered to carry our baggage to his hotel. Going along with the suggestion, we took a short walk to what could best be described as a cramped but clean hole in the wall. We had planned to stay two nights in Venice. However, we arrived in the rain and left in the rain after one night. Consequently, my impression is necessarily superficial. No romantic gondola ride, no sightseeing, except a lot of shops that sheltered us from the rain. From what we did see of Venice, subsidence affects many buildings also in need of a good sand blasting. I had to see Venice to fully appreciate the River Walk in downtown San Antonio, Texas.

The light rain and overcast sky accompanied us through Austria as we made our way to Vienna. The weather softened the landscape along the Austrian Riviera that borders Yugoslavia and made this trip aboard a comfortable Austrian train a delightful experience. In addition, a fascinating Austrian woman, involved in some sort of world peace organization, joined us in our compartment to give us interesting information about Austria and her work. Her view of Mikhail Gorbachov's initiatives seems the same as ours—hopeful, but skeptical.

Rome was intriguing, Venice was unique, but Vienna was love at first sight. Gracious attendants staffed our hotel, a converted palace. This city's class is expressed in its architecture, its music, its sense of neatness and order, its shops, the personal appearance of its people, and the courteous manners of its citizens. Both Italy and France reek with nudity—especially Italy. Total nudity exists on book covers, magazines, newspapers, posters, billboards—everywhere. But we saw virtually none of this in Austria. A visit to the Hapsburg Palace highlighted our city tour. The interior, exterior, and surrounding gardens were in excellent condition. The overall layout of the building and grounds, combined with a superb blend of architecture, art work, and furnishings showed the perfect taste of a master planner—an Italian, no less. Seeing such a harmonious blend caused both of us to conclude that the isolated placement of such treasures in modern homes or museums is often distasteful, if not profane.

The music of Johann Straus and some of his contemporaries filled our second night in Vienna. A marvelous orchestra performed in the "new hall"—only one hundred and sixty years old but not the one in which Straus performed. The music we have loved for a lifetime took on a whole new admiration in that setting.

Downtown Vienna has wide expanses of walkways such as those in Barcelona. Nita and I ate our way down a couple of them. During the second day, a brass band appeared about two blocks from our hotel and played American standards, attracting a large, appreciative crowd.

While doing our laundry at a self-service shop, we met two backpackers who were just graduated from Yale. They told us about a youth hostel in the Alps that also accepted families. Since Switzerland was the next country we were going to visit, we decided to stay there in the little town of Lauterbrunnen.

With the strains of Strauss music still running through our minds, we left for Lucerne, arriving late at night. The next day, we took a three-and-a-half-hour boat ride through spectacular mountain scenery down the entire length of Lake Lucerne and then rode the train back. Mowed meadows graced the hillsides, as it was haying season. Distinctive cottages dotted slopes, and elegant hotels hugged the coastline. At a sheer cliff, sky divers floated back down to lake level.

Since Lauterbrunnen was off the main rail line, we had a car all to ourselves except for two back-packers from the states who had met during spring break. She wanted to tour Europe but didn't want to go alone, so she persuaded the young man to go with her. Being quite congenial, they were good company. Later, I said to Nita, "Can you imagine the conversations that took place in their respective homes before these kids left on this trip?"

Lauterbrunnen entranced us. A barn had been converted into a hostel that would accommodate a substantial number of backpackers. We had one of the two upstairs private rooms, but shared a bathroom and kitchen with everybody else. In this case, "everybody else" consisted of six young girls and one young boy who came just to hike in the mountains and enjoy the scenery. The village straddled a rushing river in a narrow valley. We had a good view of the high waterfall that fed the river as well as Jungfrau glacier between the mountain peaks. The cool fresh mountain air accorded us the best night's sleep of the whole trip. All of this for six bucks apiece.

On our way to Geneva, we stopped at Montreau for a tour of Chillon Castle, one of the most completely restored castles in Europe that's essentially a museum full of furniture and war materiel of the thirteenth to the fifteenth century. François de Bonivard was imprisoned in a dungeon here from 1532 to 1536. Lord Byron, the British poet, immortalized him in his poem "The Prisoner of Chillon." As I viewed the pillar where Bonivard was chained, from somewhere in my distant youth came some of the closing lines of the poem after his release.

My very chains and I grew friends,

So much a long communion tends

To make us what we are—even I

Regain'd my freedom with a sigh.

And I thought of the millions of people who yearn for freedom today but wouldn't know what to do with it if they had it.

At Montreau we also laid to rest a myth that French people are pompous and dislike Americans. When we checked our baggage at the train station, we were having difficulty getting directions to Chillon Castle.

Standing nearby, a Frenchman waiting to retrieve a shipment for his business addressed us in flawless English, "Get yourselves a cup of coffee at the restaurant across the street, and I will pick you up in fifteen minutes and take you to the castle."

We did and he did. He kept up a friendly conversation for the entire drive, stating that it would take about two hours to make the tour. He graciously offered to pick us up at the end of two hours and return us to the train station. We thanked him but opted to take a bus back to pick up our luggage. We encountered many friendly people of this sort during our two-week trek across Europe.

In France as elsewhere you tend to get back what you radiate.

After spending the night in Geneva, we took a fast train to Paris and thence toward Verdun for Nita's long-awaited pilgrimage to the battle site where her father was gassed and wounded in World War I. Because of this meaningful trip, an incident at Chalons that we otherwise would have shrugged off because of our holiday mood almost turned disastrous. We had to change trains at Chalons and had a three-hour layover. The posted train schedule showed the train to Verdun to leave on both track two and track three. The ticket agent insisted that we should wait on the platform by track two. I verified this with another agent since this was the last train to Verdun that day, emphasizing that we needed to be certain about which platform to take. I also explained the importance to my wife that we get to Verdun. I thought that their knowing that Nita, the daughter of an American soldier who helped save France, might strike a responsive chord.

While waiting on platform two, we were dismayed to learn that the train to Verdun had left on track three. In complete frustration, I could neither hire a taxi to take us the remaining seventy-five miles nor secure a hotel room for the night. The train clerks seemed to be totally indifferent to the predicament in which they had put us and offered no solution. Nita was crying, and I was angry.

I expressed my displeasure to one of the clerks saying, "You people may not care about the problem you have caused us, but if there are any people in this organization that do care, they are going to hear from me!"

Then I got out my camera, attached the massive zoom lens, and made a big production of photographing the ambiguous schedule.

While we were waiting for a train to take us back to Paris, one of the men finally came over and said, "Your taxi is ready."

I asked, "What taxi?"

"The one to take you to Verdun."

"How much is it going to cost?"

"Nothing. We will take care of the expense."

"Put it in writing, because I don't want an argument with your driver when we get to Verdun."

He did, and we ended up with a pleasant ride through the night in a brand new Volvo that took us to the door of our hotel.

Verdun isn't just a city. It is an experience. No words or pictures can adequately describe the spirit of the place and the overwhelming emotions that torment the visitor. Verdun is beautiful, but somehow it still seems to reek with horror and death. Trees have reforested the hills, once denuded by endless shellfire. Yet neither the trees nor the

Remains of a church at Montfaucon

grass can hide the ugly pockmarks of explosions or the outlines of abandoned trenches.

We took a taxi to the American sector to see the names of the Red Diamond Division on the huge monument overlooking a field of endless crosses. On an overcast day with rain beginning to fall, we stepped out of the taxi to approach the monument, which housed a chapel. How symbolic!

Nita, inside the American Monument Chapel

In the fall of 1918, a quagmire more than thirty feet deep filled much of this area because of the constant shelling and rain. The United States committed a million men to the war and 122,000 became casualties, including Nita's father. More than a dozen villages and thousands of men were pulverized out of existence, their final resting place "known only to God." Only three gaping craters marked the former town of Fleury. The very air seems to be the breath of a million ghosts. The hardship of the men who fought there was complete. The rain, the mud, the stench of dead bodies, the stench of human waste—these alone were sufficient for perfect misery. But added to that were the terror of poison gas, hand-to-hand combat, and constant shelling of heavy artillery, which gave a new description to survivors: shell shocked. Yet they fought, bled, died—and won.

Neither Nita nor I are very prone to tears, but neither of us could contain them. As a final gesture Nita picked a bouquet of poppies by the roadside.

We left Verdun on a somber note. The trip back to Paris ended on the left bank of the Seine in the middle of the Latin Quarter about three blocks from Notre Dame Cathedral. St. Mihiel Square, where our hotel was located, contrasted sharply with Verdun. Greeting us as we emerged from the subway, a kaleidoscopic scene jolted us into another world. A small crowd watched a man put on a fire-eating demonstration. A ring of adults appeared to be taking in a lecture from one in its members. Nearby, students sat cross-legged in a circle in a rap session. Dress ranged from chic to sloven with dogs and motorcycles interspersing the crowd. Of course, the omnipresent sidewalk cafes provided a culinary vantage point for onlookers.

Our hotel window looked down on this scene of contrasts. Nita chose all the hotels for our trip. Her spirit of adventure is securely intact.

Naturally, we took in the Louvre, or rather it took us in. Four months would be required to see all the masterpieces there if only thirty seconds were spent in front of each one. After a few hours, the museum became just as blur of bygone grandeur, landscapes, and portrayals of human tragedy in its various forms. Since I have not been trained in art appreciation, the originals did not impress me any

more than the countless reprints I had seen for many years. People don't appreciate what they don't understand, and I'm no exception.

A night boat trip on the Seine via the Eiffel Tower took us through the most dramatic man-made scenery of our entire trip.

It's easy to see why people fall in love with Paris. When I left Nita at the airport the next day, neither of us wanted to leave France or each other.

The Eiffel Tower

Gaeta, Italy, July 13, 1989

While Nita flew back to Houston, I took a train to Italy via the Swiss Alps. After a night in Milan, I spent a few hours in Florence.

After seeing Vienna, Florence struck me as being just old and unkempt. Tourists packed the city and swelled the busy streets with countless motorbikes, creating greater hazards for pedestrians than cars. I wandered through the huge Palazzo Piti whose gardens extend over several acres on a hillside. It shows evidence of considerable neglect, a condition that seems to characterize many of Italy's national treasures. The artwork inside the churches bore the same extreme opulence that I have seen throughout Europe. Only the designs are different. A stranger to Christianity who judged it by its art might conclude that Mary, not Jesus Christ, died to save mankind.

I went on to Pisa, but without Nita, neither city seemed quite as exciting. Naturally, I went to see the Leaning Tower of Pisa, an architectural delight.

Arno River at Florence, Italy

After dinner, I returned to look at it under the special illumination. Before leaving the city, I went back a third time to climb to the top for an excellent view of the city. Seven bells, one for each note in the musical scale, crown the tower. Just as I reached the top, the largest bell, suddenly began an ear-splitting peel. For an instant, I thought, "This is it! After leaning like this for eight centuries, the tower is going to topple while I'm on it!" I liked Pisa and would enjoy a return trip.

The Leaning Tower of Pisa

The night before my departure from Pisa, I went to the train station to check the train schedule for the next day. One clerk was available. I asked him, "What time does the train to Formia leave tomorrow morning?"

He said, "You have to ask at the next window."

"There's no one at that window," I protested.

"There will be at eight o'clock in the morning."

"Can't you tell me tonight?"

"No. You have to ask at the next window."

I wondered if train clerks arrive on the job insensible, or whether they receive on-the-job stupidity instruction. In any case, they've taken exasperation to the Olympic level.

I arrived back on *Belknap* in time for dinner and no longer had to start every conversation with, "Do you speak English?"

Gaeta, Italy, July 23, 1989

The news hit the newspapers this week. *Belknap* and two other ships are going to Sevastopol, Russia. We leave Saturday and will arrive at this city on the Black Sea August 4. A Soviet ship will make a reciprocal visit to Norfolk. The crew has known about this exciting trip for several weeks. *Belknap* will be the first American ship to visit any Soviet port in fourteen years and the first ever to visit a Black Sea Soviet port.

The ship has been a zoo ever since I came back on board ten days ago. The ship is docked next to the USS *Shenandoah*, which is a huge tender with a large crew of both males and females. It seems strange to see women stuffed into men's clothing coming and going on *Belknap*. The wardroom galley is undergoing an overhaul. So is the head nearest to me. The nearest functioning head is three decks down. Just what I need—to walk out of a shower dressed in a towel and meet a female Sailor. Since they dress like Sailors and cuss like Sailors, I guess it really doesn't matter.

During one of my classes last week, an announcement came over the 1MC system in a slow voice that just trailed off, "Flooding, flooding, flooding." Then came a garbled attempt to give the location. Silence. Again the voice intoned, "Flooding, flooding, flooding." Pause. "I don't know how to do this." The whole class just cracked up. I laughed too until I learned that it was my head flooding my sleeping area! But in spite of the botched announcement, quick action prevented any damage. However, the incident did trigger a training session that night on the proper procedure for using the 1MC. I have asked a lot of people what 1MC means, and no one can tell me for sure. Earlier in the day, someone announced the arrival of an admiral by referring to him as a commodore. The XO shot out to the quarterdeck where the announcement originated to try to correct the embarrassment. It was not a good day for the lieutenant J.G. in charge of these guys. He lost a few pounds off his posterior. But one man's tragedy is often another man's humor. We tried to console the young officer by assuring him that if he embellished the story enough, it would make a great saga when he gets out of the Navy and returns to college.

Yesterday, I finally made it to Pompeii, just outside of Naples. Four officers from *Shenandoah* took the same train, so we stayed together. Two were women. All four seemed rather ordinary in civilian clothes. Since they were recent arrivals, I got to introduce them to the best pizza place and the right ice cream place when we returned to Gaeta late in the evening.

Pompeii, Italy

We only spent the afternoon in Pompeii, which would take two or three days to really absorb with a good guide that knows his archaeology. Parts of nearly all of the buildings that have been excavated still stand. It's a large compact city whose streets generally are wide enough to accommodate two chariots abreast, which have worn deep grooves in the stone pavement. It must have been a magnificent city, when Mt. Vesuvius destroyed it with its eruption in 79 AD. Some of the stately houses would cost a million dollars or more to build today.

The huge stadium would be usable today if it were cleared of

Pompeii Stadium

brush, vines, and grass. It appears that one of the theaters is being used. A brothel, along with residential sexually explicit statuary and wall paintings, attests to the character of Pompeii's citizens. The downstairs portion of the brothel remains fully intact. A lewd painting depicting various types of sexual activity adorns the door of each room. One room had the name of a patron with marks indicating that he was a charge account customer. Early Visa? If so, Mt. Vesuvius effectively canceled the debt.

The street here was about eight feet wide. A hotel, with a bar next-door, sat directly across from the brothel. Nothing has really changed since 79 AD—just the technology. When archaeologists dig up our civilization 1900 years from now, I wonder if our pornography will be considered priceless art.

The Temple of Jupiter, the Temple of Vespasian, and the other temples give mute testimony to their pagan and emperor worship. Deeply worn stone temple steps indicated they must have taken this practice seriously. These temples, along with other large public buildings comprise the center of a huge business district.

A number of bodies have been created from molds formed by volcanic material that encased the actual people and animals that died there. These are rather arresting scenes. Having seen pictures of these people over the years, I didn't think seeing them would particularly move me. I was wrong.

Gaeta, Italy, July 24, 1989

Slave who died at Pompeii

The chaplain had a congregation of one yesterday—me. Because of a recent series of negative incidents, my attitude toward Italians had begun to turn sour. The chaplain has been in Italy a long time and encouraged me see their methods and traditions in a different light and rekindle some brotherly love for my fellow man.

After leaving the chaplain, I took a four-hour climb to the other side of Mt. Orlando by way of a part of Gaeta that I had not seen before. My route took me through deep shades of the forest devoid of sounds, except the songs of the birds, leaves rustling in the wind, and the rhythm of my own footsteps. I encountered several old ruins with construction identical to that which I saw in Pompeii. Nazis probably built some of the newer structures now in a state of disrepair. At the top, a cloudless day afforded a spectacular view of Gaeta. Descending the mountain by a different route, I ended up in the cool salty waves of Gaeta Beach. Following classes today, Mr. Mike Cuoco, one of the local citizens whom I had met weeks before, took a senior chief petty officer and me to the mausoleum on top of Mt. Orlando. He is one of the very few people that can get permission from the city to enter the mausoleum, which is not open to the public, because

Italians deface the structure to try to take souvenirs.

A replica of the statue of Gen. Lucio Munazio Planco occupies the center of the rotunda. Originally, his brother and two sons were also

Mt. Orlando Mausoleum

entombed there. Conquering armies long ago stripped this double-walled structure with the outer wall being about eight feet thick. A reticulated pattern formed from a hard concrete-like substance that no one seems to know how to duplicate characterized the interior of the walls. The top of the building afforded a 360-degree panorama of this entire Mediterranean area. At one time, a lighthouse occupied the top of it. The Italians built a new lighthouse on the seaward side after World War II.

Mr. Cuoco took us to his home for refreshments and talked at length about the connection between Gaeta and the United States. Only 23,000 people populate Gaeta, but about 20,000 people in Cambridge, Massachusetts can trace their roots to Gaeta. The frigate USS *Capodonno* (FF-1093) wears the name of Mr. Cuoco's cousin, a Congressional Medal of Honor winner killed in Viet Nam. He took us to the Plazza Enrico Tonti and showed us a marble slab that noted Tonti's 1648 birth date and credited him with being in LaSalle's party when he explored the Mississippi Valley. Since Mr. Cuoco has more relatives in the U. S. than in Italy, he seems to know more about American history than do many Americans. As we parted, he gave the senior chief and me a copy of an old painting of Pope Pius IX boarding the USS *Constitution* (Old Ironsides) in August 1849. It marked the first time the Pope ever set foot on American property, and it happened at Gaeta.

Gaeta, Italy, July 25, 1989

Today, Mr. Cuoco introduced me to Mr. Mariano Mandolesi, the owner of a metal working shop who sold me a silver-plated seal of Gaeta.

General Mark Clark awarded him the Bronze Star for his service as an Italian Partisan during WWII. Like many Partisans who refused to be Facists, he joined the Communist Party, but quit after his brother visited the United States and got a good look at capitalism.

Agean Sea, August 1, 1989

If *Belknap* were a zoo when we were next to the tender at Gaeta, it has turned into a jungle. Wet paint is everywhere inside and outside the ship. Men who normally run high tech equipment have been pressed into work details to make the ship look its best for the Sevastopol visit.

On a mirror-slick sea, the *Belknap* is taking on fuel and supplies from the port side of USS *John Lenthall*, while the frigate *Kaufman* is taking on fuel and supplies from the starboard side. What an amazing operation. Three ships with about 150 feet between each pair cruise at precisely the same course and speed. After completion of refueling, *Belknap* will break away from the oiler at a fast speed while playing a segment of the "William Tell Overture," music commonly associated with the Lone Ranger.

Supplies coming aboard at amidships include 15,000 cans of soft drinks and the ingredients for 15,000 hot dogs—all in anticipation of Russian visitors to the ship when we reach Sevastopol.

Sixty interpreters and other civilian specialists as well as specialist naval personnel have crowded onto an already packed ship. Two Navy bands have boarded, two members of which are women assigned to *Kaufman*. They come over in a small boat during the day to rehearse. One of the bands practiced on the flight deck during the refueling operations.

The death of Marine Lt. Colonel Robin L. Higgins, whom the Iranian-backed Hezbellah says they executed yesterday, has created

Sixth Fleet Band

an air of uncertainty for the ship. Liberty has been cancelled for the entire Sixth Fleet in the Mediterranean. Since *Belknap* is the flagship, the possibility exists that we will turn back to join the rest of the fleet.

Classes have become chaotic. Students cannot show up consistently because of extra duties imposed upon them. Some look very sleepy. In spite of it all, we finished two basic skills classes last Thursday and started two more the next day. One of my students commented to me about his changed attitude since he enrolled in both basic skills and freshman composition last June. He used to spend his spare time on board watching inane movies and hanging out in bars ashore. Since he has rediscovered his thought processes, he has little interest in either. Statements like that keep teachers in the profession.

Aegean Sea, August 2, 1989

We're only twenty miles outside the Dardanelles and will reverse course shortly. *Belknap* has been recalled to take charge of the Sixth Fleet. Consequently, the ship has abandoned preparations to visit the Soviet Union and has begun to transfer all extra personnel for the

Russian visit from *Belknap* to *Kaufman*. Operations began at first light, utilizing the captain's gig, a launch, and a rubber boat from *Kaufman*. Of course, the change in plans disappoints the crew. The assassination of one man triggered World War I. The big question now is, "What will Col. Higgins' execution trigger?"

Off Rhodes Island, August 3, 1989

Belknap is preparing for any eventuality by test firing the weapons systems during GQ drills to be certain that they work properly. They remain loaded and ready. There has been some talk of removing me from the ship, but no one seems to know the naval instructions for dealing with a civilian in these circumstances.

I remarked to one of the officers, "It is my understanding that I am supposed to debark at some neutral port."

Laughing he said, "Well, Jim, that's right. But how high a priority do you think that would be?"

Everyone has enough to do without this concern. If I have to be in a firefight, I guess this is as good a place as any. The ship is scheduled to rendezvous with the aircraft carrier USS *Coral Sea* later today off the coast of Lebanon.

Off Lebanon, August 4, 1989

The gorgeous day, which has just ended, belied the ominous purpose of our being here. Brilliant sunshine sparkled like diamonds on tiny wavelets driven by a cool breeze that contrasts sharply with the ship's interior. As dusk fell, the thin crescent of a moon hung near the evening star low in the west, making visible the major constellations such as Cygnus, Cassiopeia, Sagittarius, and the two dippers. A day that ended so quietly began with a deadly purpose. A GQ drill again sent the crew to battle stations to test-fire some of the guns. The old military routine of hurry up and wait seems to be settling in. When we left the Dardanelles, we hurried to get here. Now we wait.

Off Lebanon, August 5, 1989

Perhaps blind John Milton observed correctly, "...they also serve who only stand and wait." While staff officers work long, hard hours and lose sleep, the ship's crew, having readied the ship for battle, looks at 360 degrees of blue water and waits. For what? No one seems to know.

Waiting allows time to think, and thinking can be as dangerous as firing missiles. Why are we here? Ostensibly to avenge the death of an American, prevent the death of a hostage, and gain the release of all hostages. There have been hostages for a long time. Why now?

What is America's responsibility to its citizens held captive in foreign countries? If the citizen were there in the capacity of the U. S. Government, it would seem logical that the United States should protect the citizen or punish those who harm him. Conceding the point that punishment is merited in that case, what form should the punishment take? What about the citizen who voluntarily enters a country openly hostile to Americans? Should he not be responsible for his own decisions? Why should we call out the Sixth Fleet and risk widespread destruction because of the voluntary action of one man? Why do we try to hold Middle East hostage-takers accountable, but ignore an obscure people who murder a missionary in South America? Is the concern for the Middle East hostage a ploy for some other reason to flex our military might? It is human nature to have two reasons for some of our actions—the real reason and the one that sounds good.

I don't know the answers. I am just an English instructor with a fair acquaintance with history.

The stars shine brilliantly tonight. May their brilliance illuminate the thinking of our national leaders.

Off Lebanon, August 6, 1989

Today was another beautiful day for the "cruise ship *Belknap*." With no work scheduled, the crew rested and enjoyed a "steel beach picnic." The report that the crews of the two ships at Sevastopol are having a great time makes us all a little envious.

We ate all day—breakfast at the usual hour and brunch from 10 a.m. until noon. About 4:30 p.m., the mess cooks along with the captain and XO started barbecuing chicken and ribs and grilling frankfurters for the picnic. The Navy band, known as The Diplomats, performed on the flight deck while the captain and his other cooks

"Chef" Captain Signer with his cooks

served food on the fantail.

Some of my students, who are fire control operators, gave me a briefing on the firing of missiles and the five-inch gun. The electronics boggle the mind. How did men so young learn so much so soon? The push of a button brings up the exact latitude and longitude of the ship as well as the location, speed, and direction of the target. Either missiles or torpedoes can be fired from the same launcher. Once a torpedo separates from the booster rocket, it descends by parachute and homes in by the sound of the target, whether ship or submarine.

The initial excitement from the prospect of using this firepower is gone. We sense no danger and anticipate nothing but cruising in a circle until the Powers-That-Be get through arguing.

Tonight tissue clouds, scudding under a half moon, soften the ship's features as it glides through a moonbeam cast on a gentle sea, inviting a long vigil somewhere topside.

Off Lebanon, August 12, 1989

Calm seas, sunny day, and starry nights—what more could one ask for? Information. How astonishing to learn that the presence of thirty American warships off the coast of Lebanon ceased to be news in the United States a day or two after *Belknap's* aborted Soviet trip!

Negotiations supposedly proceed at the highest levels in various nations. No one aboard this ship admits to the faintest notion as to where these negotiations will take us. In the meantime, our gun crews stay on alert around the clock.

Two days ago, security personnel conducted a training exercise off the ship's fantail. About twenty men took turns firing at floating targets with M-60 automatic rifles. Also breaking the routine, two Hornet fighter planes from the USS *Coral Sea* made several passes at the ship, dropping their ordinance squarely in the ship's wake about three hundred yards astern.

During one of the nights, I watched signalmen practice semaphore with red flashlights on the signal bridge. After observing them for a few minutes, I took the flashlights and sent my first semaphore message in more than forty years. Some things are never forgotten.

One of *Belknap's* crewmen who made the Sevastopol trip has returned rather unimpressed. Still obsessed with their "Great Patriotic War" (WWII), the friendly Soviets took him on tours to WWII monuments. Sevastopol, devastated during the war, now has buildings resembling American slums, only cleaner. The city had no shops, no discos, no bars, and only three restaurants—nothing to interest a Sailor at night. He went to a butcher shop but quickly left because of the odor. Apparently, the arms race of the last forty years has brought the Soviet economy to the verge of bankruptcy. Hence, the real reason for Glasnost and arms reduction.

Off Lebanon, August 16, 1989

Both President Bush and congress are out of Washington. Who is conducting the talks at "the highest level?" Because of the proliferation of messages, flag officers just eat, sleep, and stand watch—all of which complicates their lives because of their imminent transfer to the battleship USS *Iowa* as *Belknap* will soon go into dry dock.

Several visiting helicopters bring on board people, mail, and supplies. Last night the aircrew was so tired from flying all day that its chopper remained on its pad where the ship normally receives incoming cargo. Consequently two twin-rotor choppers from *Shenandoah* delivered mail and provisions to our bow from *Monongahela*. Last week, an eight-bladed chopper exchanged some personnel while hovering over our bow. It has the power to lift an army tank. The blades were so long that it first appeared that their tips would come through the ports of the pilothouse. For these operations, fireman and medical personnel are always suited up and on standby.

Off Lebanon, August 17, 1989

For the second time in three months another pizza/bingo party took place on the mess deck. Interspersed with bingo, prizes were given for silly accomplishments—the one who had the most tattoos, the most hair on his chest, or some other nonsense designed to promote levity. I wasn't in the game and had just stopped by to pick up some pizza and a Coke when they called for the oldest man on deck. I got lucky. One hundred fingers pointed as one hundred voices roared "Mr. Lee!" My prize was a blank tape.

My work here is just about completed, and I will be leaving soon. However, it would be interesting to stick around for the final outcome over the hostage crisis. I am ready for Texas but share the crew's disappointment over the aborted trip to Sevastopol.

Postscript: After I departed *Belknap* on August 17, she played a role in the Malta Summit between U.S. President George H. W. Bush and Soviet Leader Mikhail Gorbachev on December 2 and 3, 1989. President Bush was berthed aboard *Belknap* for the two-day meeting, but he actually met with Gorbachev aboard the Soviet cruise ship *Maxim Gorky*. The *Belknap* was decommissioned in 1995 and was sunk as a target on September 24, 1998, off the east coast of the United States.

USS Stein (Photo courtesy of Elsirac Enterprises)

USS *Stein* FF-1065

Northwest of California, September 17, 1989

Shortly before departing *Belknap*, I watched the staff officers transfer to the USS *Iowa* while in the harbor at Antalya, Turkey. They will remain on the battleship for eight weeks while Belknap undergoes repairs in dry dock at Toulon, France.

I left the ship at Augusta Bay, Sicily, where the ship off-loaded its ammunition prior to going into dry dock. Then I flew out of Sigonella, Sicily, on a C-2 Navy plane to Naples where a bus picked up about twenty-seven Sailors and me for a trip to Gaeta. After a train ride to Rome and a night in a hotel there, I flew back to Houston. Five days later, I got a call from the PACE coordinator in San Diego asking me to take my present assignment. The seventeen days at home just flew by. However, I did manage to clean up all accumulated mail, take care of most of Nita's "honey-dos," and spend a day water skiing.

The crisis in the Mediterranean now seems far removed both in time and distance. It's odd that something so dramatic should now be

The author "coming out of the whole" at Coleta Creek near Goliad, Texas

out of sight and mostly out of mind. The focus now is on the biggest naval exercise since the end of World War II.

The USS *Stein*, a fast frigate attached to a battle group led by the battleship USS *New Jersey*, will undergo training exercises somewhere off Alaska for the next six weeks to keep the Pacific Fleet combat-ready under arctic conditions. Consequently, the crew will be confined to the ship until we reach Chin Hae, Korea, where I will leave the ship six weeks from now. It's a good thing that I like the ocean.

Off Oregon, September 18, 1989

I not only like the ocean, I like this ship. Being smaller than *Belknap* it has more pitch and roll with just one engine and two boilers. But when we got underway Friday, the ship left the dock surprisingly fast because the power to weight ratio is higher than that of the *Belknap*. Designed by one of the enlisted men, a huge white flag with a beer stein in the middle of it fluttered from the yardarm. The ship was not named for a beer stein, however. Rather, that honor went to Marine Cpl. Tony Stein who single-handedly wiped out several pill boxes and machine gun nests manned by the Japanese at Iwo Jima in WWII for which he received the Congressional Medal of Honor.

Sea lions

Since the crew will not see their families again for six months, the San Diego pier witnessed many tender partings. Some relatives raced the distance of the channel to wave farewell from a distant promontory. One family, including their dog, stood on the water's edge several miles from the pier holding up a sign reading, "We love you, Senior," a reference to a senior chief petty officer. Proceeding out the channel, we passed four sea lions basking in the sun on one of the starboard channel buoys.

Farther out, dolphins gave us a brief escort. Now that we have moved into colder waters, killer whales keep us company.

So far, we have had overcast skies, chill winds, some drizzle, and a calm lead-grey ocean. Two nights ago during underway refueling, alto-cumulus clouds occasionally parted to frame a beautiful full moon.

Aleutian Islands, September 26, 1989

A full semester compressed into six weeks, requires class periods to be extended accordingly. I teach ten hours a day and then read student compositions outside of class. A considerable improvement over what I had on *Belknap*, the teaching space is big enough to hold all my students without anyone having to sit on the floor. Besides, I have a private office with a typewriter.

The young commanding officer and his XO made it a point to welcome me aboard before getting underway. The CO is rather informal with his door always open, and he has given me the full run of his ship—just as the commanding officers of *Belknap* did. I take some of my meals in the chiefs' mess instead of the wardroom, since the Educational Services Officer is a chief petty officer. Little time exists for games, but another chief and I have taken on all comers in spades and remain undefeated, except for one game.

A few days ago, brilliant sunshine and bright stars, turned the ocean to a deep blue. The clean, crisp, clear air sharply contrasts with the perpetual milky haze hanging over the Mediterranean. Saturday, I awoke to the announcement that the weather decks had been secured due to high winds and rough seas. For two days we steamed through a storm with twelve-foot swells. Although a number of people got seasick, I loved the ride. This ship just knifes through the water. In high seas it dives into a swell, shudders momentarily, and drives on through, throwing spray over the bow and obliterating the view of everything in front of the pilot house. At night, phosphorus in the water makes the spray luminescent, creating an eerie glow, another contrast to the water in the Mediterranean and Caribbean.

Yesterday, we went through miles of man-of-wars. These stinging creatures have always been a nuisance on Padre Island along the Texas coast, but I didn't know they were in the Pacific. This could be a spawning area. Small chunks of tar from the *Valdez* oil spill lay scattered among the man-of-wars. In any case, this is no place to fall overboard.

Prior to entering the storm, a Sailor from the USS *Cimarron* did fall overboard during a refueling operation. Another frigate in our group recovered him in less than ten minutes. When ships refuel, another ship follows at about a thousand yards just in case someone does go over the side. A daytime recovery in calm seas is not difficult, but someone going overboard at night would be lucky to be seen.

Aleutian Islands, September 28, 1989

Heavy seas and high winds continue to be the prediction, but not much rough weather has materialized. We have been taking twenty degree rolls, but if things had really gotten rough, we would have cut through the Aleutians at Unimack Island and continued down the island chain in the Bering Sea where we will eventually go anyway.

I relearned a lesson from my WWII Navy years: Never place your hand on a hatch frame when traveling through rough water unless the hatch is securely fastened. I got back all my fingers, but they did smart for awhile. During the worst of the weather today, writing on the board with my right hand while hanging onto a nearby Coke machine with my left hand during twenty degree rolls, proved to be a bit of a challenge.

Last night one of the chiefs took me into the Combat Control Center and explained some of his duties. I learned that for twenty to thirty years the United States has had a system of cables established in the Pacific and Atlantic Oceans that can accurately give the positions of ships and submarines.

About eighty U. S. ships comprise the deployment for this WESTPAC exercise. Eventually, allied ships will swell this number to about 120. Although no one here expects a major conflict between the U. S. and Russia, preparedness apparently guarantees that result.

Off Amchita Island, October 2, 1989

None of the predictions of cold weather and really bad storms have materialized. Temperatures have ranged from 42 to 50 degrees. However, we have encountered some high winds, and at forty-two degrees, "the wind's a whetted knife." We have passed into the Bering Sea via the Strait of Adak, between Adak Island and Kanago Island, which could not be seen because of overcast skies and fog. Because we are crossing the International Date Line, Tuesday will not exist. Therefore, I am holding classes on Saturday in order to stay on schedule.

Northwest Pacific, October 7, 1989

Rock and roll took on a literal meaning this week. A few days ago we encountered one of the storms that had been predicted when we left the Gulf of Alaska. This little breeze got our attention, giving us rolls of thirty-six degrees. I don't mind swinging through a seventy-two degree arc when I am on the bridge, can see the water, and watch how the ship takes it. In fact, it's quite exhilarating. Below deck the situation is very different. Teaching is a challenge, eating is an adventure, and showering is downright dangerous. Some of the crew got seasick, but the sea and I are still getting along well together. However, all of us took steps to keep from rolling out of our bunks. We were taking eighteen-foot swells that buried the ship's bow and then seconds later sent it skyward sixty feet. Welcome to the real Navy! After two days of that, the sea got relatively calm again, going from lead grey to sparkling blue under sunny skies. Right now, Typhoon Colleen is trying to seduce us. So far, the lady's advances have amounted to nothing more than mild flirtation, thanks to a course change. Having seen forty foot waves in the Pacific before, I have no desire to see them from a ship this small.

Aside from teaching, the last three weeks have been rather boring in some respects. As part of a large battle group, we undoubtedly play some important role, but we have not seen any amphibious action or very many of the other ships involved. In actual combat one of the functions of this ship is to transmit radar signals to simulate a carrier and thus attract hostile fire power intended for the real carrier. That's a happy thought!

Spotting dolphins, sea gulls, flying fish, or albatrosses highlights my day. However, I never get tired of just watching the ship cut through the water and observing the ocean's shifting appearance. It never seems to stay the same from hour to hour. Yesterday, an oil tanker cut across our bow about ten miles ahead, leaving traces of oil. You don't realize how much the ocean is polluted until you see debris hundreds of miles from land. In order to control some of the damage, the Navy has banned the dumping of plastics into the ocean.

Northwest Pacific, October 9, 1989

The seas are calm again. Evidently we finally escaped the clutches of Colleen, but not before she gave us some severe rolling and pitching. We suddenly took a forty-degree roll two nights ago that caused a crewman to get a brain concussion. Plans to transfer him to the battleship *New Jersey* for treatment were scuttled due to high winds and advice from their doctor that we were doing everything that could be done for the man. He's going to be o.k.

Two basic skills classes have been completed. Because they have been replaced with only one, I now have free mornings and welcome the relief from so much pressure.

Today, we officially left the Third Fleet that operates out of the San Diego and became attached to the Seventh Fleet that operates out of Yokosuka, Japan. During the night a number of Japanese ships joined our group. Forty-five years ago we would have been shooting at each other.

Since leaving San Diego, the routine of shipboard life inspired creative grooming among the crew that started a contest for mustaches. A few sport shaven heads. The crew looks like a fierce bunch of pirates. We are still two weeks away from Chin Hae, but all of us are ready for it.

Off Japan, October 13, 1989

When I was on the signal bridge two nights ago visiting with one of my students, he asked me if I would like to talk to the battleship *New Jersey*. Although a former Navy quartermaster, I hadn't used Morse code in decades. But after running through the code with a flashlight, I felt confident that I could do it. So for the next few minutes, I shot the breeze via flashing light with a young signalman on New Jersey who said he plans to become a U. S. Navy Seal.

For about a week the entire crew received battle rations. For me, peanut butter and bread became a mainstay. Wednesday, we came back to regular rations in style—steak and lobster, both excellent.

Far West Pacific, October 14, 1989

Warm water, clear sky, hot sunshine—what a gorgeous day! We are about eighty miles west of Okinawa, just south of Kyusyu, which is south of Japan's main island, Honshu. That has been the story of this voyage—always close to something, but never there.

We are close to a great number of ships, however. WESTPAC ships came together in close formation this morning with ships stationed 600 yards apart—off bow, stern, and both sides stretching from horizon to horizon. Battleships, carriers, cruisers, destroyers, frigates, amphibs—they were all there, the biggest assembly of ships since World War II. One of the chiefs promised to send me a picture of the formation.

East China Sea, October 15, 1989

Some nights at sea have a hypnotic effect on me. Last night was one of them. Streaks of stratus clouds hovered over patches of puffy lower-lying clouds, filtering the rays of a full moon over a calm sea. At the forward part of the signal bridge, the ship's noise fades to the sounds of just the wind and the waves crashing against the ship's bow, resembling the sound of combers breaking on the seashore. It is so peaceful and relaxing that I don't think I would ever tire of it. Reluctantly, I sacked out about 1:30 a.m.

While on the signal bridge, I had a long chat with one of the chopper pilots. He told me that he had a near disaster two days ago as he was taking off from the battleship *New Jersey*. Because of wrong information given him regarding wind velocity and direction, he went into a spin right after take-off but recovered about twenty feet off the water. Although the Navy conducts constant training and drills to prevent accidents, some do occur. Injured men and damaged equipment don't contribute to successful missions.

Sea of Japan, October 17, 1989

We took on fuel and other supplies in mounting seas and drizzling rain yesterday. It has occurred to me that a ship's personnel do at sea on a very large scale what a housewife does—clean house and shop for groceries and other supplies for the home. Within a few days, the whole shebang ends up in the ocean.

I have my orders to leave the ship October 29, departing for the states from Pusan. Except for my wedding anniversary November 4, I would be tempted to stay aboard until we reach Subic Bay. One of the chiefs assured me that I would not like being there because of all the immorality. Maybe so, but people usually find what they are looking for.

The chief who made that observation is in one of my college classes. Last week, I asked the students to write a five-hundred-word essay in which they either affirm or deny that the Bible should be taught as literature in college. One chief petty officer approached the subject with some trepidation because he had never read the Bible. Once he got started, he read further than required and is still reading.

The Executive Officer asked me to assign my students the task of writing something about their involvement in, or impressions of, WESTPAC for publication in the ship's newspaper, which would be circulated among the families of the ship's personnel back in San Diego. One young man wrote a touching soliloquy about his love for his wife, how he missed her, and how he looked forward to returning home even though he was excited about seeing new countries. The first batch of mail from San Diego brought him a Dear John letter. She wants a divorce. He chose me to unload on. It seemed like a good time to just shut up and listen. He didn't need any platitudes from me. For many naval families, a six-month separation constitutes a strain and hardship unknown to and unappreciated by most American civilians.

Off Pohang, Korea, October 23, 1989

For several days we have been positioned in this small area covering the amphib operations going on around us, just lazily cruising back and forth along the coast. Amphib ships have changed considerably since I served on an old World War II LST. Part of this operation includes a new boat, an integral component of an amphib operation. Small LCACs can take a tank ashore at thirty knots—considerably faster than a World War II LST. The concept is similar to a swamp buggy. Two engines drive the fans that propel the vessel. Two other engines enable it to hover over water or land. The noise from these engines can be heard for miles.

Being nearly dead in the water is a welcome change from a month of rolling and pitching. It's great to be able to jog again, even in a small area. Graced by a beautiful Korean sunset yesterday, we had a steel beach picnic consisting of burgers, hot dogs, and chicken.

The crew has been picked to paint a Korean orphanage while in port. Some of the crew of *Belknap* did similar community work in Mediterranean ports, a part of the Navy's way of building goodwill in ports throughout the world. Usually, the crews volunteer for the activity because it gives them a chance to interact on a personal level with people in foreign countries.

Delta Flight 1720, Portland to Dallas, October 29, 1989

I departed Chin Hae, Korea, last Friday. While in port, I invited myself aboard an old WW II LST under the Korean flag. One of the officers took me on a tour of the pilot house, control tower, and signal bridge—scenes of my former duties as a Sailor. These areas had been significantly modified. However, some of the twin 40 mm guns were still in place. Scheduled for decommissioning next year, the ship brought back a flood of memories.

The next morning I got my passport stamped at Masan and then took a taxi to Pusan to pick up my plane ticket for departure the next day. My driver spoke no English, and I speak no Korean. After driving some distance, we came into a small town. Pointing to a store ahead, I spoke the international word "Coca Cola." He smiled and nodded agreement. Returning from the store I handed him his Coke, and he handed me a beautiful metal-encased letter opener. Then I remembered that if a Korean receives a gift, he must give one in return. Of course, the value of his gift far exceeded the value of mine, but it was all he had available in the car. Somewhat embarrassed, I graciously accepted his letter opener.

The forty-mile taxi ride to Pusan gave me an opportunity to see something of the Korean mountainous countryside with small ter-raced plots for farm use. Just outside of Pusan, wetlands, the home of many migratory birds, stretch extensively. Smoke from burning rice fields hung over much of the country. I noticed this when we were involved in a week of amphib exercises off Pohang, but the industrialization of the south coast of Korea surprised me.

Hyundai, the company that built my taxi, also builds buses, trains, and missiles. Good roads, modeled after American, link up the towns. Manufacturing everything from missiles to clothing, Koreans seem to be a people in a hurry to move ahead. Their school system reflects this same industriousness. High school students go to school from 8:00 a.m. to 6:00 p.m. six days a week for four years. And only ten percent of the schools have organized sports.

American influence permeates everything in Korea—clothing, music, TV programming, advertising, roads, and architecture. Downtown Pusan looks much like any large American city without zoning restrictions. An industrial supply store may share a common wall with a fine furniture store. Such was the case for about a three-mile stretch down an eight-lane thoroughfare in Pusan. Prices for anything did not tempt me.

About two blocks from the waterfront, I wandered through some side streets and encountered what I always thought would be typical of an Asian seaport—junk souvenirs, over-priced merchandise, cheap-looking women, and loud-mouthed Sailors nursing a bottle. Here was a place where anything could happen and all of it bad. It looked like an ideal spot for an anti-American terrorist to toss a grenade. Further on, an open air produce market blended the smell of fresh vegetables, spicy prepared foods, and fish—including piles of dried squid. The prettiest thing in the entire area, a little tan and white puppy, just cocked his head and gave me a quizzical look.

Coming to Pusan a day ahead of my scheduled departure proved to be a wise decision. I expected to just pick up my prepaid ticket back to the states at the downtown office of the airline. But both my prepaid ticket and reservation were with Delta Airlines in Seoul! My travel arrangements didn't include a flight from Pusan to Seoul. The Koreans spoke almost no English. I spent hours in their office, on the phone to Seoul, and on the phone to the travel agency in Killeen, Texas, that finally solved my transportation problem. I wanted to show my appreciation to the long-suffering Korean airline clerk and invited him out for some refreshment. He took me to a bar and ordered some kind of alcoholic drink, which arrived with something that looked like dried squid. He explained that mixed drinks always came with food to keep people from getting tipsy. Americans should take note.

Before an afternoon departure the next day, I went for a long Sunday morning walk. All of the American ships had left, and it appeared that I was the only westerner among thousands of Koreans. Being much taller than the Koreans, I stood out, and each one I met seemed to stare at me. I was the oddity. Then it hit me. The only thing connecting me to my world on the other side of the planet was a passport, an airline ticket, three credit cards, and about four hundred dollars in cash. Just paper and plastic, but what vital paper and plastic! American citizenship never looked better. And nothing I have seen in the last six weeks looked any better than the snow-capped Rockies below this airplane.

Postscript: The USS *Stein* was decommissioned on March 19, 1992. Mexico purchased the vessel on January 29, 1997.

USS John F. Kennedy (Photo courtesy of Elsilrac Enterprises)

USS *John F. Kennedy* CV-67

Off East Florida Coast, January 15, 1990

Since leaving Norfolk twelve days ago, this aircraft carrier has cruised up and down the East Coast of the United States conducting day and night air operations involving nine squadrons, including two squadrons of F-14 Tomcat fighter aircraft. It's been a full schedule.

F-14 Tomcats taking off for night training

With my bunk located directly under the flight deck next to the motors that operate the third of four arresting cables that stop the incoming planes, some of my first experiences startled me. Cable three, the preferred touch down point on the flight deck for the thirty-ton screaming Tomcats, is positioned about eight feet overhead, a disquieting attention-getter. Upon touchdown the pilots give the engines military power (full throttle) until the plane's tail hook engages the cable. This insures a safe take-off if the plane's hook fails to engage the cable. Once the cable disengages, the whining machinery drags the cable about four hundred feet along the deck to get it into position for the next incoming aircraft.

Four steam-powered catapults—two on the bow, two on the angled deck—propel the planes along a 150-foot track from zero to 160 knots within three seconds, giving the ship a loud jolt, as the aircraft becomes airborne. "Who has woe...who has redness of the eyes...?" Not only he that tarries long at the wine, but also he that tries to sleep in all this commotion. Old timers tell me that I will adjust, and change does tend to keep people young, healthy, and free from boredom.

Having recently arrived from a frigate, I find the immense size of an aircraft carrier overwhelming. Ocean swells that would have sent the USS *Stein* into fifteen-degree rolls have virtually no effect on this ship. I sense movement by looking at the sea. Yet its massive screws, twenty-one feet in diameter, can propel the carrier in excess of thirty knots.

Holding a ship this size at anchor also requires outstanding engineering. Anchor chains, weighing 123 tons, hold in place two bow anchors weighing thirty tons each. Just one link weighs 367 pounds. The brake controlling the anchor's descent uses a drum about eight feet in diameter and two feet in width. A brake band encircles the drum and operates much like a windmill brake. Two other brake systems back up the primary system.

About 5,000 Sailors make up the population of this sea-going island. Highly motivated students in four two-hour basic skills classes fill up my teaching day. Seeing young men take pride in academic achievement continues to be very satisfying. Since safety and successful missions depend upon their job skills and dedication, I guess it's only natural that this attitude spills over into the academic area.

January 16, 1990, Mayport, Florida

Last night the officers performed one of their periodic "Fo'c'sle Follies." "Fo'c'sle" is what Navy people call the ship's forecastle, a huge area housing the anchor chains and capstans. Songs and skits, intermingled with ribald humor, poked fun at everyone from the admiral on down. It's a way of letting off steam. On long cruises, the ship may stage a talent show or smoker to foster good morale.

Between my early afternoon class and evening class, I took a quick tour of the Mayport area, including long, white, beautiful, but cold beaches. An important naval base, Mayport hosts two carriers and several smaller ships at this time. Jacksonville, some twenty miles away, straddles the St.John River, which played a vital part in America's history. Surrounded by lush forests, the wide river instigated a major ship building industry when wooden ships ruled the seas. Early on, the river attracted more tourists than the Mississippi River. Jacksonville, now an important financial center, sprawls over more than 800 square miles.

January 17, 1990, Mayport, Florida

This is a now-it-can-be-told story. The Florida Times-Union printed a picture of the USS *John F. Kennedy* in today's edition with the following caption: "The aircraft carrier USS *John F. Kennedy*, escorted by tugs and a helicopter for security and safety, arrived at Mayport Naval Station basin yesterday afternoon for supplies, giving some of its 5,000 officers and enlisted personnel liberty. The *Kennedy* was to have served as the centerpiece of a drug interdiction operation in the Caribbean, but Columbia objected to the operation." Whether Columbia changes its stance remains to be seen. Meanwhile, the carrier awaits new orders.

The crews of all naval vessels receive constant reminders to say nothing about the ship's mission or its schedule. But then the men call home and learn that the ship's movements have been on the nightly news. It only takes one news leak to abort a carefully planned, expensive operation. News leaks in Washington harassed President Reagan's administration; it appears that President Bush will have the same problem.

The *Kennedy* command primed two fighter squadrons for the aborted operation, the Swordsmen and the Tophatters. Having observed its 70th anniversary last year, the Tophatters are the Navy's oldest aviation squadron. Strangely, no one in the squadron, or even the entire Navy, seems to know how the Tophatters came by that designation. The Swordsmen squadron splashed two Libyan MIGs in a four-on-four confrontation in the Mediterranean last year. All the squadrons designed patches especially for the anticipated drug interdiction. The Swordsmen's patch reads, "Deep-Six a Doper" and "We Smoke Dopers." The mere presence of one of these hot fighters on the wing of a dope-laden plane would be enough to intimidate the drug runners.

This morning a teen-age enlisted man was cleaning the chief petty officers' head when I greeted him with, "Hello, how are you doing?"

He glumly replied, "My father always told me that nothing comes free."

"What happened?" I asked.

He said he had gone to a strip joint for the first time in his life the previous evening. One of the young girls asked him if he would like to see her dance. He allowed as how that would be all right with him. One dance led to another and he began to wonder why she was doing this when she could be making money. When he got ready to leave, he found out she had been making money. It cost him five bucks a dance. Today, he was cleaning toilets and pondering the loss of his money—and his innocence.

January 19, 1990, Mayport, Florida

The USS *John F. Kennedy* has a new admiral on board to take command of Carrier Group four. The XO had given strict orders to keep the hanger bay quiet during the ceremony taking place one deck up. Because of all the foot traffic through the hanger bay, someone decided to maintain quiet by closing the huge division doors to isolate the space. The button that activates the doors also sets off an ear-spitting blast sustained for a full minute. At that precise moment the chaplain began his invocation. He got as far as, "Our Father...." The dignitaries at the ceremony will never forget this memorable occasion—neither will the Sailor who pushed the button!

Early today, I finished in the middle of the pack of some of the crew in a 5K run. Some of these men are serious runners. The ship's captain finished third. Later in the day, I added mileage to my legs by walking a long stretch of Jacksonville's clean, white beach. A few surfers braved the chilly water. A few joggers plodded back and forth. A few lovers strolled together. A few loners like me just soaked up the serenity. At water's edge just the screech of seagulls mingled with the roar of breakers, a welcome contrast to the carrier's harsh sounds.

January 19, 1990, Mayport, Florida

Today's activities focused on a four-hundred-mile round trip to the Kennedy Space Center, which also held the expectation of interesting sight-seeing for my first trip to Florida. But sight-seeing turned out to be 400 miles of Interstate 95 flanked by pine trees. Near the space center, ravaged orange groves attested to last month's killing freeze.

Located amid one of America's largest wildlife reserves, the space center harbors wild life ranging from alligators and turtles to blue herons and bald eagles, all of which could be seen on a tour around the environs. Of course, the rocket displays and indoor films offer an impressive insight into the history, methods, and rationale of

America's space program. It's a great time to be an American!

January 25, 1990, Caribbean Sea

A January week spent in Florida sounds like a tourist's dream. Most of the *John F. Kennedy* crew spent the week in Mayport, Florida, trying to go somewhere else. The ship did sponsor two picnics with plenty of beer. Except for my trip to the Kennedy Space Center, attending a "real" church on land highlighted my week.

Arriving an hour early at a church near the beach, I soaked up the morning sun along the deserted shore where dolphins humped their way through a school of fish that served up themselves to diving pelicans. The balance of nature always fascinates me.

January 29, 1990

Leaving Mayport Tuesday, we headed toward the Caribbean for war games with three other carriers and their support vessels. The ship resumed day and night flight operations. Last night, this carrier fired two surface-to-air missiles. The day before, F-14's fired Phoenix missiles, the Navy's most sophisticated air to air weapon. All missiles scored direct hits.

The war games in progress essentially involved our pilots who also searched for submarines. This routine training exercise took place south of Puerto Rico, which is also north of South America. In view of President Bush's imminent talks with South American heads of state in Columbia and the threats on his life by the Colombian drug cartel, the question naturally arises, what support, if any, will these carriers render in that February meeting?

Tomorrow, the question becomes academic for me since I will fly off the carrier to Puerto Rico where I will take a commercial jet to my next assignment out of California after a couple of days at home in Texas.

My students in the high school refresher courses weren't ready for classes to end last night. I am really proud of these men who try so hard to improve their language skills. Most moved up one to three grades, but one man tested in at seventh grade level four weeks ago and tested out at 12.9

San Juan, Puerto Rico, January 31, 1990

Two days ago the ship launched a C-2 aircraft with me aboard going from zero to 160 knots in less than three seconds. That's about two G's, which is not as much force as that developed by a typical dragster through the quarter mile, according to two pilots who discussed it over dinner one evening. Passengers in the plane face rear-ward, wearing seats belts, shoulder harness, noise reducing helmets, and life vests. The plane, known as a COD, doubles as a cargo carrier and has two tiny windows in the passenger space. Consequently, the only sensation of speed at take-off comes from the momentary pressure against the shoulder harness.

After landing at Roosevelt Roads and learning that the BOQ had no vacancies, a Navy driver took me to San Juan. Wanting to avoid heavy traffic because of rain, the driver wound through some of the more impoverished areas of Puerto Rico, finally emerging onto a coastal road leading to a long stretch of plush hotels and high rise condos. I checked into one of the hotels to the strain of a Latin combo playing off the lobby, ate supper, and headed for the beach.

The rain had stopped. Occasionally the crescent moon, ac-companied by Orion and Pleiades, pierced the low-hanging clouds carried by a cool breeze over a deserted beach stretching endlessly in both directions. Combers breaking through the ebb tide completed the harmony of sight and sound. My best night's sleep in four weeks followed a long leisurely stroll along the beach. Tourists, arriving on the heels of the hurricane season, frolicked in full swing in San Juan. Tattered awnings and taped windows attested to a recent visit by a hurricane. Otherwise, the balmy island contrasted considerably to the weather I left in Texas a month ago. Today, the same beach that enchanted me last night begs me to stay longer, but duty calls—and so does my flight out of here.

Postscript: The USS *John F. Kennedy* was decommissioned on March 23, 2007, and joined other mothballed vessels at the Inactive Ships Maintenance Facility in Philadelphia, Penn.

USS Gridley (Photo courtesy of Elsilrac Enterprises)

USS *Gridley* CG-21

February 20, 1990, San Diego, California

Officially, the USS *Gridley* became my new assignment today. In reality, I am attached to YRBM37, a Navy berthing barge for the entire six-week' class session. While in dry dock, *Gridley* will be undergoing repairs for more than a year. Crew's quarters, ship's store, galley, and other crew support facilities on the barge are similar to that on board the guided missile cruiser. The major difference from my perspective is a bone fide classroom. Classes run from 8 a.m. to 8:40 p.m., with breaks for meals five days a week. Considering the papers I must grade, that's a bit rugged, but it does leave the weekends free to get reacquainted with Southern California.

This tour of duty offers no interaction with the crew except for the students in my classes. That's probably just as well. During my first meal, a lieutenant sitting directly across the table from me asked, "Where are you from?"

"Texas," I replied.

"I don't like Texas."

Smiling, I said, "Really? Texas is a pretty large state. Which part do you not like?"

"I don't like the people."

I thought he was kidding. He wasn't, and the other officers remained silent. So I won't bother to press my luck with any of them. Rather, I will devote myself to teaching, sight seeing, and physical fitness.

A room equipped with exercise machines lies adjacent to the living quarters on the barge. In addition, the naval base has a fully equipped gym located about a mile away. I can get a pretty good workout in an hour by running to the gym, working out with weights, and then running to the ship.

The Navy permits basic skills courses to be taught during working hours. However, college classes must be conducted during non-working hours. Since there are neither ocean-going duties nor standard watches for the crew, the schedule easily breaks down into day sessions for the basic skills students and evening sessions for the college classes.

One straight "A" college student made my time here a little more interesting. He grew up in Ohio and had a visit from some relatives during my time on the barge. He and his wife invited me into their home for dinner one night during a visit from his folks. They presented me with the only buckeye I have ever seen. All are down-to-earth, friendly people and the Sailor's wife attends some of the classes along with him.

February 24, 1990, San Diego, California

San Diego is one of my favorite towns, and I am glad to be able to spend this time where I went through naval boot camp in 1944. I revisited Camp Decatur. The "grinder" where I spent many hours of marching to the music of John Philip Souza seems much smaller. Nearby, the mockup of a destroyer has been added to give new recruits a taste of shipboard life. The scene brought back one nearly forgotten funny incident.

Some of my fellow recruits had a hard time adjusting from civilian to military life and talked after "Taps". The drill instructor trying to get some sleep admonished them to be quiet. The whispering continued in the dark barracks. Finally, the DI bellowed into the dark to nobody in particular, "All right! Hit the deck!"

Raising his head, the red-headed culprit asked, "Who?"

The DI said, "You!"

He made the recruit get fully dressed and then pack up all of his gear sea-going style by placing all his clothing and personal items into his sea bag. Next, using his rope, he had to lash his mattress, pillow, blankets, and hammock into a long roll that wrapped around his sea bag. His tied-up belongings looked like a small life raft. Then, while everybody else went to sleep, this guy got to march around the grinder carrying a fairly heavy load. Thereafter, we had a quiet barracks after "Taps".

Old Town San Diego holds some rather dramatic memories. I celebrated V-J Day there on August 15, 1945, the day the Allies accepted the surrender of Japan in World War II. What is now the Gas Light District was the central business district in those days, and revelers packed the streets, making automobile travel impossible. To the amusement of everybody watching, one inebriated Sailor vainly tried to direct traffic.

I had recently completed four months of quartermaster training at Gulfport, Mississippi, and was ready to join the fleet for the anticipated invasion of Japan when two atom bombs ended the war. Without the time spent in additional training, I might have been assigned to an amphibious ship to assault Okinawa, the last big battle in the Pacific. The LST to which I subsequently reported saw action at both Iwo Jima and Okinawa. Among other responsibilities it received casualties from the beaches and got the soldiers and Marines patched up enough to be sent to a transport for return to the states. At Okinawa, a Kamikaze plane attempted to sink the ship, but the ship's twin 40mm and 20mm guns splashed it off the port side. The crew used to hold an annual reunion, but very few of us are left.

The barge for the *Gridley* crew is moored close to a busy street strewn with broken glass along the curb. Thieves simply smash the windows of cars parked there and steal their radios. A streetcar line connects downtown San Diego with Tijuana, Mexico. I made one brief trip to Tijuana just to look around. It looks about the same as the towns across the Rio Grande from Texas.

I used one Saturday to visit La Jolla Beach and almost didn't recognize it. In 1944, it was just a rocky beach with a pier and bathhouse. My salient memory of the beach was getting slammed against the boulders in the surf while rescuing a little boy who had been caught in an undertow. Now the place is fully developed suburbia with interesting marine life for visitors to see along the shore.

The old "clang, clang" trolleys that I remember are gone. Now, streetcars combined with city buses afford cheap, reasonably fast transportation anywhere in the city. I make extensive use of the system every weekend and some nights, often going to Anthony's Fish Grotto, a restaurant right on the waterfront, to enjoy their excellent clam chowder while watching sailboats during the sunsets. The same management has another restaurant, which is a bit more upscale, right across the street. Here, I renewed my friendship with one of my former students from Westbury Christian School and her boyfriend. With so much to talk about, we stayed until the restaurant closed. She has lived in California for several years.

I spent another evening at Groce's Restaurant, which is owned by the widow of Jim Groce who died in a plane crash in Natchitoches, Louisiana in 1973, the year that his song "Bad, Bad Leroy Brown" was a number one hit. The jazz band really livens up the place about 8:30 p.m.

February 26, 1990, San Diego, California

My daughter Gail came from Los Angeles for a weekend visit. She had traded her BMW for a Jeep Wrangler, which is the "in thing" at this time. We rode in it to the President Richard M. Nixon Library at San Clemente where we read his version of Watergate. Gail collects autographed books, and I bought her one autographed by Nixon. With her transportation, we also took in the immense Hunington Gardens.

As is my custom, I saw a great deal of San Diego by long walks through Old Town San Diego, along the ocean front, and around the zoo, which is one of the best in the country. In high school, my biology teacher assured me that the Piltdown Man really did exist. At the zoo, I photographed a framed explanation that suggests that Piltdown Man was a hoax, thought to be perpetrated by Sir Arthur Conan Doyle.

A historical hoax.
Explanation is in the framed texts.

Gail had never been on a warship. Since work on the USS *Gridley* had been suspended for the weekend, I secured permission to take her aboard. A ship this size is a bit overwhelming when viewed from the keel. Then climbing up to a catwalk, we entered the vessel near the pilothouse. None of the shipshape orderliness to which I was accustomed presented itself. Black grime covered everything that was in some state of repair. But Gail enjoyed the visit, and could see that the ship would again become a formidable fighting machine in a few months.

Because the weather had turned a little chilly, we welcomed the heaters at an outdoor restaurant where we had lunch. Later I bought her a sweater. We spent the night in a hotel and watched an Andy Griffith movie. Gail had lived far away from Texas for ten years, and mostly, I just enjoyed being with her.

A couple of weeks later, I took the Amtrak to Los Angeles to spend another weekend with my daughter. She lived in a rather secluded apartment overlooking Beverly Hills. After we visited a local museum and she showed me the sights around Beverly Hills, we took in the movie *No Way Out*, starring Kevin Costner.

March 4, 1990, San Diego, California

My world is getting smaller. Tonight I had dinner at the home of one of the staff officers I chummed around with when we were assigned to the USS *Belknap*. His next assignment will be the Pentagon. While attending the theater at Balboa Park the preceding Sunday afternoon, I caught sight of a lieutenant who recently arrived from *Belknap* for an assignment in San Diego.

Back in January while I was aboard the *Kennedy*, another *Belknap* Sailor hailed me from across the hanger deck. Then last weekend, the *Stein* returned from its WESTPAC, and I renewed my acquaintance with some of that crew.

Postscript: The USS *Gridley* was decommissioned on January 21, 1994, and subsequently sold to International Shipbreaking Corp. at Brownsville, Texas for scrapping.

USS John F. Kennedy (Photo courtesy of Elsilrac Enterprises)

USS *John F Kennedy* CV-67
Deployments 2 and 3

Norfolk, Virginia, April 26, 1990

Many friendly familiar faces greeted me as I returned to the USS *John F Kennedy* today for a four-week teaching assignment consisting of four classes of Basic English involving about sixty students. The E.S.O. is making a concerted effort to get a G.E.D. for all Sailors who did not graduate from high school.

Off the U.S. East Coast, May 4, 1990

The policy of frequent emergency drills aboard Navy vessels paid off today. While linked up to the USS *Platt* for refueling, the ship had to do an emergency break away. Two days earlier the crew had gone through a break away drill. Apparently the ship lost control of the port rudder when a crewman doing an electrical repair failed to follow established procedures and inadvertently disconnected the power to the rudder. Trained reaction prevented a collision at sea and the two ships resumed refueling in a matter of minutes.

The number of ways a ship's personnel can be injured and the equipment damaged aboard a warship are practically unlimited. Even discounting the fact that the ship is a floating ammunition dump and fuel storage facility with thirty-ton jets landing at high speed, countless obstructions and projections afford constant opportunity for cuts, scrapes, bruises, and fractures. Yet this 5000-man crew is remarkably free of injuries. But in spite of the constant attention to safety, some accidents do occur. The body of one crewman missing since February surfaced when the ship pulled away from the pier at Norfolk last week. Apparently, he fell overboard when nobody was looking. A few weeks ago another crewman nearly lost a finger when his wedding ring got caught on a piece of metal. Such occurrences are rare and mostly could be avoided by following established rules and procedures. The accidents on this ship probably are no more numerous or severe than they are in any other city of 5,000 population.

Today I witnessed my first burial at sea. The ashes of two former chief petty officers were brought on board and committed to the Atlantic Ocean during a memorial service conducted by a chaplain. Wearing dress whites the commanding officer, as well as other top ranking officers, participated in the ceremony. Following a 21-gun salute by seven Marines in dress blues, a first class petty officer played "Taps."

Last night the C.O. told the crew via closed circuit that the *Kennedy* would engage the French carrier *Fuch* in some mock battle exercises off Puerto Rico in three days. Meanwhile, flight operations, along with fire drills, casualty drills, and man-over-board drills, continue both day and night.

Although the weather is an important factor, it doesn't seem to slow down flight operations. High winds and rain a few days ago got a lot of people wet, but otherwise had little effect on the men or the aircraft. This week Carrier Group Commander (CAG) Mike Johnson made his 1200th carrier landing, his 100th on the JFK. And Cmdr Edward Fahy, commanding officer of VA-46, made his 900th carrier landing. These feats are rather remarkable considering that some have described a carrier landing as a controlled crash landing. Both men received recognition in the May 9, 1990 issue of the *Bird Farm Bulletin*, the ship's newspaper.

Approaching Cmdr. Johnson, I asked, "How about taking me for a ride in your F-14 Tomcat."

"I can only do that for an important newspaper reporter."

"Hey! I'm an important newspaper reporter. I write articles for the Bee County Picayune."

Laughing, he said, "I know about the Bee County Picayune. I got some of my training in Beeville, Texas!"

Pilots need to fly a minimum of about twenty hours per month just to maintain proficiency. For combat readiness, they need about thirty hours. That's a fact of life the American taxpayers need to take into account when trimming the defense budget. Logic seems to dictate a combat ready ship and crew or none at all.

One pilot described a carrier night landing as the hardest job in the world. But even with the physical and mental stress that goes with flying high performance aircraft, the pilots say they would rather be in the air than anywhere else. An aircraft carrier exists for that purpose.

I guess the Navy is corrupting me. Today an officer made me a cup of cappuccino with sugar and cinnamon. Normally, I avoid both coffee and sugar. Food aboard this carrier is good—sometimes outstanding. This week's fare included prime rib, oyster stew, and clam chowder. Fresh fruit and vegetables are abundant.

North of Puerto Rico, May 9, 1990

Having finished flight operations with the French aircraft carrier northeast of Puerto Rico, we are steaming back to Norfolk under cloudy skies and moderate seas. Even moderate seas create no sense of movement on this huge ship. Without seeing the ocean, the sensation is about the same as being at a pier.

The air operations with the French went according to plan. Except for a few passes by French fighter craft, none of the mock combat was visible to the ship's crew. Although we did get within 500 yards of the *Fuch*, haze and cloudy skies precluded picture-taking opportunities. An exchange of personnel between the ships enhanced the goodwill between the two fighting units.

Norfolk, Virginia, May 12, 1990

Our passage up Hampton Roads to the pier at Norfolk was almost routine. But enroute, a sailboat decided to cut across our bow. After three blasts on the ship's horn and a course correction, the ship managed to miss the boat. I saw the whole episode unfold from the seventh deck of the ship's island. Even at that height, I could see only a few feet of the boat's mast as the boat slipped past our port side, a very dangerous proximity. Each of the twin screws on *JFK* weigh 69,000 pounds. Had the sailboat been sucked into those screws, both boat and crew probably would have been destroyed, resulting in more headlines about "another Navy accident" with the usual charges of malfeasance and stonewalling.

The 1MC on a carrier is especially loud so messages can be heard over flight deck noise. As nearly as I can recall, the commanding officer addressed the departing sailboat as follows: "This is the captain of the *John F. Kennedy* speaking. That was a remarkable display of damn poor seamanship. Good day!"

I wonder about the mentality of anyone who would play "chicken" with an aircraft carrier. Sailboats have the right-of-way over most power driven vessels, but not warships.

We are berthed a pier away from the battleship USS *Wisconsin*. This is the ship that was scheduled to be permanently homeported in Corpus Christi. That seems uncertain in view of today's newspaper headlines proclaiming massive cuts in next year's Navy budget.

USS Wisconsin

A few piers away rests the USS *Iowa*, which went through de-commissioning ceremonies the day we pulled out of port for exercises in the Caribbean. The last time I had seen that ship was at Ankara, Turkey when Vice Admiral Williams, Commander U.S. Sixth Fleet temporarily transferred his staff to it from *Belknap*.

New York, June 24, 1990

After completing my last Basic English assignment aboard the *JFK*, I returned to teach another four–week session of Basic English classes. What follows is a synopsis of that four-week period while the ship was in New York. The ESO still had a number of Sailors who needed to get their G.E.D.s. Since we conducted all classes during the day, I had weekends free to sight-see the city and took in as much as I could.

Starting at the lower end of Manhattan Island, I criss-crossed the town from south to north and west to east seeing places I had always

USS John F. Kennedy entering New York Harbor

heard about. After spending some time at the New York Stock Exchange I went to the World Trade Center and took an elevator to the roof of one of the buildings to get a panoramic view of New York. Enroute I noticed one of a number of rather disheveled men asleep on a sidewalk bench. This one had a book lying on his chest entitled *How to Win Friends and Influence People* by Dale Carnegie. Passing him I thought, "This guy may be down on his luck, but I'd give odds that he won't stay there."

I was fascinated by the distinctive character of the various sections of Manhattan, such as China Town, which contrasted with places like the Fifth Avenue shops, Grand Central Station, and the United Nations.

One Saturday my E.S.O., a warrant officer, and I were on our way to the Museum of Natural History when a parade of homosexuals who called themselves Act Up blocked our street crossing. I had encountered this same noisy, profane, and slovenly dressed group the day before when they also blocked my crossing and had a police escort. One of the men from the group accosted the E.S.O. in his dress white uniform and offered him some literature. When my friend politely declined, the homosexual called him a pervert before rejoining the parade. For a couple of nights, the Empire State Building was bathed in pink lights.

While *Kennedy* was in port, a plain-clothes man and woman from the New York Police Department spent some time aboard for security reasons. I made their acquaintance by offering them a cup of cappuccino from the ship's wardroom. Later they invited me to join them and some of their friends for dinner at an upscale restaurant and refused to let me pay for my own dinner. Over the years, I've heard many comments about the aloofness of New Yorkers, but I've never met a more gracious group of people than those from the NYPD.

Without sea duty distractions, my students did quite well. After completing the grammar section of the course, the student customarily writes a 250-word essay to demonstrate his grasp of the subject matter. Typical of many high school students, one young man said, "I don't know anything to write about. You gimme something to write about."

"OK," I said, "Where are you from?"

"Georgia,"

"Did you live in town or on a farm?"

"Farm"

"Did you have any cows?"

"Yeah."

"Write something about cows."

It turned out that he grew up on a dairy farm and wrote a fairly decent essay about the process of milking cows. He mentioned getting the cows into the stalls, cleaning their udders and hooking the prongs from the milking machines to the cows' tits. He made a few minor errors, so I asked him to correct them and re-write his paper saying, "By the way, cows don't have tits. They have teats."

"They have what?"

"Teats."

"That ain't what we called 'em."

"That's not what we called them on the farm where I grew up either, but that's what they are. The word is in the dictionary, t-e-a-t. Look it up."

I don't remember that young man's name, but I'll never forget the punch line to his corrected essay: "So you see, there's more to milking cows than just playing with their tits."

USS O'Brien (Photo courtesy of Elsilrac Enterprises)

USS *O'Brien* DD-975

Hawaii, July 30, 1990

Upon completing my assignments with the USS *John F. Kennedy*, I returned to Texas and soon got a call from the San Diego Office of Central Texas College to return to San Diego for an assignment aboard the USS *O'Brien*.

Tomorrow morning this ship, a Spruance class destroyer, will inport at Pearl Harbor, ending a six-day voyage out of San Diego. Being one of the newer warships in the fleet, *O'Brien*, powered by gas turbines instead of steam, compares in size to *Belknap*. Before a steamship can get underway, the boilers must be fired up hours in advance. This ship can get underway within minutes and can go from zero to thirty knots within three lengths of the ship. Equipped with cruise missiles, the ship also packs weaponry more powerful and sophisticated than *Belknap*.

I welcome a change from the aircraft carrier I just left. A crew of three hundred friendly people contrasts sharply with a crew of five thousand where I was just a number. Living accommodations include a three-man stateroom with an ample office.

Classes got off to a good start albeit somewhat frustrating. I teach two different college writing college courses, but the college sent me four different textbooks, three of which I had never seen before. Students taking the same subject ended up paying different prices for their books. One syllabus was out of date, and I had to completely write two others. All this along with registration and organizing the classes! Anyone who lacks creativity and adaptability has no business being a PACE instructor.

After onloading ammunition, including cruise missiles, just outside the harbor at San Diego, the ship immediately initiated drills of various sorts. A submarine accompanies us and the helicopter pilots have really been logging long hours in anti-submarine warfare drills. The sonar techs stay glued to their screens. The ship conducts GQ drills daily. The new personnel on board plus the short time the ship has been on extended sea duty makes the drills even more urgent. The first GQ drill out of San Diego required eleven minutes to get the ship watertight with battle stations manned. The crew now has it down to six minutes.

The sea has been pleasant all the way. Low swells have given the ship three to five degree rolls most of the time. Even so, a few guys got seasick. I wondered if it weren't psychological because a rocking chair will create that much motion.

Yesterday, a sizable group met in my classroom for church service, my first day just to relax and enjoy the trip. This ship doesn't have a chaplain, but one of the officers serves as a lay reader. People attending the service, including the commanding officer, were a cross section of the Protestant world. Church is the one place in the military where men can abandon the caste system. Following church service, we had a cookout on the main deck. Then the sun came out for the first time since we left California. I stood on one of the bridge wings for a long time just soaking up the sun and watching the flying fish. Later, I took a turn at steering the ship. I think I surprised the Officer of the Deck by knowing how to handle the helm and give the proper response to his commands. It's fun to renew old quartermaster skills. When I was on the aircraft carrier, I did some sun lines with a sextant. This ship's quartermaster has invited me to do both sun and star sightings when we leave Pearl Harbor.

The ship receives a daily printout of weather maps similar to

Relaxing on the Port Bridge Wing

the ones on commercial television. One of the charts showed the area from California to Hawaii, clearly revealing the overcast that we experienced most of the way, along with two typhoons southeast of us. Tonight darkness fell over a sparkling blue ocean with just enough whitecaps to break the wide expanse of water. The remaining cloud cover softened a brilliant moon. I would never tire of such nights at sea.

This ship has the best weight room of any ship on which I have served. Lifecycles and rowing machines make up for a lack of jogging space. In addition, plenty of free weights augment the universals along with popular omnipresent rock music.

Western Pacific, August 5, 1990

Seven young men just proved again that there really is a sucker born every minute. We just crossed the International Date Line. Ten minutes earlier the Officer of the Deck announced over the ship's 1MC that we were approaching the line and invited the ship's personnel to assemble on the foc's'le to take pictures of the "line" as we crossed it. And there they were—these seven guys—with cameras and binoculars ready to record the big event. People on the bridge and bridge wings had a hard time controlling hysterics.

Although Sunday has officially ended, we will consider the entire day Sunday and begin Tuesday at midnight. The whole crew needed a day to relax. Arising early this morning, I spent a pleasant time in the XO's chair on the port bridge wing watching the sea gulls, flying fish, and one albatross frolic over a calm ocean under a bright sun.

Following breakfast, I attended a church service and then spent an hour and a half in the weight room. After a leisurely lunch, the ship's captain, the command master chief, and I served as judges for a kite flying contest.

About a dozen entrants participated, but only three kites ever got off the deck. The shirtless spectators enjoyed their efforts and provided a lot of good-natured kidding. Then at four o'clock, we had another cookout on the fantail.

The ship is at Condition Three, meaning that we could respond immediately to any hostile move against the ship with all weapons manned and ready. A call to GQ would send the rest of the crew to their battle stations and close all watertight hatches. Such precautions prepare the crew for anticipated conditions in the Persian Gulf.

Two other situations have stressed out the crew the last few days. One of our evaporators malfunctioned, thereby restricting our water supply. Water has been turned off at certain hours, preventing anyone from taking showers last night. Only a shipboard fire presents

Kite judging contest

a more serious condition than the loss of water. The men in that division have worked around the clock to restore the evaporator to its normal function. They solved the problem early today, but one of the generators went out, knocking out some lights, the surface radar, and shutting down the evaporators again. The electricians took care of this problem very quickly, restoring all systems to normal.

Last Tuesday and Wednesday I got to revisit Hawaii. First, I had lunch at the Royal Hawaiian Hotel at Waikiki and then headed for the beach at Hanauma Bay where I spent the afternoon just walking the beach, taking pictures, and watching the waves break over the rocky point.

The next day, I took a trip around the Island of Oahu, something I had not be able to do on previous visits. The ship provided a bus for anyone who wanted to go. Surprisingly, few accepted the opportunity.

The ride through a rain forest took us to Pali Point, which provided a breath taking panorama of the terrain far below. King Kamehamea's last battle to win complete control of the island took place here. He demanded that the opposing leader, his cousin, surrender and join his army or be destroyed. The opposing faction chose to

Pali Point

Punch Bowl

Punch Bowl Monument

leap off the cliff.

A trip around Oahu had to include a stop at the Punch Bowl, an extinct ancient volcano, now a national cemetery for military personnel and other notable people. Ernie Pyle the famous World War II war correspondent rests there. The memorial includes diagrams of the most significant battles with the Japanese in WWII.

The famous Blow Hole stretches out just around the corner from the small secluded beach used in filming the beach scene in the movie *From Here to Eternity* starring Burt Lancaster and Debra Kerr. The calm ocean today minimized its display.

Some of the ship's crew swam at Waimea Park. I used my time there to soak up the scenery and enjoy some macadamia nut ice cream. Continuing our tour of the island through sugar cane and pineapple

Blow Hole on Oahu

fields, we stopped for fresh pineapple at the Dole plantation store.

As we left Pearl Harbor the next morning, we passed within about eight thousand yards of Kauai, one of the wettest spots on earth. Dense clouds the same size and shape of the island hung over Kauai in an otherwise cloudless sky. Before leaving the area, the ship conducted some gunnery exercises. A jet fighter flew over the ship several times towing a target. The CIWS hit the target every time and finally shot it down. The ship also fired one of its Sea Sparrow missiles. Besides Tomahawks and Sea Sparrows, the ship also carries harpoon missiles. Fifty cal. machine guns, along with 25mm guns capable of blowing a small ship out of the water, round out the arsenal. Also, the crew is becoming proficient in the use of small arms. All of these weapons, plus the ship's helicopter, make *O'Brien* a powerful force for a small ship.

We are about 2400 miles from the Philippine Islands and about the same distance from Hawaii on an ocean that continues to be unbelievably smooth. Today, not even white caps break the horizon. We haven't even seen another ship since leaving Pearl Harbor. How awesome to be so utterly alone in God's great universe, except for about three hundred other men!

By night, the ocean shimmers under a full moon intermittently filtered by a thin veil of clouds. At night, the ship's wake looks like a long glistening snow bank and sounds like a giant waterfall, drowning out all other noise. But the ideal perch for night watching is the XO's chair on the port bridge wing. Here the dominant sounds come from gentle waves crested by the ship's bow as it plows through the water, creating phosphorescent streaks of light. Seated here with my feet on the rail, I just let the sights and sounds of the night engulf me. Sometimes I doze off to wake up to the same enchanting scene. This is peace. This is tranquility. This is serenity. This is too good to last.

We have had five thousand miles of remarkably smooth water, for we avoided two typhoons to our southwest as we left California, and currently, the weather map shows two more northwest of us. But I have seen the Pacific in the doldrums—slick as glass. In the days of sailing vessels, ships becalmed there for extended periods, faced a threat to survival. But by contrast, sometimes this ocean can be as hostile as a jilted mistress. I once passed through this same area in a typhoon so devastating that old Navy men still talk about it because the typhoon sunk some ships. Fortunately, I rode out that storm on an aircraft carrier. When it comes to danger, good fortune has almost always favored me.

Since the ship's destination is the Persian Gulf, I may need some more good fortune. According to the news arriving here, the situation in the Persian Gulf rapidly deteriorates. President Bush has ordered naval, air, and land units to that area. It's merely coincidental that this ship is going to Bahrain at this time, but I'm sure America's enemies would not believe that. The ship carries out daily drills designed for the kind of hostility expected in the Gulf. The crew can now set GQ in less than half the time required two weeks ago. Understandably, each news bulletin keenly interests the crew. Six hours constitutes a night's sleep for many.

One of the ship's cylindrical life rafts accidentally fell overboard yesterday, giving the crew an unexpected man overboard drill, the "man" being the life raft, which weighs about five hundred pounds and has no hooks or rings for easy retrieval. Using a cargo net, the deck crew struggled for an hour or more to bring it back on board. The raft was supposed to open automatically and inflate upon hitting the water. In a real emergency, it would have been useless. Consequently, the ship will check all rafts at Subic Bay.

Western Pacific, August 13, 1990

Another cookout took place on the fantail yesterday. Prior to that, the crew engaged in a skeet-shooting contest. Later some of the gunners practiced on the 50-cal. machine guns and 25mm guns. After dinner, a basketball tournament took place on the helicopter hanger bay. Three men per team faced off in a very confined area, but that didn't quell anyone's exuberance.

Philippine Islands, August 15, 1990

Shortly after dawn today, the first Philippine Island appeared off our starboard bow. By mid-morning, Luzon the scene of bitter fighting in World War II passed to starboard as the ship entered the San Bernardino Strait. Here Navy pilots sunk a Japanese battleship, one of the largest ever built. It is somewhere about a thousand feet below. The battle lasted two days.

San Bernardino Strait presents an interesting challenge for the navigator and quartermaster. No channel buoys mark the shipping lane, and currents contribute to the problem. Some ship captains have avoided the strait by taking the long way around these islands, especially in the old days before radar and satellite navigation. Getting caught in here in a sudden storm could spell disaster without modern navigation devices. Transmissions from both civilian and military satellites can fix the ship's position to an accuracy of three feet.

Subic Bay, Philippine Islands, August 16, 1990

We arrived in Subic Bay early this morning in a squall spun off from the storm brewing behind us. Even so, we had calm seas. Traveling all the way from California in smooth water has been an unbelievable experience. As we pulled up to the ammunition pier, the rain ceased and the sun dissipated the clouds and mist to reveal mountainous islands of profuse dark green foliage overlooking the aquamarine bay. The Philippines—land of a thousand islands—literally has seven thousand islands. What a tragedy that such sparkling beauty masks the poverty and political unrest that afflict the people here.

Positioned in a valley right off the naval base, much of the town of Olongapo has been placed off limits to the ship's crew. Going ashore to get my overseas I.D. issued, I had the good fortune to meet a chief petty officer that has served here for four years as a Navy diver. He provided me with a map and showed me which streets to avoid. My trip ashore only slightly acquainted me with the naval base and didn't acquaint me with Olongapo at all because a torrential rain returned.

The additional ammunition onloaded this morning suggests a change in mission for this ship. Originally, *O'Brien* was to replace a ship already in the Persian Gulf so that their crew could go home for a while. Complementing the ammunition onloaded at San Diego are more small arms ammo and additional cruise missiles in case Hussein doesn't get his act together.

As I write this, three drills are in progress: a major fuel oil leak, a fire, and a security alert. The guys who are ashore tonight really need to be ashore. For most of the last two weeks, the ship has been at "condition three." Some personnel are always at their battle stations. Lack of sleep has almost left both officers and men in a fog. The routine has taken a heavy toll on my classes. Most of the students stand two six-hour watches per day; work another six hours; and then eat, sleep, study, and go to class during the other six hours. Out of forty-eight students that started the courses, only twenty-eight remain, projecting the worst completion percentage I've ever had. And we are only half way through the courses.

Mail call highlighted my day—five letters and a newspaper from Nita; two letters, a care package, and a zany tape from my daughter Gail; and the return of lesson number one of an algebra course I'm taking by correspondence from Southwest Texas State University. Mail call: It's the tie that binds.

Subic Bay, P.I., August 19, 1990

This ship doesn't depart on Monday after all, but I do, assuming that space is available on a MAC flight out of here back to the states. I would prefer a commercial flight out of Manila today, but no U. S. civilians are authorized to fly out of Manila by a directive from the White House. This sudden turn of events disappoints me, but I really have no business being a part of this ship's future.

Naturally, the ship's new orders also disappoint my active students, but their days and nights will become even more hectic. Neither they nor the ship's command need to be distracted by college courses at this time. College has suddenly become relatively unimportant. But most of the students have made it clear that they would like to restart the classes with me as the instructor when circumstances allow, an unlikely event.

The fringe of the storm that followed us into Subic Bay still hangs around. Rain cancelled a picnic planned for the ship's crew on Grande Island. Officers have canceled golf dates. No horseback riding, no water skiing, no nothing we anticipated doing here except dodging the rain on trips to some indoor activity on the naval base. Some of the men have gone into Olongapo with reports that it has all the characteristics of a Mexican border town, only worse. P. I. is a beautiful country, and it's a shame to be stuck with three or four streets in an obscure town. So far, my big excitement ashore has been a phone call to my answering machine in Houston followed by a Coke with French fries at the Exchange. Oh, I did get to watch an episode of Batman while getting a haircut!

Honolulu, Hawaii, August 20, 1990

Today is my second August 20, 1990 as I crossed the International Date Line on a Philippine Airline 747 last night. While my military flight in a C-12 (Beech 200) lifted off the runway at Cubi Point Naval Air Station at Subic Bay, I saw the USS *O'Brien* heading out of port for a fast trip to the Persian Gulf. Two days ago the Navy changed the ship's mission and departure time three times within a few hours. Plans to escort some amphibs coming down from Japan were scrubbed upon learning that the USS *David R. Ray*, the ship *O'Brien* was originally supposed to relieve anyway, had developed some serious mechanical problems and needed immediate relief. *O'Brien* was supposed to take on additional personnel to become the command ship of a destroyer squadron. The captain commandeered my classroom for office space.

My attempt to leave Subic Bay via a MAC flight proved fruitless. The possibility existed for a flight in about a week. I didn't relish the idea of living in the BOQ with nothing to do but watch the remnant of a typhoon. Consequently, I got a written waiver, took a C-12 flight to Manila, and boarded the commercial flight back to the states. Tight schedule. It took all morning yesterday to work out the details, and my flight was already boarding when I arrived at the gate. I never would have made it, except for a stroke of luck when the C-12 landed. Some Filipino from the American Embassy offered to take me to the International Airport.

Last Saturday night I finally got off the naval base for a brief venture into Olongapo. The ship's personnel had a 10:30 p.m. curfew and a stern recommendation to avoid going alone into town. Therefore, I gladly accepted the invitation of two officers to a little party at the Cubie Point Officers Club celebrating the recent promotion of one of the men. But first they wanted to go into town for a beer. We dodged rain for two blocks amid countless sidewalk vendors, taxis, and streetwalkers—all vying for our attention but none receiving it. Olongapo looked like a poor Tijuana.

The guys had their beer at a bar where a number of very congenial girls played pool. Three of them stopped playing and became uninvited guests at our table. One kept insisting that I buy her a drink. I shoved one of the officers unopened beers her way. She refused it, saying she wanted a mixed drink. It's an old scam. Buy the lady a drink consisting of colored water and the bar is five bucks richer. I gave a firm, clear response: "I don't drink. I'm not going to buy you a drink. I'm just here because my friends are here." It took a while, but both she and the unhappy bar tender finally got the message and left me alone. The situation was similar to the Filipino bar scene in the movie *Nowhere to Run*, except these dancing girls wore more clothes.

As we left the bar to return to the base, torrents of rain suddenly descended and then stopped just as suddenly, drenching us to the skin. When we arrived at the officers club, we looked like we had swum across the bay instead of arriving in a taxi. This whole incident reminded me why I nearly always travel alone.

Postscript: The USS *O'Brien* was decommissioned on September 24, 2004, and subsequently sunk as a target in 2006.

USS Cushing (Photo compliments of Elsilrac Enterprises)

USS *Cushing* DD-985

Los Angeles, California, August 21, 1990

My daughter Gail was waiting for me at the L. A. International Airport after I cleared customs last evening. As soon as we had completed our hellos, she handed me a message to call the PACE coordinator in San Diego. It seems my presence is needed aboard the destroyer USS *Cushing* (DD-985) next Sunday. Destination? Persian Gulf! The Navy's ways sometimes "are past finding out." That's today's schedule. Who knows where the ship will actually go or how long it will take to get there? I'll simply teach the courses as best I can and try to find a friendly debarkation port before the ship gets in a shooting match with Iraq. I'm not sure why another destroyer is needed in the Persian Gulf. It seems to me that the Navy already has enough firepower on station to level the whole Middle East.

USS Cushing, North Pacific, September 1, 1990

After a six-day visit at home, I boarded this ship in San Diego. Faulty generators delayed our departure, but we have had four days of smooth seas and the ship now undergoes its first underway refueling.

I'm already familiar with *Cushing* because it's a Spruance class destroyer like *O'Brien*, which I left at Subic Bay. But at first, I experienced some apprehension about being assigned to an eighteen-man berthing area because the twenty-man berthing area I called home for two months on the USS *John F. Kennedy* was such a disaster that I finally appropriated a folding cot and slept in my classroom. However, only one congenial and very sharp officer, a medical doctor, shares it with me. When his name revealed his Polish ancestry, I grinned and asked, "Do you know any Polish jokes?"

"Do you speak Polish?"

"No."

"How does it feel to be dumber than a Pollock?"

Touché!

We are in company with three other ships: The USS *Sacramento*, an oiler; the USS *Fletcher*, another Spruance class destroyer; and the USS *Downes*, a frigate that accompanied the USS *Stein* when I traveled with that ship.

Two other civilians are on board, one a tech rep checking out electronic equipment, the other a lady scientist from some naval research facility. She experiments with a new type of scrambler for sending messages. Mealtime is about the only time I see either of them. The lady sleeps in sick bay.

The ship's captain and XO are quite friendly. The first day at sea, the captain called an orientation session for all "riders" such as civilians, air detachment personnel, and other non-crew members. Referring to us as special guests, he did not want to address us as "riders." He designated me to come up with an appropriate name, so I canvassed the group who suggested "Party Animals." Knowing the Navy's affinity for acronyms, I added "Lost at Sea." Thus we became known as P.A.L.S., which somewhat amused the captain.

The smooth seas that blessed my last ship for some eight thousand miles have also blessed this ship. The difference is that we are heading north into cold water. A jacket feels good. Nights are spectacular again. A waxing moon, heavy clouds, and crisp air delight the senses. The helicopter crew welcomes a bright moon for its anti-submarine drills. The usual shipboard drills have also been in progress—fire, man overboard, abandon ship, general quarters. Only the GQ drill really ties me down because all watertight hatches must remain sealed.

North Pacific, September 3, 1990

We have been on a heading of about 282 degrees since leaving San Diego. That's almost a straight line to Rat Island at the end of the Aleutian chain. Before leaving Texas, I understood that the ship would go to the Persian Gulf. Consequently, I brought no cold weather clothing, not even pajamas. Not much storage space exists on a Navy ship, so I travel with a minimum of baggage. Yesterday, I got rather chilled because much of the ship's temperature ranges from cool to cold. My stateroom buddy lent me some thermal underwear. Today I will see what warm clothing the ship's store has to offer.

A water shortage mandated that all showers be secured. Therefore, I haven't worked up my usual sweat in the exercise compartment.

Off Amchitka Island, Bering Sea, September 5, 1990

Following several days of stormy seas and overcast skies, the weather turned pleasant today. Bright sun put the temperature in the fifties, and what had been a thirty-knot wind has become a zephyr. Coming off our port beam yesterday, the wind caused the ship to carry a ten-degree list. Swells of ten to fifteen feet approaching head-on kept the forward main deck awash, casting spray back to the pilothouse. Predictably, the pitching, rolling ship causes some of the crew to get seasick. Because the ship handles the rough seas so well, I enjoyed the ride. Today, the ship's motion is barely perceptible. In spite of the pleasant weather, the atmosphere turns to a milky haze a few miles away, blocking visibility of nearby islands.

World news remains sketchy, but it appears that the Middle East crisis has become a stalemate. The economic sanctions against Iraq may eventually work, but by that time Kuwait likely will be ruined by vandals, neglect, and exploitation by Iraq. In the meantime, many displaced persons experience much worse conditions than the citizens of Iraq. There has to be a better way to handle the situation.

A submarine has joined the battle group, giving the ship's helicopter training in anti-submarine warfare. For about four days, various sea operations will take place in the Bering Sea and then the ship will head for Japan for more training exercises. The ship set the last GQ in four minutes, the best time of any ship on which I have served—an indication of an efficient crew. That speaks well of the ship's command, especially since the captain has only been the commanding officer for one month.

As we passed through Amchitka Strait into the Bering Sea late today, the Islands of Amchitka and Semisopochnoi flanked us. Both islands are of volcanic origin and appear to be barren except for some tundra and a few small patches of snow on the mountains. An

Moonrise over Amchitka Island

Sunset behind Semisopochnoi Island

unforgettable sight presented itself with a simultaneous sunset over Amchitka and a full moonrise over Semisopochnoi. The setting sun hanging just below the tip of Amchitka cast a shimmering golden shaft across the calm ocean all the way to the ship. As it sank below the horizon, lavender hues shrouded Amchitka while remaining daylight highlighted the wave crests with streaks of gold, contrasting with the blue in the shallow swells.

I have never before seen such a combination of colors in nature. Had an artist captured this scene on canvas, I would have assumed that he gave it his own interpretation. Transfixed by the sunset, I almost failed to notice the moonrise behind me. Poised just over the mountains of Semisopochnoi and casting a sparkling white beam across the blue water, the moonrise enchanted me as much as the sunset. I photographed both islands at several timed settings and hoped at least one would turn out even with the ship's movement.

Northwest Pacific, September 11, 1990

We transited Oglala Pass two days ago, leaving the Bering Sea after several days of anti-submarine exercises. Yesterday we officially crossed the Date Line, losing Sunday, and got our first unrep since leaving San Diego. The supply ship USS *Sacramento* also gave us a vertrep, using helicopters to deliver goods to *Cushing*'s fo's'cle— good timing since the ship had little milk on hand. But somehow the supply department has arranged to keep our meals filled with fresh vegetables, even lettuce. The supply officer says the key is to keep vegetables at about 52 degrees in a sealed environment. He says that automatic defrosters on home refrigerators cause rapid deterioration of vegetables. Anyway, we get a wide assortment of fresh vegetables twice a day. All other ships on which I have served have always had peanut butter available in the wardroom. Not this one. Instead, we have tuna salad available twice a day, a tradition started by some former captain of the ship. Tuna makes a good alternative in case the main dish doesn't appeal. With limited physical activity, most of us need to be careful about our calorie intake.

Periodically, an announcement typical of all Navy ships comes over the speaker system "to dump all trash overboard." This simple routine triggered a philosophical thought. A ship not only accumulates the usual household trash, but the men accumulate quite a lot of mental trash, such as vulgar language, degrading movies, and all sorts of annoyances arising from interaction with each other. The best Sailors are the ones who don't accumulate much mental trash at the outset. And they periodically "dump overboard" whatever mental trash they do accumulate. Call it imperturbability, forgive and forget, or whatever, it enables a person to tolerate close confinement for extended periods. "Dump all trash overboard." I like the idea.

Northwest Pacific, September 17, 1990

Today we are about fifty miles off the northeast coast of Honshu following an uneventful trip from the Aleutian Islands. Since moving about twelve degrees latitude farther south, we're back in short sleeve shirts are again. Although cloud cover has been the norm for the last week, the seas have been calm. Long, low swells give the ship a slight roll and no pitch while we travel in a circle waiting for a joint exercise with Japanese naval vessels.

These have been the days when basic values manifest themselves during free time—the exhilaration of cold mist on the face, the physical "high" from crisp clean air that truly invigorates the lungs, the rhythmic surf-sound of waves washing the ship's hull. As the Psalmist says, it has been a good time to "be still and know that I am God." The harmonizing of body, soul, and nature holds a memory to cherish and recall in whatever days of stress that lie ahead. I sometimes wonder if these long periods at sea are meant to mold me for some purpose yet to be revealed.

Yokosuka, Japan, September 24, 1990

We arrived here two days ago after a relatively smooth voyage all the way from San Diego. About a week before our arrival, we did have to take evasive action to avoid Typhoon Flo, a very powerful storm that struck Japan. We changed course from southwest to southeast in order to swing around the storm. In doing so, we only had two days of ten-degree rolls.

Yesterday, I went to church on the big naval base and then spent the rest of the day checking the base's facilities, which include gyms, weight rooms, and courts—anything for physical activity. Since Yokosuka homeports the Seventh Fleet, other facilities incorporate a large naval exchange, a movie theater, and laundry facilities.

Today I attempted to get my passport stamped. No luck. Japanese holiday. I had the same problem about this same time in Korea last year.

After studying a map of Yokosuka, I headed out the main gate to see what the afternoon would turn up. My wanderings took me to a beautiful park laced with waterways and waterfalls. Families filled the park where little children, some of them naked, played in water warmed by the brilliant sunshine. A band shell looks across a grassy knoll into Tokyo Bay.

The Japanese battleship *Masada* has been embedded in concrete by the beach adjoining the park since 1926. Using *Masada* as the flagship, the Japanese devastated both the Russian Baltic and western fleets in the Battle of the Yellow Sea on May 27, 1905. As a result, Japan became a world naval power that persisted until her defeat in World War II. The Japanese take pride in this old ship.

Leaving the park, I wandered through the business district for a lesson in economics. I had heard about high Japanese prices but wasn't prepared for the details. Before leaving the naval base, I traded a $100 check for 13,400 yen. At a department store, a ladies sweater that I thought Nita might like caught my eye. I needed three times the amount of yen in my wallet to buy it. A sampling of other merchandise discouraged any other purchases. I traded back my yen for about $95, the best bargain of the day.

The very heavy traffic in Yokosuka, as well as the naval base, flows on the left side of the road. I guess I knew that at one time, but I had forgotten it. As a pedestrian, I have to really be alert to what I am doing, especially when jogging.

Masada

Yokosuka, Japan, September 25, 1990

After classes today, I took a walking tour of Yokosuka beginning with the immigration office where I got my passport stamped, proving my legal entrance into Japan. Making my way through town, I arrived at a museum on my list of things to see. I encountered an English-speaking native who told me the museum was closed on Monday. "But this is Tuesday," I protested.

"Monday was a holiday," he replied, "so it is closed today."

Ah, so, *arigato gozaimashita.* (Thank you very much.)

Taking one of my famous "short cuts" back toward the center of town, I ended up on a circuitous route through a residential area of mixed-quality homes interspersed with a few shops. The closely spaced houses were small by American standards. At the end of a dead end street, I found Ryu Honji, a Japanese temple on my list to see later. This sort of good fortune smiles on me frequently.

Before dropping off some film to be developed and returning to the ship, I went back to the water park to see a presentation of music and the beautiful "dancing waters." After dinner, I returned for a night performance. A stunning display of colored lights complemented the water movement, carrying out the visual effects of the music.

Without even trying I could come up with the names of at least a dozen people who would have reveled in tonight's performance. It has been said that, "He travels fastest who travels alone." It is also true that he travels loneliest who travels alone. Tonight's spectacular is forever tucked away in my memory, but with whom can I really share it?

Yokosuka, Japan, September 26, 1990

Dancing Waters

Dancing Waters

Rain aborted my plans to visit some Japanese shrines in the Kamakura area today. When the rain turned to light drizzle, I decided to have another try at the Yokosuka museum that had been closed on my last visit.

The Miura Peninsula, the site of Yokosuka, encompasses the entire subject of the museum. Geologic formations from the Early Miocene Period—about 18 million years ago—with fossils dating from the Paleozoic Period, and artifacts from man's incursion onto the scene form the basis of the area's history.

Even though explained in Japanese language, extensive aerial photographs and scale models of the peninsula enable the visitor to grasp the essentials. The museum devoted one section of a room to Admiral Perry and the part he played in opening up Japan to the rest of the world one hundred and fifty years ago. Much of the culture on display comes from that era—a fishing boat, a typical Japanese house, tools, and clothing. A hand-cranked wringer similar to the ones used on American washing machines a generation ago separated cotton from its seed. Although the Japanese demonstrated expertise in making high quality swords, their agricultural implements went begging. They made shovels of wood with metal only on the cutting edge.

So much water surrounding the Miura Peninsula on the island of Honshu required an extensive display of marine life. The sight of a spider crab whose fore limbs measured eleven feet from claw to claw astonished me.

Besides the marine life, Japan has 110 of the 450 known mammals in the world. Most intriguing, a little brown raccoon dog standing twelve inches tall does have the face of a raccoon. A protected species, it kills rats and snakes, but otherwise its timidity makes it a prey to other dogs.

Delightful attractions of butterflies, fluorescent rocks with special lighting, and glowing insects filled one room. The "glow worms" recalled pleasing memories of Waipu Caverns in New Zealand that Nita and I visited several years ago.

The top floor of the museum offers a beautiful panoramic view of Yokosuka and Tokyo Bay. A hedge formed by unusual cedar trees about eight feet tall and two feet in width enclose the grounds below. The trees looked as if their limbs had been twisted into a spiral by some giant who then changed the shaped from cylindrical to four-sided. Not only were the displays highly interesting, but so was the building itself, being modern and immaculate. And best of all, I got lucky again. I had it all to myself.

Yokosuka, Japan, September 27, 1990

Most Japanese people that I encounter on the street tend to look right past me with expressionless faces. But if I ask them for help or directions, they go out of their way to be quite friendly and accommodating. In fact, if I stop one person, two or three others will usually get into the discussion attempting to be a part of a solution. Today I had an encounter that will astonish me for a long time.

As planned, I took the train to Kamakura to visit some of the dozens of shrines there. Uncertain which way to go as I stepped off the train at Hasse Station, a well-dressed young woman approached me and indicated that she wanted to look at my map that showed the locations of the shrines in both English and Japanese. After I indicated where I wanted to go, she smiled and motioned for me to follow her. Although we didn't speak each other's language, we managed to exchange names. Hers is Haruka. Walking briskly we arrived at Hasedara, the first shrine on my list. Here, she began a series of surprises. There was a small admission fee, which I attempted to pay for both of us, but she insisted on buying her own ticket. Outside the main building that housed the eleven-headed Hase Kannon, the goddess of mercy, she purchased a flower arrangement and placed it before a small shrine already bedecked with several bouquets. Next, she assumed a standing prayer posture before another small edifice where she deposited coins through slats. After watching her deposit a coin, I started to follow suit with one of mine. She stopped me and insisted that I deposit one of hers. Then she turned to a large, brass incense burner and placed her face in the vapors, all the time smiling and using her hands to concentrate the smoke around her body.

When she completed this ritual, she took me inside the temple where she again stood quietly in prayer before this ornate, thirty-foot image. Leaving there we went outside to see the magnificent view of the Miura Peninsula where she used my camera to take my picture and then indicated that I was to take her picture. Outside the temple, a table displayed some souvenirs where I tried to buy some postcards. Again she stopped me, indicating that I should get them at the next shrine, the Great Buddha. But before leaving the table of souvenirs, she bought what I assume is a good luck charm and gave it to me. It is a little spherical clay bell attached to a pale blue cord. A card written in Japanese accompanied it. I will have to get it translated.

Next, we walked rapidly to the Great Buddha. Immediately inside the grounds several long-handled dippers aligned a covered fountain. Taking one of the dippers, she poured water over my hands and then over her own hands. Then she offered to dry my hands with her scarf. I chose my own handkerchief. Impressed by this ancient idol of forty-two feet, I waited for some people to move so I could photograph the Great Buddha alone. Meanwhile, she went to the souvenir stand and returned with a package of postcards. I tried to pay her, but she refused. Then smiling and bowing as only the Japanese can, she turned and walked right out of my life as suddenly as she walked in.

The rest of the day was anti-climatic. For twenty yen I went inside Buddha where there was really nothing to see. Naturally, my curiosity took me into a forbidden area behind one of the buildings

Great Buddha

from which one of the attendants politely retrieved me.

Then I opted to hike the two miles to the next shrine, Hachimangu. Dating from the eleventh century, it's the oldest and most famous shrine. Since Hachiman was a god of war, Shogun Yaritomo dedicated the shrine to his military prowess. Every September a major festival here includes the exciting sport of equestrian archery. Fortunately, I had seen some clips of this spectacular event on TV a few nights ago.

By the time I finished my visit to Hachimangu, daylight had turned to twilight. So I backtracked toward the train station via the cherry tree lined walkway leading to the shrine. I left much to be seen. I must return, but when?

Yokosuka, Japan, September 28, 1990

Today I took my first organized tour of Japan sponsored by the ship's Welfare and Recreation Department. The tour encompassed the area around Mt. Fuji. We stopped first at a peace park honoring Japanese soldiers killed in various battles—Korea, Okinawa, India, Thailand, and others. More than a thousand men are buried there.

Japanese Memorial Park with Mt. Fiji in the background

The centerpiece of the park set on a hillside embraces a huge monument. A long road flanked by manicured landscaping and small stone monuments at various intervals, leads up to a white building. A large enclosed shrine for worship rests at the foot of the hill. Lesser buildings, including a smaller shrine at the tip of the hill, occupy that area.

We saw five lakes around Mt. Fuji, all of which are year-around resorts and require reservations made well in advance. The lakes are fairly small, with the two-and-a-half-square-mile Lake Yamanaka being the largest.

This trip presented Mt. Fuji from all sides and several elevations, offering truly spectacular scenes with another mountain range as a backdrop to the heavily forested slopes and valleys through which we drove. People climb Mt. Fuji only in July and August. At the "fifth level" where we ate lunch, the climb takes nine to fifteen hours, depending upon which trail is taken. Overnight accommodations are available. The Japanese have a saying that, "He who climbs Mt. Fuji once is wise; he who climbs it twice is a fool."

Acting upon the tour guide's advice, I ate my first Japanese meal—sopa. Consisting mostly of white noodles about eight inches long and a half-inch wide they float in a cup of brown broth along with assorted bits of vegetables. A nearly boiled egg completed the mixture. I ate this concoction with chopsticks. Eating eight-inch long, slippery noodles with two sticks violates all rules of American table etiquette. And the broth? Drink from the bowl, of course. This experience convinced me that the only practical way to eat sopa with chopsticks is nude and alone.

We stopped at another shrine, Sengen. This is a Shinto shrine to Konohasakuya, goddess of fire and childbearing. Considering this a strange duo, I asked the tour guide whether the goddess was for or against childbearing. He didn't know. Supposedly she protected the area from volcanic eruptions of Mt. Fuji. Since the shrine was erected in the seventeenth century and Mt. Fuji last erupted in the eighteenth century, the shrine must not be very effective. Two fierce looking archers guard the gate to the temple. Gate guards at temples always wear angry visages, which are supposed to keep evil spirits away.

The childbearing bit about the shrine reminded me of all the wooden dolls that I had seen at various places. The tour guide said some of these are Kokeshi dolls. Ko means child and the dolls are in memory of the "children who disappeared." It seems that many years ago some families were unable to provide for all their children and some died from sickness or starvation. When nothing else could be done for the children, the family sadly left them to nature.

Shiraito Falls, our last stop, supposedly contain hidden treasure. Although many people have looked for it, none has been found. Superlatives really don't do justice to these falls. With an overcast day, the falls caught no sparkle from the sun. Mt. Fuji boasted no snow this early in the year, but a doughnut shaped cloud crowning the summit eventually drifted lower to look like a giant smoke ring.

Wanting to mail a postcard from this place, I asked directions to the post office. I didn't want to overshoot it, so to stay on course I kept asking people how much farther to the post office. Suddenly a little man pulled up on a scooter, flashed a smile, and said, "Mail man!" I handed him the card and one hundred yen. He gave me twenty yen in change, shorting me ten yen. Just glad to get the card mailed I didn't say anything. About ten minutes later after I had returned to the tour bus, this guy putted up again, flashed a smile, and dropped ten yen into my hand. I thought he went to a lot of trouble for the equivalent of six cents. But the Japanese seem to value highly both honesty and sincerity.

A group of teenage girls also loitered in the parking lot. Suddenly, they lined up in front of the Sailors who weren't even in their uniforms. Another girl with about six cameras hanging around her neck started taking pictures. Then the girls, laughing and waving, ran off to their own bus. The guys loved it.

Leaving there, we returned to Yokosuka by way of beautiful Lake Kawaguchi that perfectly reflects Mt. Fuji on a sunny day. Alas for a cloudy day.

Yokosuka, Japan, September 29, 1990

The eighty-mile trip to Tokyo today, with traffic jams around Tokyo, has given me a new tolerance for Houston traffic. The clouds of yesterday had turned to light mist, exacerbating the traffic jams. A young lady from the Family Services Dept. on the naval base guided our tour. First, she took us to Meiji Jingu, a 175-acre park in the middle of Tokyo. The shrine expresses appropriate recognition to the father of Japan, Emperor Meiji and Empress Shoken. Meiji, the emperor from 1868 to 1912, brought Japan out of the Shogun era to create a modern state. Unfortunately, the old Shogun war spirit settled into the Japanese army and drew the United States into World War II, during which American bombers destroyed much of the park along with most of Tokyo. Immediately following the war, people from all over Japan donated one hundred thousand trees and shrubs to restore the park. The shrine, originally built eight years after Meiji's death in 1920, has also been rebuilt. In addition to the elaborate shrine, the park has many buildings for various cultural and sporting activities.

We stopped next at Tokyo Tower, a 333-meter high structure used for radio and TV broadcasting that looks much like the Eiffel in Tower in Paris. The observation platform affords a stunning view of Tokyo and Tokyo Bay. Other levels feature a wax museum and holographic display. The museum depicted one very diabolical contraption, an ancient torture device whereby a terrified victim was placed on his back under a giant spike-studded wheel. As the wheel turned, it slowly shredded the victim.

The tour bus dropped us off at the Ginza District for shopping.

Prices here were about triple American prices. I settled for a Coke and doughnut, followed by an I-was-here picture of me.

We stopped last at the Asakura Kannon Sensoji Temple. A five-story pagoda jammed with people served as the centerpiece of several buildings. I bought a Kokeshi doll to add to Nita's doll collection from around the world.

Yokosuka, Japan, September 30, 1990

I was supposed to take a tour of Disney World today, but yesterday's light mist turned to rain. Having never gone to Astroworld in sunshine in Houston, I saw no point in going to Japan's Disney World in the rain. I made a good decision by trading my ticket for another trip to Tokyo.

When we reached Meiji Jingu, all the Sailors took off and the young tour guide became my personal tour guide. I had an opportunity to question her at length about Japanese history and Shintoism. She explained and demonstrated the whole ritual that the girl in Kamakura had shown me. First she washed her hands and dried them on a towel brought for that purpose. People are supposed to pour water from a dipper into their cupped hand so as to rinse out their mouths. She skipped that part. Proceeding to the main shrine, we passed under toris, having somewhat the appearance of giant football goal posts. The greater the numbers of toris in front of a shrine, the greater the importance of the shrine. Standing before the shrine, she clapped her hands two times. This is to get the attention of the god. Bow twice to show respect for the god. Toss money through a slotted box. Fold hands, close eyes, and make a wish. After we walked back down the steps, we came to an incense burner where many people

Smoke at a Japanese shrine

were coming and going. Everybody fanned smoke onto their bodies, concentrating the smoke where the body has a problem. The incense is supposed to heal. One lady smiled sheepishly at me as she fanned smoke across her posterior. Others simply put their faces into the smoke because they want to improve their looks.

As best I could tell, the people were worshipping Meiji, or at least asking him for favors. I asked my escort about this and she said that Meiji was a Shintoist who worshipped nature. The gods reside in the trees, paper, etc. She said that most Japanese are a mixture of Shintoism and Buddhism. These religions have priests, but they are only called into use for deaths, weddings, and trouble of some sort.

At the Ginza District, I decided to have one good Japanese meal before leaving Japan. I bought my escort's lunch and let her choose the menu for both of us. Served with tempura and side dishes, we had more than either of us could eat. I even managed a proficient use of chopsticks. The out-the-door price came to about $15.00, proving that you can get a good meal at a good price in Japan if you know how.

The return trip to Yokosuka took us through Yokohama, a major city and shipping port. The Yokohama-Tokyo Bridge exhibits an engineering masterpiece built on the order of the Golden Gate Bridge. Located nearby, the steel-structured Marine Tower looks like it's made of crystal under its colored lights.

At Sea, October 7, 1990

We have been at sea for a week undergoing war games with several Japanese ships as part of our group. The "enemy" has sunk us twice, which doesn't say much for the longevity for this type of ship in case of war. However, in a real shoot-out, we would be in company with ships designed to take out aircraft. This ship has other purposes.

We left Yokosuka a day early, which created a small problem for me. I had left some negatives with a photo shop for reprints and was supposed to pick them up at 10 a.m. We departed at 8:30 a.m. Fortunately, my congenial tour guide agreed to pick them up and mail them to me.

My stateroom buddy took a fall upon arriving in Yokosuka. An orthopedic doctor took one look at him and sent him back to San Diego. My side of the berthing compartment has filled up with civilians who came on board to run tests on new submarine detecting equipment. Between the traitorous Walkers who delivered top secret codes to the Soviets and the Japanese firm of Toshiba who sold our technology for quiet submarine propellers to the Soviets, the Navy has been hard pressed to come up with new sub-detecting systems at an estimated cost of about $2 billion. One of the civilians is a woman. The last woman left us in the Aleutians and flew home from an air force base there. All of these people will soon transfer to the USS *Fletcher* that has been with us all the way from California.

I have finished my math correspondence course and need only to take the final exam when I get back to Texas. My ex-roommate and one other officer were helpful tutors. Some of the officers got into the Navy with their math degrees. Ironically, it has been so long since some of them have used their math skills that they had no idea what they were looking at when they peered over my shoulder. It's an old story: Use it or lose it.

Off Northwest Honshu, October 8, 1990

After leaving Yokosuka, we went down the coast of Honshu for more combined naval exercises with Japanese ships. The warm latitudes inspired some sun bathing and shirtless jogging. Yesterday, we had a steel beach picnic—grilled hamburger and hot dogs with all the trimmings. The crew enjoyed a trap-shooting contest off the fantail. My team of four was winning until four guys from the engineering department shot a perfect score.

During all this activity, some hot jet jockeys flying A4 and F18 fighter craft made several passes at the ship at about 500 knots. One pilot came in at deck level and then stood his plane right on its tail. Just before he became a mere speck directly overhead, he executed a perfect Immelman turn for us admiring lesser mortals.

Continental Airlines Flight 8, October 13, 1990

I have done a lot of living since arriving at Otaru, Japan, two days ago. Going ashore I traded some dollars for yen at a bank. The bank clerk amazed me by using an abacus, a calculating device used by the ancient Greeks and Romans, with the speed and accuracy one would expect from an electronic calculator.

Next, I turned my attention to securing my travel arrangements back to the states. A radio message to the ship had instructed me to pick up my prepaid ticket and itinerary at Japan Airlines. Remembering the travel fiasco in Korea about a year ago, I immediately went to Chitose Airport to pick up the ticket. It was Korea revisited! My prepaid ticket was in Tokyo. Japan Airlines had only a reservation from Sapporo to Tokyo. After more than an hour of discussion and phone calls to Tokyo, I was sent to the Continental Airlines office in downtown Sapporo. The man I needed to see was out for the day. Would I please return tomorrow? The lady clerk seemed genuinely distressed at my plight and sent me away with an excellent brochure and map of Sapporo.

I returned the next day on the same train with two chief petty officers and some of their buddies. They were headed, as they put it, to the "cheapest, sluttiest bars in town." We parted company at the train station where I began a walking tour of the city, using the maps and brochures given me the day before.

First, I wandered through the grounds of Hokaido University and chatted briefly with one of the professors in the literature building. I learned the hard way that the tops of all doors in the building are approximately eye level to me. I knew that the Japanese are generally short, but it never occurred to me that a university building would be designed for their exclusive use.

Next, I picked up my airline ticket without further ado. The Continental Office faces Sapporo's famous Clock Tower across the street, a little wooden two-story museum in the heart of the city. Built in 1878, it originally housed a boy's school that formed the beginning of Hokaido University. Dr. William Smith Clark of Massachusetts State University of Agriculture served as the school's president. At that time, the faculty consisted of Dr. Clark and two other Americans who gave the school its direction and character. The school emphasized both agriculture and military discipline. Japan was just emerging as a modern nation under Emperor Meiji, and the Japanese people still revere Dr. Clark's memory. He instilled the motto "Boy's be ambitious" into generations of students, some of whom probably confronted men of my generation in combat on islands in the Pacific. Hokaido University still places considerable emphasis on agriculture, but the old military spirit seems to have been drummed out of the Japanese, thanks to forty-five years of protection by the United States. However, the Japanese constitution does allow a Self-Defense Force (SDF). Twice, I have seen Japanese warships demonstrate competence on joint maneuvers with the U. S. Navy ships. I have also seen F18 fighter planes at Japanese airfields. They also possess modern tanks and well-trained ground troops. Their SDF appears too small to mount any kind of offensive. Because of this and their constitutional limitations on the military, they will send money to support the containment of Iraq, but they won't send any of their troops abroad.

I came next to the botanical gardens, which were not created for tourists. I have seen more interesting plants at San Antonio, San Diego, and Bellingrath Gardens near Mobile, Alabama. Rather, these gardens are an adjunct of Hokaido University for research and teaching. For once, since coming to Japan, I didn't feel illiterate. Since scientific names identified all species, non-scientific people of all languages are equally ignorant. This museum presented another interesting aspect of Japanese lifestyle. Peoples around the globe have always used available materials for clothing, shelter, and tools. Learning that the Japanese wove cloth from elm bark, boots from tuna skins, and entire houses from reeds fascinated me.

Odori Park completed my stroll for the day. This wide boulevard, beautifully landscaped with flowers and fountains, stretches about a mile long. Annual snow sculptures here attract thousands of visitors to see what thousands of Sapporo citizens have constructed. It's too early for snow here, Sapporo being in about the same latitude as New York. But gorgeous flowers lined the entire strip, especially roses of several varieties and colors.

The next day, good fortune smiled on me again as I took my seat on the crowded train from Sapporo to Chitose Airport. This time the smile enhanced the poise of a young Japanese beauty. Having been a university exchange student at Bloomington, Illinois, she was one of the very few Japanese people whom I had met who spoke English fluently. On arrival at the airport, she helped me get checked in before she even bought her own ticket. There must have been at least a dozen people who have graciously gone out of their way to accommodate me one way or the other while I was in Japan. I am in their debt, but since I can't repay, I'll simply have to pass it on.

Shortly after take-off from Chitose Airport at Sapporo, I drifted off to sleep. Awakening a short time later, I glanced out my window at an unusual sight. The configuration of clouds above the aircraft created a single sunbeam across an otherwise dark ocean below, making ships visible only when the shaft of light passed over them. It appeared as if we were carrying the sunshine with us, which suggests another bit of philosophy: Carry the sunshine with you.

Postscript: The USS *Cushing* was decommissioned on September 22, 2005 and sunk as a target in July 2008 off Kauai, Hawaii.

USS Orion (Photo compliments of Elsilrac Enterprises)

USS *Orion* AS-18

Santo Stefano Island, Sardinia, Italy, November 20, 1990

I just finished a cold shower. No hot water. It's been that kind of a day—a long day. Here I shiver in a two-man stateroom waiting for my only clothes to get dry in the laundry. Fortunately, both the bathroom and the laundry lie directly across the passageway from me.

A series of uneventful flights brought me to this solitary naval outpost, but left my luggage in New York. With five take-offs on four different airlines, I suppose lost or delayed luggage should be expected. It should arrive tomorrow evening.

The flight from Rome to Sardinia revealed an unusual sight. A thick blanket of undulating clouds below the aircraft had the configuration of ocean swells six to ten feet. In all my flying, I have never before seen such formations. When the plane dropped through the clouds to land, modern navigation really demonstrated its worth, for we were right on top of the rugged granite mountains of Sardinia.

The urgent call to me Friday requested that I be in Norfolk for briefing on Monday to get here ASAP. It turns out that time was not that critical. The crew of *Orion* has Thursday and Friday off for Thanksgiving, and no classes are held on Saturday and Sunday. I certainly could have used those extra days in Texas. However, Sardinia has a rich history, so maybe I can spend the time learning some of it.

Santo Stefano Island, November 25, 1990

During the last five days, I have become organized and oriented to my new environment. After my first night, I was surprised to learn that my two-man stateroom already had two officers assigned to it.

But they both live ashore and don't sleep here. One is transferring December 3 anyway. When I arrived, the room smelled like the inside of a gym locker. The officers of this ship are supposed to clean their own rooms. I addressed the long neglect by cleaning all surfaces and shampooing the carpet. In the process, I rearranged all the clutter. With ample storage, a lavatory, and a desk, the room is quite livable. Also, for a change, I have a classroom dockside that has plenty of tables, chairs, chalkboard, and lockable file cabinets for my teaching materials. Except for the noisy generators outside, this could spoil me.

Soon after my arrival, I saw a suicide prevention class in progress. Surprised that one of the ship's crew had taken his own life, I wanted to know why. It seems that diversions here are extremely limited. The ship seldom leaves the island. A gym, bowling alley, snack bar, commissary, and small Navy Exchange provide the main entertainment to occupy the men when they are off duty. Two World War II LCMs modified to haul passengers in all kinds of weather offer the only way off the island. Off duty activity revolves around the boat schedule, for going to either of two small towns—Palau on Sardinia and La Madd on La Maddalena Island. The shops there close from 1 p.m. to 5 p.m. and then close for the night at 8 p.m. Coordinating the boat schedule with these stores' hours isn't always easy, and there's not much for the men to do when they get there, except eat and drink. Larger towns are available by bus, but Saturday is the only practical time to try to go there. Since I teach basic skills classes from 7:30 a.m. to 5:00 p.m., I have four weeks of isolation to look forward to. I can see how a maladjusted person would have trouble coping with two years of this.

The driver who brought me from the airport says summer conditions are better. Expensive yachts from all over Europe tie up at the various islands. People flocking to the beaches overrun the whole area, and in Italy, that means topless beaches. Unlike much of the Mediterranean, clear, unpolluted water and the air surround Santo Stefano Island, which provide excellent conditions for wind surfing and water skiing. The men who have their families here seem to handle their tour of duty very well. Predictably, the crew gets a lot of movies.

Typical of ships this size, the wardroom is quite informal, and the officers have been reasonably friendly. A previous PACE instructor left a bad impression in several ways. I sense that some of the officers have a wait and see attitude toward me. Not a big deal. Four women are on board—three officers and one civilian. Because of the holidays, I have seen very little of them as well as some of the men.

I have seen my two roommates twice.

The USS *Orion*, a submarine tender commissioned in 1943 at the height of WWII, is in pretty good shape for such an old ship. It saw action in the Pacific. The father of one of the warrant officers was one of the original crewmen. This ship can repair just about anything on a submarine and manufacture any obsolete replacement parts. Its defensive weapons are negligible. It might be able to ward off an attack by a small terrorist boat.

Yesterday, I jogged around and over Santo Stefano Island. The view from the top is worth the climb. Stretching to the north toward Corsica Island, La Maddalena Archipelago defines the southern reaches of Bonifacio Strait. Situated on the coasts, the towns of Palau and La Madd project a charming array of buildings with walls of salmon colored stucco and roofs of red tile.

After church today, I took a walking tour of Palau. The road I chose looped around the top of the mountain and back to the other side of town. The islands of La Maddalena to the north contrasted with the rain shrouded mountains in the Sardinian interior. Rugged granite outcropping mingled with thick evergreen brush dissuades anyone from leaving the road. But numerous abandoned rock fences lacing the terrain suggest a land of antiquity that indicated much different usage. The fences must have enclosed some kind of livestock at one time. Many areas of Texas now infested with mesquite and other brush because of overgrazing were once prairies with grass belly high to a horse. I suspect something similar happened here. Still, the landscape is pretty. Oncoming rain hurried my five-mile trek, and I finished the day in the gym's weight room.

Two submarines lie alongside the ship undergoing service. The sub's command of the nuclear powered USS *Pittsburgh* allowed me on board for a brief tour. It's a formidable fighting machine capable of doing major damage with either torpedoes or missiles. Since subs may eventually go to the Persian Gulf, the *Orion* crew feels that it plays a part in Desert Shield. Although a large vessel, space on the sub restricts movement as I always thought it would. I wouldn't even want to ride on one, but many men who serve on them wouldn't choose anything else. Several ex-submariners are currently in the highest echelons of the Navy.

Santo Stefano Island, November 26, 1990

Classes in basic skills began as scheduled today. As usual, I have four classes of guys anxious to improve themselves by giving full effort to the time in class. I can't imagine stepping back into a classroom where the primary objective is just to get the students' attention.

Out of hundreds of Sailors that I have taught, only three have given me any trouble. I expelled them from class permanently. Those who were left got the message without further comment. If public school teachers had the same authority, most of the disciplinary problems in American schools would end. But it will never happen because it seems that America has more lawyers than the rest of the world combined. I think that if students are not interested in academics by the time they reach high school, they should be placed in a trade school that addresses their other interests until such time they do have an interest in academics. Navy students have proven that the time to teach is when a student is ready to learn. Many of them admit to being indifferent to learning and discipline in high school and only went to school to play sports or to be with other teenagers. Now they're ready to learn and progress rapidly.

Santo Stefano Island, December 4, 1990

I just finished breakfast with the customary side order of cactus passing for national news from the States. The officers watch the news from home with a mixture of ridicule and amusement. The so-called news is about as objective as the propagandistic military commercials. TV scenes of crying reservists shipping out elicit derisive comments in the wardroom. Teenage girls, crying because daddy won't be home for Christmas, evoke laughter because many Sailors routinely miss Christmas with their families.

In August, more than seventy percent of Americans knew why the military is in the Persian Gulf. Now, thirty percent of that group has forgotten. All wars have been fought for at least one of three reasons—economic, political, or religious. A war with Iraq would be no different. Just different technology. Anyone old enough to vote should know that Americans are not a patient people. Long, drawn out sanctions against Hussein likely will work to our disadvantage, not his. It is no of consequence to him if a few thousand of his citizens die for lack of food or medicine. Indeed, this gives him a propaganda advantage.

Meanwhile, high fuel costs have driven Continental Airlines into bankruptcy. Some other airlines could follow suit. The Philippine economy is in shambles. Japan is hurting. Brazil is struggling to survive. Repayment of Brazilian debts to the U.S. is out of the question for the foreseeable future. Kuwait is a ruined nation. And fifty percent of the Americans don't know why the military is in the Persian Gulf.

Santo Stefano Island, December 6, 1990

Life has become rather routine—eat, sleep, teach, workout at the gym. The cold rainy weather discourages much outside activity. The water got so choppy one day that the ship's command secured the boats to Paulau and La Madd. Sunday the weather turned cold but sunny, so I used the occasion to visit the old home of Giuseppe Garibaldi whom Italians hold in highest esteem for his political and military contributions to the country. Located at the end of a four-mile walk through La Madd and across the causeway connecting La Maddalena Island to Cappresa Island, his house is now a museum. The road from the causeway to Garibaldi's house winds through a forested national preserve where a small stream parallels part of the road. Snow capped Corsica affords a backdrop across Bonifacio Strait.

At the museum, I had the Italian guide all to myself since this definitely is not the tourist season. Between his limited English and my limited Spanish, we got along just fine. The house reflected artistic taste, military achievement, and affairs of state. Even though his home is so isolated from the rest of Italy, Garibaldi obviously enjoyed a comfortable lifestyle for the late nineteenth century. Three special wheel chairs that helped him cope with rheumatism in his declining years confirmed his medical problems. And a special brace helped him with an old bullet wound in the foot. He, his three wives, and some of their children lie buried in above-ground vaults beside the house.

The return trip lost some of its luster at the causeway. Winds approaching gale force whipped sea spray across the narrow road, making walking somewhat hazardous. The cold turbulent water below looked anything but inviting. I got back to La Madd just in time to witness a wedding procession of about fifty cars with blaring horns.

Santo Stefano Island, December 9, 1990

The crew held its Christmas party ashore last night—eating, drinking, and dancing to loud rock music. I opted to stay on board, do some letter writing, and watch the Army/Navy football game. We lost 30 to 20. One of the officers kept changing the channel to a hockey game, which really didn't interest me.

Perfect weather settled over the island yesterday but availed little because both towns shut down for a religious holiday.

Both subs left the past week, so now the crew works on the up-keep of the ship itself.

News from home is the best morale builder for isolated servicemen. Mail call this week brought me several letters and birthday cards from Nita and Gail. Both had good news for me. Gail has adjusted to her move from Los Angeles to Dallas and her new job. Nita says our cotton farm at Ackerly harvested a bumper crop.

Santo Stefano Island, December 13, 1990

My birthday last Monday passed almost without incident. During my mid-morning classes, hail pelted our metal building. Just when I thought the noise could be no louder, a bolt of lightening struck a wire about eight feet from the classroom door, the first time I have ever seen lightening and heard thunder simultaneously. Among other things, we lost the telephone system on the island. Repair date? Who knows? This is Italy.

The ship's command chose that same night to shut down all electricity in the forward part of the ship for the periodic preventive maintenance schedule on the electrical control panel. No lights in my stateroom, bathroom, or wardroom. With flashlight in hand, I made my way aft to one of the lighted shops where I got into a game of spades with some enlisted men until after midnight. I had a good partner. We didn't just win. We demolished all opposition. Happy birthday!

Santo Stefano Island, December 19, 1990

I'm getting "short"—a Navy term for someone about to leave. I depart this ship after my last class ends at 5 p.m. two days from now. Timing is critical. All final test scores must be computed, recorded, and duplicated. Other reports must be completed and distributed. All books and teaching materials must be boxed and placed in the post office for insured shipment. Having accomplished all of this I will be ready to walk off the ship with bag packed the night before to take a boat to Palau for transportation to a hotel in Olbia. My flight leaves at 7:25 a.m. the next day. If I spend another night on the ship, Navy transportation could get me to the airport about forty minutes before flight departure. Too risky. I don't have a ticket in hand and still have vivid memories of the ticket foul-up in Korea and Japan. I have no desire to spend Christmas alone in Olbia, Sardinia.

During the last week two subs came alongside for service--the USS *Minneapolis-St. Paul* and the USS *Dallas* of Red October fame. Even so, some maintenance on *Orion* continues.

Last Monday evening the ship's chaplain took me to his home on La Maddalena Island for Italian pizza and a short visit with his family. As he has moved around the world, his sons have had outstanding educational opportunities besides the benefits of wide-ranging travel. His furniture bore the evidence of fifteen moves—and counting.

Their apartment was quite nice by Italian standards, but low thermal output and vaulted ceilings contributed to a chilly atmosphere. Electric space heaters trip circuit breakers, so some Navy people use space heaters fueled by bottled gas. The Italian authorities frown on this practice. But then it doesn't take much to make an Italian bureaucrat frown. Italians cope with the heating problem by essentially living in only the kitchen and living room, the same way everybody did when I was a kid in West Texas.

To me, the evening was my one big soiree in Sardinia.

JFK Airport, New York, December 22, 1990

My Pan Am Flight 2067 to Houston just got delayed because of weather. I wouldn't say that New York was fogged in when my flight from Rome arrived. However, it was the first time I ever saw the ground a split second before the landing gear touched the runway.

Something out of the ordinary had to happen. The departure from the USS *Orion* went too smoothly. I decided to take an earlier LCM from Santo Stefano Island to Palau than I had intended. I didn't want to take a chance on being stuck on board the ship during a security alert drill and miss my transportation to Olbia. Good decision. I was told to meet my driver at 8 p.m. He was told to meet me at 5:30 p.m.! He just happened to come by the fleet landing as I stepped off the LCM. Normally, he has a van full of people. This time, I was the only passenger. First, he took me to the airport where my prepaid ticket really did await me. Then he took me to a hotel. He accepted my thanks and a cup of cappuccino. When I left the hotel this morning, the desk clerk said the cab fare to the airport would be 11,000 lire. No problem—until I reached the airport and the driver wanted 14,000 lire. I was short 500 lire. At that precise moment one of my students taking the same flight walked up and bailed me out. At JFK my luggage came off the aircraft first, and I breezed through customs, all too good to last.

I left Sardinia with mixed feelings—glad to get off an isolated, barren island and get home for Christmas, but longing to return and explore Sardinia fully in warmer weather. But as Robert Frost says in his poem "Two Roads," I likely will not pass this way again. The sunrise over Cappresa Island is always worth getting up for. The sunsets over Sardinia are sometimes simply enchanting. Tinting the western clouds a soft pink, the sun casts a surrealistic effect over the entire La Maddalena coastline. The gray granite, green brush, and salmon-colored buildings turn to a blend ranging from pale rose to violet.

As usual, my students sent me off with a sincere "thank you." I overheard one say, "I learned more about English from this man in four weeks than I learned in four years of high school." I think that says more about his new-found willingness to learn than my ability to teach.

A little while ago, I got a chance to repay some of the kindness shown to me in Japan. An Iranian traveling with his wife and daughter spoke just enough English to let me know he wanted to call his son in Houston, but didn't know how to place the call. I placed the call for him and then found out that his son had purchased tickets, which were to be picked up at the Pan Am counter. Again, he didn't know what to do. After securing his tickets, I escorted them to their departure gate. Nice people. They were as grateful for this small favor as I was for the same kind of help I received in Japan.

Postscript: The USS *Orion* was decommissioned September 3, 1993, and sold to North American Ship Recycling, Baltimore, Maryland on 27 July 2006.

USS Austin (Photo compliments of Elsilrac Enterprises)

USS *Austin* LPD-4

Norfolk, VA, January 23, 1991

This ship just set the sea and anchor detail and will be underway by 0730. First stop is Morehead City, North Carolina, to pick up about 550 Marines. Originally the ship was supposed to engage in naval exercises with the French and Spanish with the first port call at Rota, Spain. In view of the hostilities in the Persian Gulf, who really knows what to expect?

The USS *Austin* is an amphibious transport dock, which is known as the Navy's pickup truck. It has two helicopter landing pads for transporting troops and materiel ashore. For example, in 1983 it removed the dead and wounded from Lebanon when terrorists blew up the Marine barracks there. A large ship more than 550 feet in length, it carries a crew of about 350 men and is named after Austin, Texas. In fact the quarterdeck sports an "Austin City Limits" sign.

I came on board at 2220 last night, checked into my two-man stateroom, and got to sleep after midnight. Reveille at 0500 came too soon. The late arrival was my fault. Yesterday morning my passport appeared to be missing. After conducting a "thorough" search for it and having Nita leave work to look for it at home, I flew to Washington from Norfolk to get a new passport. After a call to Central Texas College's travel agency to arrange an airline ticket and calls to Senator Lloyd Benson's Washington and Dallas offices to expedite the issuance of the passport, I caught the flight out of Norfolk with three minutes to spare. Five hours later I was back in Norfolk with the new passport. When I unpacked last night, imagine my consternation to find the old passport buried among my clothing. It was supposed to be in my attaché case. I have no idea when or why I put it with my clothing.

Briefing at the Central Texas College office in Norfolk began early in the day and continued into the evening, thanks to my unnecessary trip to Washington. I received my military I.D. card and, for the first time, a Geneva Convention I.D. card. The PACE coordinator said it would keep me from being shot as a spy in case I fell into the wrong hands. Happy thought.

South of Bermuda, January 25, 1991

The brilliant sunshine and biting cold air of Wednesday turned into overcast and drizzle yesterday. Marines laden with all their gear, including M-16 rifles, snaked up the brow looking like a long line of oversized ants. Before long, various vehicles jammed the cargo deck—HMM Vs, small amphib tanks, amphib troop carriers, LARCs, and even an LCU, which was floated aboard. HMM Vs have replaced the old WW II Jeep. LARCs recover and repair damaged vehicles once they hit the beach. Although this ship carries no helicopters, we are in company with the USS *Guadalcanal*, which carries a CH-46 Sea Stallion, a Huey, and a Cobra. The twin-rotored CH-46 carries troops and equipment. The others bristle with guns and missiles. The USS *Charleston*, a cargo ship, accompanies us.

The logistics of an amphib landing require an incredible undertaking. Everything has to be planned and accounted for in advance: Food, clothing, shelter, vehicles, spare parts, communication equipment, maps, ammunition, weapons to meet any contingency, and on and on—all in preparation for a very dirty business. But after the captain indicated over the 1MC that we likely would not go to the Persian Gulf, many of the Marines expressed disappointment. Some have friends who are already there and they want to be with them. During Translant, the Marines have little to do, so they practice small arms fire on the flight deck, clean and re-clean their weapons, conduct training exercises, and do physical exercises.

During the night, moderate seas began to give the ship a 10-degree roll. Thus, many disciples kneeled before the porcelain god in earnest supplication for relief. Fortunately, I was not numbered in that congregation. However, having been seasick aboard a flat-bottomed LST in a

Marines cleaning weapons

typhoon right after WWII, I certainly empathize with these forlorn souls.

Mid-Atlantic, January 28, 1991

We have passed through two time zones and will pass through another one tonight. Yesterday (Sunday) and today have been ideal days at sea, so we bared our chests to the sun, jogged, played catch, and generally goofed off topside. We are now in the same latitude as Florida, having veered south to avoid the rough seas characteristic of the North Atlantic at this time of the year. Tonight an almost full moon shines brightly, making few constellations visible. How incongruous that the glory of heaven encompasses the weapons of hell.

Several reservists are on board, both Navy and Marine. I was listening to two reservists complaining about having been called up. One had only a six-day notice. The Persian Gulf crisis has been building for five months, and I wondered why he had not gotten his affairs in order. I don't believe any person is ever prepared to really live until he is prepared to die. Finally, I asked this guy why he joined the naval reserve in the first place. He said, "For $150 a month." Verily he has his reward. Now it's time to do his duty. I have no sympathy for him. Every man on this ship is a volunteer, including me.

Mid-Atlantic. January 30, 1991

Last night the captain confirmed what he previously intimated—no combat assignment for this ship. The ship mostly will perform the operations scheduled for it before the Persian Gulf crisis. That makes the war even more remote since we get very little news. However, the little bit of news we received today got our attention. Iraqi engagement of our ground forces was evidently a disaster for Iraq, but 10 Marines were killed. Even so, it appears that we will do some exercises in the Med, visit some ports in the Med, and go home in July. I was scheduled to leave the ship April 19, but I'm sure that port visits and some of the ship's activities will retard that date. Anything could happen in the next three months to alter any of these plans. The versatility of this ship, its crew, and equipment make it very useful for a variety of changing world situations. For example, Navy SEALs and Marine Force Recon practice procedures for boarding ships bound for Iraq, just one of many things these men are trained to do. Force Recon is similar to SEALs but date back to Carlson's Raiders of WW II fame. SEALs were organized in the 1960s.

Last night capped off another beautiful day. Scudding, low-hanging clouds alternately obscured and veiled an almost full moon, creating an enchanting effect. Few things on earth are more beautiful than such a night on the ocean. Reluctantly, I turned in well after "Taps".

February 1, 1991

Today I got a chance to use some of my old signaling skills. The USS *Charleston* came alongside to practice the old method of passing people from one ship to another. Thanks to helicopters, that system isn't used very much, but it's necessary to maintain that proficiency as a back-up system. Anyway, I used the semaphore flags to talk to the signalman about some missing testing materials. They didn't have them.

Inevitably we had to turn northward to reach Rota, Spain so seas are getting rougher to the discomfort of some of the crew. Many find it hard to sleep in a rolling ship. I think some of that has to do with attitude. It isn't that big a deal. A windbreaker feels good again, but the nights continue to be spectacular.

Off Rota, Spain, February 3, 1991

Choppy seas still accompany us, along with a stiff, cold breeze, but bright sunshine and cumulus clouds have returned after a day of overcast. Although it's Sunday, not too many people are out on the weather decks. Small arms qualification filled the main activity. I qualified for the 45-cal. pistol and M-14 rifle. Hitting the target from the rolling flight deck wasn't all that easy. I'm pleased to know how to use the weapons, but I can't envision a scenario where I would ever need to.

Mediterranean Sea, February 7, 1991

Having departed Rota about noon yesterday, we skimmed the southern coast of Spain toward Gibraltar Strait, arriving there a little before sunset. Dolphins, the Sailors good luck sign, crossed the bow as we left the Atlantic. As Trafalgar, Spain faded off the port quarter, Tangier, framed by the gray mountains of Morocco, appeared on the starboard bow, giving a simultaneous view of two continents.

Dozens of small fishing boats bobbled along the starboard side while westbound ships of all sorts passed to port. The scene required alert navigation. The captain set the ship at Condition Three, one level below battle stations. Two three-inch fifty caliber guns were manned and ready. This old WW II weapon takes seven men, plus a passel of ammunition passers, to operate. But one shell can take out a small terrorist boat. The guns look out of place sitting thirty feet from a radar-controlled Close In Weapons System that can spew out

3in/50 Caliber Guns

50 rounds of 20-MM bullets per second.

Sailors and Marines crowded the rails to view the famous Rock of Gibraltar. Unfortunately they also got a good view of the famous milky Mediterranean haze that partially obscured the Rock. Not a Kodak moment.

Some time after night settled in, we turned northeast toward Almeria from a point off Oran, Algeria. What a poignant story from World War II its harbor holds! By a strange twist of fate, the British and French navies fought each other here instead of fighting the Germans. In late June of 1940, France had capitulated to Nazi Germany. But two powerful segments of the French fleet remained in the Mediterranean—one at Alexandria, Egypt and one at Oran, Algeria. Germany had pledged not to use the French ships in its continuing war against Great Britain, but Prime Minister Winston Churchill didn't trust Hitler. In Churchill's view the use of the French warships by Germany would have altered the outcome of the African desert battles between Montgomery and Rommel and threaten the very survival of Britain.

Through Admiral Somerville, Churchill gave Admiral Gensoul at Oran and Admiral Godfroy at Alexandria four choices: Join the British Navy, take the ships to a British port where the French crews would be removed, go to a neutral port and decommission the ships, or scuttle the ships where they were. Admiral Gensoul saw no honor in any of these options and chose to fight his old friend. When the French began to remove the tampions from their gun barrels, the British ships guarding the harbor opened fire. It was a duck shoot. In less than 15 minutes the British destroyed all but one of the French ships, including a battleship, a heavy cruiser, and a destroyer. Nearly 1300 French Sailors died. The British ships didn't even take a hit. After that, the French fleet at Alexandria was neutralized peacefully.

Our port visit to Rota turned out to be a disappointment. Tight security required all personnel to remain either on the ship or the naval base. One naval base looks about like all the others. The day before we arrived, a few thousand demonstrators showed up to protest the U. S. presence in Spain and our involvement in the Middle East War. I rode from the pier to the Navy Exchange with a chief petty officer who has been stationed there for four years and wants to extend his tour of duty there. He loves the place and said the demonstrators merely marched peacefully around a part of the base perimeter. He claimed that many, if not most, were paid to demonstrate and couldn't care less about the cause of the march. I wonder if some of the demonstrators back home aren't in it just for the attention. Anyway, both towns of Rota and Cadiz were off limits to us. The climate is much like San Diego and it would have been great to go sight seeing. Maybe next time.

Two young Moroccan naval midshipmen joined us at Rota. They will undergo training on board this ship for the remainder of its deployment. One hails from Casablanca and told me that all the cities along their northern coast would welcome tourists. The U. S. military has trained a lot of foreign nationals over the years. In the late 1970s some Iranians from the naval air station in Beeville, Texas, were guests in my home. It would be interesting to know where they are and what their political leanings are now.

Almeria, Spain, February 8, 1991

Today we offloaded a contingent of Marines in full battle dress pier side for an exercise to be completed in the next several days. First, the Landing Craft Utility was floated off and then used to transport rolling stock from the ship to the shore. Amphibious Assault Vehicles will also be used in the exercise. Some are small tanks that function on land or sea. Others look like small tanks but carry weapons and troops. Following debarkation of men and materiel, the ship moved to an anchorage about two miles off the coast.

I would like to explore Almeria, but I have no hope of doing so. This port call is strictly for business. What appears to be an ancient fort or monastery crowns the hill overlooking the city. A string of barren mountains serves as a backdrop to the city strung out along the coast. To the interior, snow caps another mountain range. High rise apartments and hotels face the beach that extends to a distant promontory jutting out from the mainland. Chilly air hung over deserted beaches. On board many of us took advantage of a beautiful day to jog and do calisthenics in the sun.

One of the Spanish-speaking crewmen tuned onto a Spanish radio station and heard the announcer say, "It's O.K. to come out of your apartments. The Americans won't hurt you." I have to believe that was a DJ joke. Nobody in a NATO country can be that uninformed. Besides, a sizable crowd had already gathered to watch the LCU take the trucks and HMM Vs from the ship.

Almeria, Spain, February 11, 1991

After a day of relative leisure yesterday, we weighed anchor and headed back to sea. It was just a fifty-mile trip to nowhere so the ship could conduct some underway drills and dump our trash. A cryptic message over the speaker system electrified the crew last evening: "This is not a drill! Man overboard! Starboard side!" People get much more serious when the real thing happens instead of a drill. Everyone mustered at his pre-assigned station to determine who, if anybody was missing. Fortunately, whatever the two stern lookouts saw, it wasn't a man overboard. To be sure, the captain required everyone to be visually accounted for twice. Meanwhile, a helicopter from the USS *Guadalcanal* stood by while searchlights from our ship played across the water with a boat crew ready to launch. In addition, one of the SEAL teams had taken it upon itself to ready one of its RHIB boats for launching. It was an excellent drill and fortunately nothing more than that.

In his nightly prayer, the chaplain gave thanks for the safety of all of us. Since we have only had one mail call in the last three weeks, he also prayed for mail. The ship's personnel packed the room at Bible study and church service yesterday—quite a change from other ships I've served on.

Off the Southeast Coast of Corsica, February 19, 1991

After another trip fifty miles off shore to dump trash and conduct underway exercises, we returned to the pier in Almeria on the 16th to reclaim our Marines who had been conducting joint land maneuvers with the Spanish armies. They came back with some strange tales. Spaniards have beer and wine with their meals, and cigarettes commonly laced with marijuana. Any of that would get a guy busted in the Navy or Marines.

Late this afternoon we transited Bonifacio Strait between Corsica and Sardinia, arriving in the Tyrrhenian Sea. Through the ship's big eyes I scanned the northern coast of Sardinia some eight miles distant to see if I could recognize Santo Stefano Island and its environs where I spent parts of last November and December. However, haze and other islands of the La Maddalena Archipelago obscured Santo Stefano. The weather is as cold and dreary as it was two months ago.

The major excitement in my life at present is the only case of strep throat I've ever had, but penicillin tablets seem to be getting it under control. My voice hasn't been much fun for my students to listen to. Quite a number of Marines have been sickly. I must have picked up the germ from them while working out in a crowded weight room.

Off the Southeast Coast of Corsica, February 21, 1991

Two days of nasty weather have hampered our amphib exercises. Before dawn yesterday the ship dropped its stern gate and floated off the LCU while a crane lifted out an LCVP into the water. In early daylight under leaden skies the AAVs splashed off the stern ramp and stretched single file toward the beach. By 0900 rain made life miserable for everyone being tossed around in choppy seas. Many of the men in these small crafts got seasick. As these assault vehicles roll out of the ship into the water, it is almost a surprise to see them float. But they do. In fact, if heavy seas cause one of them to turn over, it will right itself like a kayak. They aren't very maneuverable in water because of a top speed of seven knots. One of the main hazards to an AAV is heavy surf, which could flip the vehicle upside down on the beach. The men could still escape through the rear door, but the vehicle with its firepower would be useless.

AAV crews face another hazard when returning to the ship. If the seas are very rough, the stern of the ship could pitch high and smash the AAV as it tries to re-enter the ship. One such accident occurred on another ship some time ago, killing the AAV crew. Yesterday one of the MIKE 8 boats from *Guadalcanal* lost its bow ramp in rough seas and had to be secured to the LCU to avoid sinking. Evidently somebody forgot to do proper maintenance on the cables supporting the ramp, and when it dropped, it just snapped off the hinges and kept going. It's under about 200 feet of water. If the seas get calmer before we leave, the SEALs may try to retrieve the ramp. For reasons such as these, some of our activities have been canceled in the interest of safety.

This exercise is a drill to remove Americans from some endangered land area. The execution of such a scenario requires close coordination between amphib units, other surface vessels, and air support. *Austin* supplies the assault vehicles. The *Guadalcanal* supplies assault helicopters. The French are supposed to have one or more ships and some airplanes involved with us, but they haven't been visible. At least they are letting us practice in their territory. While our assault vehicles remain off the ship, we simply cruise back and forth off shore. As one officer of the deck put it, his task is to "stay in the box and don't hit the rocks." That's simply stated, but not exactly simply executed. Cruising at five knots in water 200 feet deep about 200 yards from shore requires very alert navigation.

Near Bonifacio Strait, February 24, 1991

During our final exercises at Corsica, the ship anchored just off the coast where the islands and mountains comprised a scenic "front yard." Marines splashed ashore in beautiful, but crisp, weather. Two days ago the ship conducted a mass casualty drill whereby a contingent of Marines "wounded in battle" was returned to the ship for medical attention. Medical personnel appropriated the mess deck for an emergency treatment center. From the removal of the "wounded" from the beach to their re-boarding of the ship for treatment, the drill went flawlessly. "Civilians" evacuated during the drill went to *Guadalcanal*.

Salt water drenched the Marines while hitting the beach in a dozen or more inflatable boats. They spent yesterday afternoon giving their gear a fresh water wash down and then hanging it on the rails to dry in the sun. Meanwhile, they disassembled their M-16s, mortars, and other weapons for cleaning. The Marines seem to enjoy this sort of thing.

We left our "battle site" yesterday, clearing Bonifacio Strait about dusk under a half moon. After getting fifty miles from land to dump trash, we turned back toward the strait to undergo a vertrep today along with the USS *Guadalcanal* and USS *Charleston*. We need supplies. We have had neither fruit nor milk for several days. After vertrep we set a course to arrive at Toulon tomorrow.

The captain conducts a short briefing for the crew over the 1MC each night. In his comments about liberty in Toulon last night he said our ship has been singled out for a terrorist attack while at Toulon. He didn't say where he got his information, but he is taking the threat seriously. Security will be conducted accordingly. People going ashore are to take obvious precautions: no drunkenness or other indecent conduct, wear civilian clothes, travel in pairs or groups, and avoid specified areas such as the Arab quarter or "Little Chicago." Lt. Klaus Guter, the head of the dental department, and I plan to buddy up for travel in the area. He and I jogged together at Rota and I like his company.

Thanks to the wizardry of some of our communications people, the British Broadcasting Co. is now on one of the radio channels in my room. News is current, but hard to understand. When they interview an American, I have no problem. Britain and America really are two cultures separated by a common language.

The ground offensive in Kuwait has begun with spectacular early success. During dinner tonight a Marine officer said, "I have been in the Marines fourteen years and every time there has been any military action, I have been on the other side of the world. Now I'm on the same side of the world as the action and here I sit eating ice cream." That predicament disappoints many of these men.

Toulon, France, March 1, 1991

The ship presently is undergoing a GQ drill. I was already out of anything to do and a GQ drill just emphasized it. My first semester classes are over, and I can't begin my new basic skills classes until I receive a grading key for the test batteries on 63 men. It should have on board when I left Norfolk. The second one should have already arrived through the mail. Ditto for the syllabuses for my college courses. Today I will try to get them faxed to the French liaison officer here. Each day of delay just adds to my time aboard this ship.

Because of security, I can't leave the ship alone during the day and the crew has to work until 1600. I have already spent two evenings ashore, but I'm really a day person, caring little for bars and restaurants. I spent my first evening ashore with three officers and one of the Moroccans. After visiting the U.S.O. and just walking around looking over the town, we stopped at a restaurant for a snack. One of the waiters told us about a nearby private club featuring a girly show. One of the officers and the Moroccan decided to go. The rest of us returned to the ship. At breakfast the next day I asked the officer how his evening turned out and got a dour response. It cost them $10.00 a piece to get inside the club. Drinks were extra and the girls never did show up. It's another old scam: "Come on in; the show will start soon." "Soon" becomes midnight, which becomes 1 a.m., which becomes 3 a.m. By that time people are so drunk or sleepy that the show, if any, doesn't matter. Meanwhile, the bar has made a lot of money selling booze. The two "victims" have taken a lot of ribbing about it with no end in sight.

There were other incidents. Three officers were still on the streets at 3 a.m. This alone announces to the world that they are young American Sailors. Three men claiming to be undercover policemen stopped and demanded to see their identification. The officers had the presence of mind to demand proof that they were policemen. One of the Sailors took off and got the real police who apprehended the impersonators. Apparently, they just wanted our guys' I.D.'s.

Some enlisted men approached the same way did not fare so well. They just handed over their wallets showing their I.D.'s. They got them back minus their money. A little ordinary precaution would have made all three incidents avoidable.

Toulon, France, March 4, 1991

The idea of faxing the test keys proved impossible. When I called John Baumgardner in Norfolk late last Friday, he just read me the keys over the phone. Since then, the syllabuses arrived along with some other mail.

Lt. Matt Maxwell, the ship's Air Boss, and I went to the opera Friday night. A twin bill, it lasted three hours and fifteen minutes. Neither the music nor the stories were familiar to us, but some of the harmony delighted us.

Saturday, Matt and I borrowed 10-speed bikes to cruise much of Toulon. A magnificent beach for swimming, windsurfing, and sailing stretches beyond the yacht harbor east of town. It's too cold for water sports now, but the ship may return here in warm weather.

Yesterday afternoon three officers and I hiked to the cable car station for a ride to the top of Mt. Faron, the site of a WW II German fortification that had a commanding view of the coast as well as the inland valley. The fortifications have been replaced with a tank, a couple of artillery pieces, and a museum giving a history of the retaking of Southern France by the Allies in 1944. For awhile we just relaxed in the snack bar and soaked up the dazzling panoramic view.

Classes resumed today: two college writing classes, one pre-college writing class, one basic writing, and one basic reading. All except the reading will run one hour a day for eight weeks. Reading will run two hours a day for four weeks followed by basic math for four weeks. Last semester we held all classes in the library. This semester classes are scattered all over the ship: library, wardroom, chiefs' mess, and first class' mess. It's a hassle, but rather normal.

Toulon, France, March 9, 1991

A rainy Saturday in Toulon, France, excites about as much as a rainy Saturday in Houston. I had hoped to hit the road again on a bike today. My classes were canceled two days this week so that my "classrooms" could be used for testing men for promotions. Chalk up two more days that I will be on this ship. I used one of those days to go ashore with Jebbour Abderrahm, one of the Moroccans. Everybody calls him Jay. First we took in the museum of natural history. Although he is quite proficient in physics and math, he showed surprising ignorance of animal life. Leaving the museum, we took the cable car back to Mt. Faron. His knowledge of French made my second trip to the WW II museum more meaningful. My knowledge of WW II and the Texas Revolution interested him.

While Jay was taking in a presentation in French that I had already seen in English, an employee of the museum practiced his English on me. Commenting on the recently concluded Persian Gulf War, he expressed his appreciation to the U. S. for stopping Hussein. He said neither the French nor the British would have done it. He said America is the greatest force in the world for peace. It's gratifying to hear that kind of sentiment from a foreigner.

Toulon, France, March 17, 1991

We have been too long in Toulon. A number of incidents point to that conclusion. Toulon doesn't have enough entertainment to occupy a month's free time. Warm weather that would open up the water sports would make a big difference. Unacceptable incidents on liberty are becoming more common. One Sailor punched out the owner of a pizza restaurant. Another one, left alone by his buddies, was hoping to acquire the company of a young lady and merely ended up drunk. Returning to the naval base alone, he got lost, climbed a fence, and ended up in the yard of the French base commandant. Realizing his mistake, he tried to chop his way out with an ax. The Frenchman maced him and sent him back to the ship in sad shape. The captain saddened him even more.

Two days ago a bunch of Marines got into a free-for-all fight. Before that, a Marine from the USS *Guadalcanal* tried to climb a rocky mountain without proper gear. He fell with disastrous consequences.

But there have been some good times. Quite a number of people are sporting red faces. They forgot to take sun block for their two-day skiing trip to the Alps. Others enjoyed a couple of days in Paris. Last Sunday, a group took in a tour of Avignon, the former city of the popes. While all this was going on, I was organizing and kicking off my second semester classes.

Yesterday, however, Lt. Matt Maxwell and I again went bicycling. This time we went west instead of east, taking a direct route to Sanary du Mer. A few people sunned themselves at Blutal Beach where we stopped for orange juice. Our return trip took a circuitous route along the coast and over a mountain through Community Forest. We biked on a beautiful day through beautiful sights. At Observatoire de la Mer massive shale cliffs overlooked the Mediterranean to the west and secluded campgrounds to the east. As we labored our way up the mountain, using the lowest gear of our ten-speeds, the sudden seclusion overwhelmed us. Except for the birds, only the occasional passing of an automobile broke the silence. What a contrast to the constant din of machinery on the ship! Intermittently breaking through dense evergreens, we took in views of deep valleys, panoramic scenes of Toulon and its suburbs, and a windsurfing regatta.

Although we had biked about 25 miles, we went back into town to eat dinner at a Vietnamese restaurant with LCDR Paul Mazich, the ship's executive officer, and LCDR Precup, the ship's chaplain. Chopsticks time again. Leaving there, we chose a restaurant at random for coffee and got lucky. Shortly after we arrived, some musicians showed up and treated us to some American jazz.

At Sea Near France, March 25, 1991

We are back at sea, cruising off the southwest coast of France, with the ship's personnel and Marines performing various drills. Since these drills mostly take place ashore or in small boats, I have little concept of what they are doing. When we left Toulon, some French officers came on board to observe the amphib exercises. The two Moroccans disappear during the day: Something about their Muslin religion requires them to fast during the day for thirty days.

The weather is cold, wet, and cloudy with seas so turbulent two days ago that many men got seasick, and many loose objects slammed around the ship. The chill winds limit outside physical training.

Now that the war in the Persian Gulf has ended, world news is not as popular as it used to be. Everyone is glad that we won so quickly, so decisively. But a sense of frustration pervades many of the Marines. These are combat professionals in peak physical and mental condition who sat out the war while women Marine reservists went to Saudi Arabia. One Marine captain bitterly complained that the man who wrote the book, *The Feminization of the American Military*, should have titled it *The Castration of the American Military*. When I left Texas, I thought this ship would end up somewhere near the action, for I couldn't conceive of 600 Marines just floating around in the Med for six months. I was wrong. I was also wrong about Hussein. I thought he would avert war by striking a deal with Congress on January 14 that George Bush couldn't refuse. It still astonishes me that one man can lead an entire nation into such a disaster.

Palma, Spain, March 29, 1991

It's a little after sunrise as I cross the quarter deck in shorts and T-shirt looking a bit conspicuous next to a Marine sentry still bundled up from the night's chilly air. Having had breakfast, I'm anxious to break the routine of jogging around the flight deck and run ashore. The ship is moored next to a doglegged breakwater extending into the bay. I climb the steps to the top of the forty-foot seawall to greet the morning sun burning off the haze over a placid sea. Completing my stretching exercises, I begin my run along the top of the wall.

Palma, not quite awake, beckons my gaze. Countless yachts decorate the waterfront lined with chic establishments along the wide boulevard. To the far right, the cathedral, Palma's most famous landmark, dominates the scene. Seaward, an empty tanker parallels my course as it departs for some probable Middle East destination. A thousand yards off the breakwater, a British naval support vessel rides at anchor. In the distance, two ferryboats bring early travelers to Palma.

The air still feels chilly as I reach the small lighthouse at the end of the seawall. Reversing my course, I pass the USS *Austin* and the USS *Charleston* moored outboard of *Austin*. Next comes the USS *Guadalcanal*, and then two Spanish oilers that have seen better days. The HMS *Ark Royal*, a British carrier with a ski jump flight deck loaded with Harrier fighter planes, completes the lineup of ships. Passing a building that houses administrative offices, U.S.O., and snack bar, I arrive at the other end of the seawall that terminates at the port gate. Again reversing my course, I face the morning sun with renewed exhilaration. After four miles and twenty-eight minutes, when my body heat offsets the chilly air, I feel like I could run forever on such a morning. But forever will have to wait since I am scheduled to tour the island of Mallorca shortly. So I return to the ship's weight room for upper body exercises before showering and boarding the bus.

Palma, Spain, March 30, 1991

A bunch of us toured the island yesterday via bus, train, and boat. A short bus ride through Palma ended at a small quaint electric train that forgot its shock absorbers. The one-hour ride crossed lush flat lands of Mallorca before ascending the mountain range that traverses the entire western side of the island. Wherever there was a meadow, yellow daffodils extended from the tracks all the way to some barrier. Poet William Wordsworth would have thought he was in paradise. Orange and lemon trees appeared ripe for picking, but olive and carob trees would have to wait awhile.

After crossing the mountain range, I loaded myself into a bus for a short trip to a dock where 149 other people and I boarded a 150-passenger boat. For an additional hour, we tossed our way to Puerto De Soller. Riding topside, I soaked up the brilliant sun under a cloudless sky. But the stiff breeze kicking up whitecaps made my windbreaker welcome.

I was well into the trip before I realized that this was really an outing for a geologist. But even an amateur could see that Mallorca is a geological oddity. Sheer cliffs dominated most of the trip. Layers of strata paralleling the water suddenly bent or inclined at a steep angle. In other places vertical strata contrasted with horizontal. This would give way to an indistinguishable mass. Caves often marked the waterline of the cliffs. High on the cliffs, huge, hollowed-out depressions suspended stalactites.

Then the cliffs abruptly changed to a steep slope carpeted with grass studded with pine trees. Weird, steep rock outcroppings punctuated deep ravines creasing the slope. Nestled in the back of the cove, a forty-foot waterfall poured into the ocean. The trip ended at the narrow beach of Puerto De Soller where the guide recommended a "typical Mallorcan meal," a mixture of rice, beef, pork, chicken, and shrimp washed down with Mallorcan red wine—all excellent.

Near the restaurant, a path led through the mountain to a spring-fed pool that eventually connected to the ocean. A small pebble-covered island offered a haven for sunbathers braving the chill wind and water. Making the trip with me were two young officers and a bosun mate. Although we had our swimsuits with us, we didn't use them.

Leaving there, a bus took us some thirty-five miles through the mountain range. Countless 180-degree switchbacks and narrow roads made it a two-hour-plus ride to Inca.

Enroute, the tour guide told us an admittedly ridiculous story, the legend of the Black Lady of Mallorca.

Many years ago, a Mallorcan man became jealous of his beautiful wife whom he falsely accused of spending time with another man. At that time, a duke occupied a monastery, which we passed in the mountains. While enroute to the monastery with his wife so that she could do penance, the jealous man pushed his wife off a

One of many switchbacks

cliff. Miraculously, she floated to earth "like a parachute." When the man arrived at the monastery, his wife was already praying there. Nowadays, tens of thousands of people make an annual pilgrimage from Palma to the monastery. They walk the 50-kilometer (30 miles) trip from 11 p.m. to 9 a.m. Thirty miles in ten hours is a good hike for a well-conditioned soldier. For a once-a-year pilgrim—well, I have to sprinkle a little skepticism on that. I suppose that there are stranger cultural traditions.

At Inca, the tour guide herded us into a shop selling a wide variety of over-priced leather goods and cheap jewelry. From there, we had a straight shot down the freeway back to Palma.

Rather than ride the bus back to the ship, my two officer companions and I got off at the cathedral. I wanted to photograph it as the full moon rose later.

The preceding night I had taken in part of the Easter pageantry. A male chorus brought back memories of all those years I sang with the Dallas Rotary Chorus. The powerful music I understood. The rest was a mystery. People holding lighted candles double lined the perimeter of the sanctuary. Priests led a procession between the two lines. Following close behind, ten other priests held a canopy aloft on long poles. Under the canopy marched another priest carrying a censer of incense. There was more.

At breakfast the next day, a Marine officer asked me about my visit to the cathedral. I told him as much as I could and said I didn't understand any of it. Then I added, "I don't think Jesus himself would have understood any of it."

The two officers accompanied me into the cathedral where another service was in progress. It seems that catholic services are always come-and-go affairs. Anyway, we marveled at the stained glass windows and the height of the walls supported by flying buttresses, an architectural device first used centuries ago to create such high ceilings. Unlike the cathedrals I have seen in Italy, France, and Yugoslavia, this one had no paintings on the walls or ceiling.

Cathedral at Mallorca

Square-rigged Galleon

Their curiosity being satisfied, the officers wanted to go back to the ship. I went with them as far as the yacht basin and suggested that they detour fifty yards to see a small, two-masted, square-rigged galleon, a beautiful brown-hulled ship trimmed in red and gold. A wooden rail supported by carved balustrades encompasses the hull. The sails are red. I would love to take a cruise of such a ship. They didn't bother to look at it.

That may be a pattern. When we rode the boat earlier in the day, I stayed topside and gave free rein to my curiosity about the trip. My friends stayed below, either bored or reading and interested only in getting from point A to point B. Life in general is like that. Some of us are interested in the trip; others merely traipse from point A to point B.

I retraced my steps to the cathedral. To my dismay a dense haze partially veiled the rising full moon, threatening to spoil a picture I had planned since the preceding evening. Light had just begun to bathe the cathedral. Light also illuminated the quarter-of-a mile long reflecting pool adjacent to the cathedral. In the pool near the cathedral, a fountain would soon send its single shaft skyward at various intervals. Pedestrians cluttered the area I wanted to photograph.

Finally, the fountain came on just as the clouds obscured the moon. I started to leave. But like a mantra, a line from Kipling's poem "If" popped into my mind: "If you can wait, and not be tired by waiting...." So I turned up my coat collar against the bay breeze, settled down on a park bench, and soaked up the serenity while I waited. Forty-five minutes passed before patience rewarded me. The moon finally struggled through the clouds as people cleared the area. Then the fountain came on. Wind diffused its soaring shaft into a fine mist, capturing the pale colors of the rainbow from the lights below.

Cathedral by Night

I started snapping pictures at various settings hoping that at least one would turn out well.

Palma, Spain, April 1, 1991

The ship's crew had another day of tours yesterday. The brochure invited us to, "Ride Spanish Carthusian horses through pine-wooded sand dunes on English saddles." A Spanish Carthusian is a magnificent, high-spirited horse. For me, it would be a unique equine experience. As it turned out, I have had better horseback experiences on father/son weekends at YMCA camps. Imagine my chagrin when a dozen of us showed up at the stables where each was given a sorrel nag whose experience was limited to following the horse in front of it and whose main interest was returning to the barn. There were a few pine trees. Sand dunes? Splotches of sand did occasionally appear among streets, buildings, broken terrain, and debris of lower suburbia. In addition, my horse and I had a major disagreement. He wanted to travel in a butt-bouncing trot, so I spent most of the trip keeping a tight rein.

Last night's affair made up for the disappointing bronc ride. In a "country castle," located about six miles out of downtown Palma, we ate a banquet while watching a medieval jousting tournament. Tiered banquet tables lined both sides of a long sand covered arena where the horses could achieve a full gallop. The colors red, green, blue, and yellow divided the banquet bleachers into four sections, the colors of each of four competing knights. The banqueters in each section cheered their own knight but booed the others.

My champion, the red knight, turned out to be the best horseman of the quartet. Before the main show got underway, he performed some beautiful routines with a Carthusian horse. The man and horse functioned as a single entity. Next, a dozen riders put their horses through a series of precision drills. I could have spent the evening just watching the performances of these magnificent animals and the talented men who rode them.

The jousting involved more than riders simply charging each other with lances and then engaging in swordplay. For example, using their lances, they had to pluck a small ring off an overhead wire and throw a javelin at a bull's eye while galloping. The "evil count" of the castle kept score.

At one time some "demons" captured the count's wife with intent to burn her at the stake when one of the knights rescued her.

The spectacle, the music, the food—all these made it an evening to remember.

Palma, Spain, April 3, 1991

Yesterday, I took another tour of Mallorca Island by taking the same road from Palma to Inca but traveling north instead of west. Between Inca and Pollensa lies some of Mallorca's most fertile lands, a truck farming area sprinkled with ancient villages named by Arabs who controlled the area from 900 AD until about 1236 AD. Prior Roman culture also left its distinction. The Dutch left their influence all over the island with their giant windmills. Only a small fraction of the 1500 windmills that once covered the island remain in working condition. But broken remains of these brick towers topped by giant wheels still abound.

At Pollensa, I boarded a boat for a short, uneventful trip under bright sunshine over a calm sea to Formentor. Here's an isolated spot for tourists who want to get away from everything. A narrow beach stretches in front of a few hotels and restaurants, most of which have not yet opened for the season. Pine trees rooted in sandstone lean precariously over the beach awaiting some storm that will bring them crashing down. Eucalyptus trees tower over a nearby road.

A bus ride through the mountains to Pollensa afforded some spectacular views of cliffs and ocean. As the bus made its hairpin turns, my window view of sheer drop offs just a few feet away added excitement to the ride. The bus stopped at the very top of the mountains for photographs.

The beach at Pollensa is much longer, wider, and sandier. But none of the few dozen people in swimsuits ventured into the cold water. Some children built sandcastles, and one cute little girl used the dock's edge to make cakes of wet sand. She "frosted" them with dry sand.

My last stop introduced me to several varieties of wines produced on the island. They tasted more like liqueurs than wines, and a person would have to be a confirmed alcoholic to drink much. Besides the restaurant, other attractions included a wax museum, elaborate swimming pool, and summertime amusements.

After a short bus ride southwest of Palma, I arrived at Palma Nova, which is reputed to have beaches superior to the one at Palma. It was just a stretch of long and narrow packed sand with sea debris at the water's edge. Out-of-shape people, probably tourists from the mainland, populated the place. McDonald's dominated the whole area with its huge restaurant, swimming pool, and assortment of amusements for older kids.

I finally found the beach I was looking for two kilometers on down the road. Magalluf's beach is a long, wide expanse of deep, clean sand washed by water as clear as the Caribbean. I have left my footprints on more than four dozen beaches around the globe, and this is definitely one of the better ones. Here I encountered CPL Scott Zoll and three of his buddies off the USS *Austin* who invited me to participate in their sun worship. Having spent the night in a first class hotel ($15.00 each for two rooms with kitchens), they were now involved in some horseplay with two little rambunctious English boys whom they were using to do some "reconnaissance" with topless girls that looked like they had just stepped out of a men's magazine. I had an interesting chat with the parents of one of the boys, as well as a couple of men from Scotland. Boats and windsurfers plied the cove. I wish I had time to go back.

Off the southern tip of Sardinia, April 7, 1991

Our last day in Palma was supposed to have been April 4. However, thirty-knot winds, gusting to fifty knots kept the ship pinned to the pier in spite of the efforts of two tugs to pull the ship away. The *Charleston*, which had been moored outboard of *Austin*, got underway before the wind reached such high velocity. We didn't leave Palma until the next morning. The *Guadalcanal* followed us later. Rough seas tossed the ship around a bit all day and night until we reached our present anchorage this morning.

Since we had to stay in port an extra day, the crew received one more night of liberty. CPL Scott Zoll and I walked the three miles to Jazz Forum in hopes of hearing some good music. The place didn't even open until midnight. Strange hours, but rather typical of Spain. Disappointed, we just walked around the downtown area until time to return to the ship.

The preceding day, I made my second trip to Bellver Castle, which overlooks downtown Palma. LTJG Todd Prideaux, my roommate, and I had gone there earlier in the week when it was closed. This time I went alone. Knowing that the castle contained a museum, I didn't take my camera, because museums usually ban picture taking. Big mistake. I could have taken pictures of some of the best Gothic architecture to be found anywhere. The castle resembled a miniature Texas Stadium. The second floor opened onto a loggia about ten feet wide. Octagonal pillars of rock forming gothic arches between themselves and also the inner wall of the castle supported the entire circumference of the loggia roof. The structure is in excellent condition, thanks to considerable restoration work.

A few dozen workers, including slaves, built the basic castle over a nine-year period beginning in 1300. Ornamentation came later. Mallorcan King James II, son of James I, King of Caledonia and Aragon, ordered its construction.

The sparse rooms contain a few pieces of furniture from an earlier period. Others contain artifacts and descriptions of the town's civilizations dating back to 5,000 BC.

We're back into a war games mode. Some Marines went ashore by helicopter today. This exercise, involving military components of Spain and Italy, will last about eight days. Next port of call is La Spezia, Italy.

Gulf of Teulada, Sardinia, April 10, 1991

For several days the crew has been making plans to visit Rome, Florence, and Pisa when we reach LA Spezia on April 16. The wife of one crewman had already purchased her airline ticket to meet her husband in Italy. Last night all such plans got canceled. We have been diverted to the Eastern Mediterranean on a humanitarian mission. No details yet—just something about assistance to refugees from Iraq, probably Kurds. I'm sure everyone in the United States knows more about the situation than we do. Anyway, most of the men are pumped up about it. It beats merely cruising the Med and playing soldier while the country was at war. Maybe this operation will assuage some wounded egos.

The new mission destroyed our current exercise. Early yesterday, Marines in AAV's and other amphib vehicles assaulted the beach. Many others had already been airlifted to make believe battle sites in a full swing operation when the word came to recall the troops. The Marines and naval support personnel rehearsed the assault two days ago, and then commenced the actual assault at 2 a.m. yesterday. Activities of the two days just blended. And now at 8 a.m., men and equipment are still being brought back on board.

These are tired people. A number of bleary-eyed Sailors have come by to tell me why they missed class for two days. Because of extended hours of work plus regular watch duty, several students have simply dropped out. But a nucleus of students always doggedly hangs in no matter what happens. Some who make it to class have difficulty staying awake. Even so, only two failed to finish the basic reading class that ended yesterday. Most of those who finished will enroll in basic math that starts tomorrow.

I'm glad that the ship has an opportunity to participate in a significant endeavor, but I'm sorry that the current operation had to be aborted. One of the Marine captains had invited me to go ashore next Saturday and fire a variety of weapons.

Between Italy and Libya, April 11, 1991

Details of our mission are still quite sparse, but Captain de Groy has told the crew this much: This ship is part of "Operation Provide Comfort." We will anchor at Iskenderun, Turkey, near Syria on April 14. Components of the army and air force in Europe are included in the operation. About 300,000 refugees from Iraq have settled in Turkey. Another 800,000 have gone to Iran. They need refugee camps, food, and medicine. Much of this material will be air dropped, and some of our Marines probably will go ashore to assist. Something of this magnitude must be making headlines in the States.

Last night, the ship underwent fuel replenishment and also took on a cargo of soda pop. The crew drinks more than one thousand cans of soda pop a day. I would like to collect the cans that are thrown into the ocean. I have suggested on other ships that the cans be saved so the ship's Welfare and Recreation Dept. can use the proceeds from their sale. I was told that this is not practical. I don't know why it isn't because crushed cans take up less space than full cans.

Iskenderun, Turkey, April 14, 1991

Shortly before 0700, the ship dropped anchor about fifty-seven miles offshore from Iskenderun. We had cruised at top speed, about nineteen knots, taking a direct route from Sardinia. Later in the morning, the ship moved to an anchorage within two miles of Iskenderun. The USS *Charleston* and the USS *Guadalcanal* are anchored nearby. The supply ship USS *San Diego* is at pier side.

Two days ago, we saw two-day old news clips from three networks detailing the plight of the Kurds. We learned from another source that some would not be friendly to Americans. In fact, one helicopter took small arms fire when it attempted to land and to provide assistance to the people. The news people seemed to make a big deal of President Bush's decision that day (April 10) to finally help the Kurds. This operation was put into motion at least a week earlier. It makes me wonder what else the news media knows that isn't so.

Security is at the highest level because of terrorist activity in Turkey. Some terrorists target not only Americans, but also Turkish officials. I don't anticipate any problems for naval personnel because no one is likely to go ashore. We could be in for weeks of boredom. But the good news is that I should be able to leave the ship two weeks earlier than anticipated.

I'm ready to go. I'm finally cured of my "strep throat," having left it in Palma. The cough and sore throat that persisted for two months wasn't strep at all. Even the doctor who diagnosed it came down with the same thing. So did many other people. I think the ship's ventilation system caused the problem. I enclosed the air vent in my room with cheesecloth, which turned black within a week. When I first moved into the room, a black film covered everything and required considerable scrubbing to remove. All the running, walking, boat riding, and train riding that I did in the fresh air at Palma seems to have flushed out my respiratory system. I feel perfectly fit again with a blood pressure reading of 110/70.

Tomorrow the ship's Marines will go ashore for transport to the Kurd's refugee site in the mountains some four hundred miles away. Earlier today they checked and packed their gear on the flight deck preparatory to departure. They comprise only a small contingent of a worldwide effort, both military and civilian, to try to alleviate the distress of the displaced Kurds. What this ship will do in the immediate future nobody seems to know.

As with other Mediterranean cities, mountains form a backdrop to Iskenderun, a city larger than I anticipated. Peaks of snow rise behind the immediate mountain range. Tonight the lights of the city form a beautiful semi-circle around us. But even the darkness fails to hide a layer of polluted air over the city. This afternoon one industrial plant completely obliterated its view with dense smoke that spread over a wide area. Trash extending many miles from the harbor litters the ocean. This indifference to pollution by so many Mediterranean cities likely accounts for the haze that hangs over the entire length of the Med.

April 18, 1991, Iskenderun, Turkey

The ship went from anchorage to pier side today, but we do not know how long we will be here. All but a very few Marines went to the beach about 0700 today via the LCU. Buses are taking them inland about 400 miles to assist in Operation Provide Comfort. The SEALs went with them. The Beach Masters (Sailors who insure the safe landing of Marines' materiel in amphibious operations) seem to be disappointed that they didn't go also. Their skills are not needed in the mountains since their function is to support an established beachhead. A number of Marine officers left in eager anticipation.

The Marines' trucks and AAVs await flat-bed Turkish trucks to haul them to their destination. Transporting the rolling stock by truck through the mountains will save considerable wear on the vehicles. Now that the Marines have been dispatched, the ship seems to be in a state of boring uncertainty. But that's typical of a military operation. Very few people are actually on the "point of the spear." All the rest provide support. So this Mediterranean Amphibious Readiness Group (MARG), consisting of USS *Guadalcanal*, USS *Austin*, and USS *Charleston* sits in a port I never before heard of and waits.

Yesterday, we took aboard an unusual quantity of supplies (more than 200 pallets) from the supply ship USS *San Diego* which has since departed. When the supply department ordered the supplies, they thought we would still have the Marines on board plus several hundred refugees. The crew worked far into the night to stow the material. Some of the crew had a 36-hour day which decimated my classes. In addition, they had to cope with fickle weather. The day started off warm and balmy. Then the wind whipped up to 50 knots, causing the ship to drag anchor and requiring the engines to power up to reduce the strain. Next, the weather turned cloudy and cold, then shirt-sleeve warm again. After that, hail and sleet pelted the ship, creating banks of sleet around the ship. Some of the busy Sailors took time out to chunk ice balls at each other. Snow covered the nearby highest mountain peak. By evening the air had warmed again under clear skies and a "Turkish moon"—a crescent with a bright planet near the lower point.

A few days ago, a dust storm reduced visibility to 1,000 yards, reminding me of life in the Texas panhandle when I was a kid. A brown film covering the ship turned to mud the next day when a rain shower passed over. Through it all, at least a dozen industrial plants blanket everything in sight with a brown haze. Land 16 miles away is barely visible through the ship's big eyes. Today would be a beautiful sunny day if there were no industrial pollution.

Liberty is not authorized for this city which doesn't look very promising anyway. In addition to the several industrial plants, oil storage tanks line some of the ocean front. The only nearby beach looks uninviting. And then there is the high terrorist risk. Sentries armed with loaded M-14 rifles, shotguns, and 45 cal. pistols patrol every exposed segment of the ship. This looks like a good time to just teach English and math—twenty-one days, and counting.

April 21, 1991, Iskenderun, Turkey

Last Friday dozens of Turkish trucks crowded the pier to take supplies to our Marines in the mountains. Each truck contained about 250 artillery shells. Quantities of other ammunition followed, along with all the necessities for a sustained operation in the field. So far, no word has been received from the Marines.

That same day, a news team from one of the networks came aboard for some interviews. I don't know whether we are famous, infamous, or just footage on the cutting room floor.

Since the crew has not been allowed into town, it gets a daily excursion onto the port facility after working hours. Some of the men jog or play touch football. But the big hit is free beer and sandwiches.

Today about seventy-two of us took a two-and-a-half-hour bus ride to the Air Force Base at Incerlik. We did some shopping at the Base Exchange and enjoyed the ride through the Turkish countryside. But mostly, the men just wanted a chance to get away from the ship for a while. Quite a number don't like the Navy in general and this ship in particular. I keep asking the malcontents why they joined the Navy since they don't like the ocean. Some say they just never expected the separation from their families to hit them so hard. All jobs have a down side. And since they are stuck with this one for a certain amount of time, they may as well accept it and make the best of it.

April 25, 1991, Iskenderun, Turkey

Our Beach Master Unit left today for Solopi, Turkey. This town, located at the juxtaposition of Turkey, Syria, and Iraq, was the destination of our Marines who left six days ago. The Beach Masters will join Navy Seabees and army engineers to construct a refugee camp for the Kurds. Evidently, even more workers are needed. There has been some talk of sending some volunteers from the ship's crew to assist in the effort. The Marine rifle companies set up a safety perimeter 15 miles inside Iraq for the Kurds and the construction crews.

The Combat Cargo Officer (CCO) attached to the ship told me that the anticipated world-wide relief effort had not yet materialized and that no coordination of effort between the Turks, Kurds, and others was in place until the Marines arrived to provide it.

The CCO also said that the Marines, using helicopters and trucks, delivered more tonnage to the Kurds in two days than the Air Force had delivered in two weeks. Tonight the ABC News of April 15 showed ineffectual air drops to the Kurds where food and supplies were destroyed as they hit the ground. Our guys are trained to get it down undamaged and avoid the clamoring crowds of people. I wonder if the TV networks will take notice of that or simply engage in more hand wringing.

The departure of the Beach Masters just decimated my basic math and basic English classes. Knowing that the classes would be over when they returned, some students asked for assignments to work on while they are in the field. Reluctantly, I parted with my students, but PACE courses are low priority compared to dislocated people.

April 28, 1991, Iskenderun, Turkey

This ship was supposed to get underway five days ago to conduct some tests on its engineering equipment and satisfy some inspectors who have come aboard. A defective valve in one of the steam lines prevented the ship's movement. The defective device looks deceivingly simple. It is a silver-plated metal ring about four inches in diameter. But it has to withstand steam pressure of 850 pounds per square inch at 700 degrees F. A steam blowout at that pressure and temperature would instantly kill anyone in the engine compartment. A blow out did occur on the helicopter carrier USS *Iwo Jima* last year and killed ten men. The part arrived today and the repair has already been made.

Now we are transferring a large quantity of the Marine ammunition to the *Charleston*, which will remain here to support the Marines. The *Guadalcanal* will also remain in port to service its helicopters that were dispatched to help in the Kurd's relief. This ship has been assigned to Operation Dragon Hammer, an annual training exercise with other ships of N.A.T.O. countries.

Judging from our change in schedule, our Marines won't be coming back any time soon. Three days ago we sent them another 25 pallets of ammunition. That was the second supplementary shipment since they left the ship. Last evening I talked to a Marine who had just returned from the mountains for a few hours. He said that our guys had established an artillery line of defense about 40 miles southeast of the Iraq border and about 25 miles southeast of Zakho, Iraq. So far, no clashes with Iraqi troops have occurred even though some are in the same area with the Marines. He said the establishment of refugee camps had gone well, but the Kurds were reluctant to come down out of the mountains.

April 30, 1991, Off the Coast of Syria

The switch from Operation Provide Comfort to Operation Dragon Hammer complicates my travel plans back to the states. I had requested transportation from Turkey ten days ago, thinking that the ship would stay in port to give any necessary support to the Marines.

Today I received my instructions via ship's radio to depart from Istanbul, Turkey. I would have enjoyed seeing that famous city which has been the crossroads of the Middle East for two millennia. These instructions crossed with a revised travel request to leave from Taranto, Italy, a city on the southern coast of Italy that I also have not seen but lacks the mystery of Istanbul.

We finally left Iskenderun yesterday to carry out the various tests of the ship's equipment and conduct some drills. Nobody was sorry to leave this particular port since we were confined to the port area. Even confirmed beer drinkers could get bored with the nightly routine of bending elbows on the pier.

Today we played "leap frog" with the *Charleston*. This is a practice maneuver to teach the junior officers how to approach another ship to take on fuel or provisions. I happened to notice the signalman on *Charleston* when he spelled out "pace instructor." It seems he somehow found out I was formerly a Navy quartermaster with signaling skills. We chatted briefly via semaphore before his ship pulled away.

May 1, 1991, Eastern Mediterranean

Today this ship, along with the *Charleston* and *Guadalcanal*, replenished its fuel supply. Plans were made to use the LCMs to transport the rest of the Marines' ammunition onto the other ships before we left the area, but rough seas made the operation too hazardous. So tonight, while the other two ships are on their way back to Iskenderon, we are on our way to Benidorm, Spain to pick up two Spanish helicopters to be used in Operation Dragon Hammer. It is a five-day trip there and a three-day trip back to Taranto, Italy. That seems like a lot of unnecessary travel for the ship when the choppers could cover the same distance in a matter of hours. Besides, we are expecting even rougher seas which could slow us down. The weather decks have already been secured due to high winds. We are still expected to reach Taranto on May 9. I hope so since I am supposed to fly out of there the next day.

I received a letter from Bob White, the PACE coordinator in Naples, today indicating that I might be needed back on the *Orion* in Sardinia in July. However, a group of ships are supposed to go to South America in July and I would prefer to be on one of them. He also indicated that an assignment might be available on *Belknap* in Gaeta, Italy in May. I have fond memories of *Belknap* and would like to return, but I need to spend some time in Texas first.

May 5, 1991, Western Mediterranean

Shortly after passing Cyprus yesterday, Captain de Gruy informed the crew that we had been directed to abort our trip to Benidorm, Spain to pick up Spanish helicopters. So we turned around and headed east toward Taranto, Italy. But a few hours later, we received orders to go to Alicante, Spain to pick up some Spanish officers and Marines. So now we are going west again.

Since today is Sunday, the crew is getting some much-needed rest, quite a contrast from last Sunday when the crew put in a thirty-six hour day transferring ammunition. I got my hour in the weight room out of the way before 0700 today, listened to a sermon that Nita sent me, and took my final exam in a math correspondence course. The lessons have been spread over four different ships. Now that the final exam had finally caught up with me, the challenge is to remember everything I had studied since last July.

The crew has been taking typhoid shots because of our visit to Turkey. Fortunately, the shot I got nearly two years ago is still effective. However, I, along with everybody else, take a chloroquine pill weekly to prevent malaria. Even after leaving the ship, I will have to continue taking plasmaquin for a few weeks. No one who takes this preventive treatment can donate blood for a year.

May 6, 1991, Alicante, Spain

We had an exciting arrival at Alicante. While steaming at 15 knots directly toward the breakwater, the ship suddenly lost power, including all electricity, lights, radar, and computers. One of the anchors was released in an effort to stop the ship. But the momentum caused the ship to pivot 180 degrees. As the ship swung around, the stern cleared the breakwater by less than twelve feet. Since the breakwater is wider at the base than at the top, the ship's screws almost collided with the breakwater.

May 8, 1991, Off Sardinia

All classes ended yesterday, and I worked until nearly midnight boxing up school material for shipment back to Norfolk. The final paperwork just seems endless. I have to keep photocopies of all records in case the originals get lost in the mail. A PACE instructor must perform the functions of a college dean, instructor, secretary, book store operator, disbursing officer, stock room clerk, and general flunky.

I got the word at noon yesterday. We are not going to Taranto, Italy. Now it's Brandisi, Italy. That's today's schedule. Who knows what tomorrow's schedule will be? I really don't care as long as I can be in Bari, Italy, to catch a plane at 1100 on May 10.

Postscript: The USS *Austin* was decommissioned at Naval Station Norfolk, Virginia, on September 27, 2006 and towed to the Philadelphia Naval - Storage facility.

USS Barnstable County

USS *Barnstable County* LST-1197

Off Norfolk, Virginia, July 5, 1991

This LST is another amphibious ship, but very different from the LST on which I served in World War II. It may be the ugliest ship in the U.S. Navy, having two huge booms extending forward beyond the bow. These are used to move a ramp about 28' by 135' that is carried on deck. The ramp can be extended from the ship to shore for loading and unloading vehicles. It just kills the deck space forward of the pilothouse. They say a woman engineer who had never been to sea designed the ship. Although this statement was made seriously, it sounds like a chauvinistic joke to me. High winds and rough seas two nights ago proved that this ship does have one thing in common with the old LSTs—a flat bottom. Naturally a lot of people turned green, especially some of the young Marines. Today is a beautiful day of bright sunshine, cool breeze, and smooth sea.

We have company, as usual—two destroyers, a frigate, and a sub. Since leaving Norfolk, the battle group has engaged in a number of training exercises. Keeping the Navy sharp justifies a basic reason for sending ships to sea for extended periods. Recent events in the Persian Gulf evidently proved the value of that policy. This crew will get back to the states a few days before Christmas after having visited most countries in South America and about eight countries in Africa. If my classes go according to schedule, I should disembark some time in September from Chile.

Henry, my roommate, is an easy going Filipino Catholic chaplain. And we have a doctor on board from North Dakota, a naval reservist who looks tired and in need of a change of scenery.

Classes got off to a very ragged start. Placement tests indicate a potential of seven classes: One semester of college composition, one semester of college sophomore literature, two sessions of basic

English, two of basic reading, and one of basic math. The problem is that very few prospective students know which classes they are eligible to attend. I do have a decent classroom that can accommodate about fifteen students. However, it is right next to the engine room and very noisy.

Roosevelt Roads, Puerto Rico, July 7, 1991

Class schedules are still up in the air. The captain routinely asked me how things were going. I told him. He said education is one of his high priorities. Action began within five minutes of our conversation. That's encouraging, but in the meantime I have lost four teaching days.

It happened again for the thousandth time. When I was visiting the signal bridge two nights ago, another guy visiting the signal bridge said, "I know you from somewhere." People who say that usually don't know me from anywhere. After introducing ourselves and comparing places and events for a few minutes, we couldn't establish any connection. Later, I happened to mention the USS *Belknap*. He said he was on the USS *Shenandoah* when it was moored next to *Belknap* at Gaeta, Italy two years ago. I looked closely at the man. He was the petty officer who repaired the broken lock on my attaché case.

Also riding the ship is a ten-piece Navy band. They performed at an on-base carnival after we arrived here yesterday. They're good and crowd-pleasing.

Today started off with a 5K "fun run." About 300 of us (mostly Marines) left the starting line at 0700. I was in the middle of the pack about 400 yards from the finish line when I stumbled and fell to the pavement, receiving abrasions on my right hand, shoulder, elbow, and knee. Immediately, two corpsmen swabbed me down with Bacitracin, loaded me into a car, and returned me to the ship where they slapped a cold pack on my bruised hand. The doc said I would feel places tomorrow that I don't even know about. He may be right, but for the moment my "wounds" are merely a minor annoyance, compared to my injured dignity. But there will be other "fun runs" in other countries.

I joined a small group of people at the Family Service Center on base for Bible study and church services both morning and evening. They are a friendly, dedicated bunch.

At Anchor off Vieques Island, July 15, 1991

We left Roosevelt Roads five days ago for training exercises with a Peruvian ship and a Venezuelan ship. Some of their personnel came on board. Some of our personnel went to their ships. A school of dolphins welcomed our arrival here where our Marines are ashore on maneuvers, having taken their AAVs with them. They came back to the ship Saturday but left again Sunday morning to repeat the entire operation. Retrieving the tanks and launching them again gave the crew quite a workout. Apparently the Peruvians and Venezuelan troops don't get very good food aboard their ships. They consider the Marines' MREs an improvement.

Before we left Puerto Rico, these South Americans jammed the Navy Exchange buying everything they could carry out—anything electronic, bicycles (multiple purchases), clothing, and household items. They appeared to be single-handedly trying to solve America's balance of payments problem.

As usual, I spent some time on the signal bridge during our last night in transit from Roosevelt Roads. The chief signalman broke out the Night Observation Device (NOD), a very effective telescope that allows the viewer to clearly see objects in the dark. The chief said that sometimes, when the ship is in port, signalmen will relieve the boredom of night watches by training the NOD on the darkened rooms of beachfront hotels. Inevitably, such high tech equipment will find its way into stores selling military surplus. The concern will not be whether Big Brother is watching you, but whether your neighbor is watching you to collect salable information.

My roommate has gone to another ship for several days, but will return this week. His absence gave me a chance to really get the room clean, floor waxed, fan installed, light fixed, and door lock fixed. Logic dictates that such routine maintenance would be performed when it is first needed. But it doesn't work that way. Someone must delegate each problem to the proper department who selects the right person who selects the right equipment and/or materials—during the respective hours that such equipment or materials can be checked out and accounted for. For example, the pieces to a metal bookcase 84" by 42" have cluttered my classroom for two weeks. When I first came on board, I requested that the bookcase be assembled so that it could be used. Finally, I borrowed a screwdriver and crescent wrench yesterday and took an hour to assemble the bookcase and attach it to the bulkhead. End of problem. I'm convinced that people dedicated to getting things done could shave billions of dollars off the annual defense budget that the military would never miss.

An admiral came on board yesterday morning and approvingly observed the ship carrying out several complex operations simultaneously. After he left, the crew had a holiday routine the rest of the day. About a dozen men got out their fishing tackle and fished off the stern. A number of barracudas swam by, but none took the bait. One man caught a small shark but threw it back when the galley crew refused to cook it. Naturally, the shark got longer as the day progressed.

Roosevelt Roads, Puerto Rico, July 19, 1991

The training exercise at Vieques Island having been completed, the ship returned here late Tuesday afternoon to give some of the crew a little rest and relaxation. I had just mailed a letter at the shore post office when I encountered a chief petty officer who invited me to join him and some of his buddies at the Chiefs' Hut up the beach. Although I had no interest in watching other people put away a lot of beer, I decided to be sociable. These men have direct control over some of my students, and I think I made some lasting points with one of them who assured me that class attendance would no longer be a problem with his men.

A huge computer-printed sign hung in the hut, which read, "Whatever is said in this room stays in this room." I asked my host if chiefs took this sign seriously. He assured me they did. The fellowship and camaraderie are genuine. Christian groups should be so fortunate.

The next day a tour bus dropped a bunch of us off in Old San Juan. My roommate and I set out to see the two old forts—San Felipe de Morro and San Cristobal. It took over 240 years to complete the ingenious architectural engineering at Morro. Now both forts only attract tourists. During all those years many people probably asked why all that time and money couldn't have been spent on social programs. In retrospect, that seems like a good question but probably a bit naive. Future historians likely will make the same observation about the present generation. Nothing basic ever changes—just the technology.

The passengers of three cruise ships in the harbor competed with us for the sidewalks, restaurant space, and the attention of store clerks. Inside the restaurant, a woman at the next table told my roommate and me that she came from Africa but now lived in Canada. Soon two American couples from the East Coast replaced her. One man had retired from the army. We spent a little time in mutual lying, bragging, and deploring.

Leaving Old San Juan, Henry and I spent the remainder of the day in Condado, a beach area of expensive hotels with casinos and extensive shops. For a long while we just dangled our feet off the seawall and watched the aquamarine waves roll in. Later, we bought some presents to send home and treated ourselves to piña coladas, sans rum. At this point, my Catholic friend decided that we were buddies for the remainder of the cruise. He's an interesting little guy, somewhat younger than I am. We do seem to have many common interests. And, like most Catholic priests, he knows a lot of jokes. He's originally from Olongopo, P.I., the town next to Subic Naval Base. The recent volcanic eruption there affected his family and many of his friends.

Naturally, we had some interesting religious discussions comparing Catholicism with Protestantism. He pointed out that traditions that Catholics observe in the Philippines were not necessarily celebrated in Spain or Latin America. When we stripped away the traditions of both groups and focused on the basic message of the Gospel, we discovered many common beliefs. People in Northern Ireland should be so fortunate. For the last 2000 years Christianity has abused and been abused. But with the rise of so many other powerful religions, it seems to me that if Christianity is to be a significant influence on civilization during the next 2000 years, churches everywhere are going to have to get their splintered act together. Having attended a wide variety of shipboard worship services, I've discovered that worshiping God doesn't necessarily require other people to be in total agreement with me in matters religious.

Yesterday the bus took a group of us through a rain forest in a slow, winding drive up a mountain through dense foliage and small waterfalls. An observation tower at the top afforded a panoramic view of mountains toward the interior and the town of Luquillo on the coast. We also stopped at one waterfall where the guys horsed around and took pictures. I got the best drink of water that I have had in a long time. Since we didn't get to do any hiking, we missed the close up observations of plants such as I had while climbing through the rain forest of Mt. Scenery on Saba Island a few years ago. However, a large quantity of white wild ginger with its jasmine fragrance enlivened my senses—just like the ginger in Hawaii, except white instead of red.

Leaving the forest, we arrived at the beach a little before noon. Here we spent the remainder of day, and most of us have red skin to prove it. Henry and I jogged on the long beach until we ran out of people, about a three-mile round trip. Then we cooled off with a long swim. An offshore reef checked the breakers, making the cool, clear water perfect for swimming. The sparse crowd on the beach appeared to be natives—primarily a mixture of Tiana Indian and African Negro.

The ship just departed from Roosevelt Roads. Two of my students (one college, one basic) had to stay behind—medical problems.

Last night I lost my roommate who went to one of the other ships in our group. So for eight days I will again have the room all to myself—all 96 square feet, including closets, drawers, two fold down tables, two beds, two chairs, a lavatory, and a wastebasket.

Caribbean Sea, July 21, 1991

Yesterday, our first abandon ship drill cut short my basic reading class. I am assigned to a life raft with Navy SEALs, the doctor, the dentist, and the chaplain. If I have to be adrift at sea, I don't suppose I could ask for better companions. The ship continues to engage in training exercises that strains class attendance. Today is Sunday and it's work as usual except for short Catholic and Protestant church services, both conducted by lay people. So far, I have not held classes on Sunday, but may have to in order to make up some missed classes due to ship's activities. Four of us showed up for Protestant services today—one naval officer, one enlisted Marine, one civilian, and one Navy enlisted man who brought the lesson. I am now the designated "song leader"—read that "soloist" unless attendance picks up.

Prior to church service, the deck division gave the ship a fresh-water wash-down. I spent the time on the signal bridge in the sunshine and fresh air just watching the flying fish skim the whitecaps. Although the smallest fish, they are the largest schools of flying fish that I have seen. They can skim the waves for a hundred feet, and then glance off the surface in a new direction. I don't see how a predator could ever catch one.

Cartagena, Colombia, July 23, 1991

A cloudy bright day turned the sea to a lead color. Except for a dark gray landmass that embodies Cartagena, the sea and the sky blended so as to make the horizon indistinguishable. The water in Cartagena Bay itself is an ugly greenish gray. Apparently the bay has little chance to wash itself out in the main ocean because it is so well protected. Perhaps it improves during the rainy season. As usual, a local pilot came on board at the entrance to the channel.

I guess we looked good to anyone interested in seeing us. We steamed into the harbor single file behind two destroyers and frigate—USS *Dahlgren*, USS *O'Bannon*, and USS *Aylwin*. Two small Colombian ships and our sub brought up the rear. Sailors in summer whites and Marines in olive and khaki manned the rails. One of the Marines fainted while standing at parade rest. Standing at attention or parade rest with knees locked for an extended period cuts off the blood circulation. I guess the young man forgot that. Meanwhile, the band played marching songs. All ships anchored a short distance from shore since the water at the available piers is too shallow to accommodate the ships. After anchoring, all four of our small boats were put into the water to be used for official transportation and to carry the crew ashore for liberty later.

I stood on the quarterdeck watching the first men go ashore. Officers who look reasonably mature in uniform suddenly looked like high school boys in sport shirts and shorts. Although repeatedly warned, orally and in writing, that forty percent of the local prostitutes have AIDS, crew members eagerly accepted the free condoms. Russian roulette probably offers better odds. All the medical research that money can buy can't offset folly.

Cartagena, Colombia, July 24, 1991

Yesterday, I took a tour bus that drove around Old Town where we stopped for a look at a 400-year-old church with a 200-year-old tree in the courtyard. Nearby, some boys holding macaws on their arms invited us to let them perch on our arms. We did. After a short visit to Old Town, we drove to the top of the mountain overlooking Cartegena, the site of another old church. As I stepped out of the bus, a young man thrust a three-toed sloth carrying a baby sloth upon me. Before I realized what was happening, he had my camera and was taking a picture of this little animal and me. Then he demanded two dollars. The tour guide made him settle for one dollar. The magic word in this country is "no."

Next, the bus stopped at an old fort built on the order of the ones I saw in Puerto Rico. Modern Cartegena actually rests on an Island, and this fort (on the mainland) protected the Old City as well as the surrounding area. The statue of a commander with one arm, one leg, and one eye who died defending the fort stands in front of it. The guide told us which battle, but he told us about so many so quickly that I don't recall which one.

The tour ended at a jewelry store in the modern portion of downtown Cartagena. Before showing off emeralds, rubies, diamonds, and other precious stones for the benefit of a bunch of Sailors, first the establishment served snacks, soft drinks, and beer. Then the fashion show started. To the strains of appropriate music, models who looked like they had worked for a health club all their lives wore black skin-tight bodysuits. Naturally, this "ensemble" effectively showed off the various pieces of jewelry. The guys must have been very interested in the jewelry, because they took a lot of flash pictures. I spent $4.23 at a store next door for a straw hat. Columbia has a blazing sun.

Today was fun in the sun when six men from the USS *Aylwin*

and I took a snorkeling tour. All the men from my ship wanted to go scuba diving. My certification as a diver expired a long time ago, and I figured that I remembered just enough to be dangerous. Besides, the water is so clear the tanks could be just an encumbrance. A fast small boat, driven by a little non-English speaking black guy, took us to an island with a coral reef about 17 miles out of the harbor. We anchored in a small cove where coconut trees served as a backdrop to a clean sandy beach. Red blooming flamboyant trees framed the ends of the beach. A young woman originally from Bogotá who had just enough Indian blood to distinguish her facial features and give her a permanent tan served as our guide. Being very knowledgeable about marine life she led us through a spectacular undersea environment reminiscent of that in the Windward Islands of the Caribbean where I snorkeled with my wife and daughter while on windjammer cruises. The brilliant Yellowtail is my favorite fish. Snorkeling uses leg muscles differently than jogging, and when cramps hit me in both legs, I knew it was time to hang up the fins. And even with the use of sun block, I still got more than enough sunshine.

We ate snacks and drinks on our way to another beach dotted with thatched huts. From the sea, it looked quite picturesque. From the beach, it looked quite impoverished. We anchored offshore to prevent theft, and as we swam toward the shore, people entered the water trying to sell us something. Some of the men snorkeled here while the rest of us just walked the beach and observed the populace.

Leaving there, we went to Boca Chica Fort for a short visit. Again, three of us just took in the exterior of the fort and the surrounding area. I have seen quite a number of these Caribbean forts, and they all have a certain sameness.

Off Cartagena, July 26, 1991

We left Cartagena before sunrise today. During the next few days, the ship's personnel will undergo training exercises off the Colombian coast with Colombian Marines, several of which are on board. By departing so early, we secured from sea and anchor detail in time for my students involved to make it to class.

Last night I went ashore with two enlisted men. We walked for about three hours just sightseeing. Vendors carrying their merchandise with them filled the sidewalks and vied for our attention. Handicrafts, T-shirts, shorts, cigarettes were for sale everywhere. "No, gracias" soon turned to just plain "No!" Visitors to this country very quickly learn that eye contact approves harassment.

Colorful buses that reminded me of the Jeepneys in the Philippines decorated the streets. So did the horse drawn carriages with

candles for sidelights. A few buses were converted fire trucks—
"bombero tourisimo." A little four-car train wound through the traffic tooting its whistle to the delight of the kids and parents riding it.
But the prettiest sight of the evening was the full moon through the
palm trees. It is hard to improve on nature. At length we made a
short visit at a disco, an obvious trysting place for available men and
women. Eventually we arrived at the beach on the Caribbean side
where breakers glistened in the moonlight. There, some girl tried in
vain to sell us pornographic key chains.

Reversing our course, we walked to Old Town, which is encircled
by a six-mile wall. Ships tied to the pier on the lagoon side served
as a background to countless sidewalk eating-places. Much of the
food looked good and smelled good, but we ate and drank nothing.
Passing a large old structure that now houses government offices, we
came to a large park-like plaza. Here, we grew a tail. Some native
began following us trying to get us to let him be our guide: "Step
over here and listen to the guitar music," or "I show you good place.
Where you want go?" We ignored him, but he stuck with us until
we headed back to the ship. It's saddening to be forced to be rude
to people, because I like to explore a country and interact with the
people. Those who only have a monetary interest in me defeat that
purpose.

Morrosquillo Bay, Colombia, July 28, 1991

After spending one night anchored at Covenas about 75 miles
from Cartagena, we anchored here for other war games. *Morros-
quillo* means mosquito, and according to a Marine captain, the place
is appropriately named. At Covenas and also here, the Marines
launched AAVs in mock attacks on the beach. Each of the dozen
AAVs contained three American Marines who operated the vehicles
and 20 Colombian Marines. After going inland, the Marines deployed
behind a defense perimeter formed by the AAVs. The men don't get
much sleep ashore because the heat hangs on until about 0200. Some
of the men sleep in the AAVs with the rear door and hatches covered
by mosquito netting.

The U.S. Marines carry water to replenish their canteens. The
Colombians make do with what's in their canteens until they find a
water source. Since the Colombians are already acclimated to this
climate, they don't require as much water as American Marines, and
they are immune to the impure water. Early today, the SEAL teams
in Zodiacs released dye markers in the bay, indicating the position
of the "enemy" who was pursuing them from the beach. Colombian
jet fighters flew repeated sorties, dropping their ordinance on enemy

positions. This whole exercise coordinated the various U.S. and Co-lombian military forces.

Caribbean Sea, July 31, 1991

We detached from the rest of the battle group yesterday to shadow a merchant ship suspected of carrying drugs. About 0600 the Italian ship Onda Azzarra came alongside a small boat about the size of a tugboat just off the Colombian coast. The captain not only refused to identify himself, but investigation revealed that the Italian ship had come from Los Angeles through the Panama Canal and was way off course. We kept the ship in sight until relieved by a U. S. fast frigate with a coast guard officer on board who was knowledgeable in maritime law.

A coastguard officer on board told me at dinner last evening that the American embassy passes requests to board foreign ships to the embassy of the foreign country. Approval, which is usually granted, has been received in as little as eight minutes. It would be interesting to know what the frigate will do with the ship. This episode took us away from the rest of our battle group and about 500 miles out of the way. During much of this time, we traveled through more high winds and heavy seas. After his experience aboard this flat-bottomed ship, the coastguard officer says he will never again complain about riding on a coast guard cutter.

Colon, Panama, August 1, 1991

After playing the game of "sea chase," we rejoined the rest of our battle group to arrive here at the scheduled time (0600) ready to enter the Panama Canal. But the canal authorities are not ready for us. So in the meantime, we drift outside of Colon waiting for the traffic to clear. The sea is calm, the air is cool, and the sky is an overcast of high and low clouds. Low, jungle-covered mountains flank the entrance to the canal, and very white, thin clouds nestle in all the small valleys. So the waiting is rather pleasant, but the delay in ar-riving at Rodman will probably cause some people to miss calling home today. We should have a lot of mail waiting for us at Rodman. That's where we will also take on new provisions, including fresh fruit, fresh vegetables, and real milk.

Rodman, Panama, August 2, 1991

The trip through the Panama Canal yesterday was the experience of a lifetime. The weather turned perfect by the time we reached the first three pairs of locks. After we entered the first lock, the gates

Traversing the Panama Canal

closed and water from the second lock flooded our position, raising us to a common level. Then we entered the second lock where water from the third lock flooded the second lock. When we were in the third lock, water from the large inland lake flooded the third lock raising us to lake level so we could proceed across the lake. Just gravitational flow eliminates the need to transfer water. The lake is considerably higher than either the Caribbean Sea or Pacific Ocean. So after leaving the lake, we were lowered by the three remaining locks. Every time a ship goes through the canal some water is drained from the lake into the ocean. Once in the history of the canal, a drought caused the lake to become too low to allow traffic through the canal. Transiting the lake in a large ship at 20 knots via a channel having numerous sharp turns marked by buoys created an exciting sensation similar to driving a car through a series of obstacles.

The many small islands dotting the lake appeared to be uninhabited. In fact, all of the jungle on both sides seemed to be the way God created it except for the canal itself. Stunning foliage among palm trees, with the darkest green fronds I have ever seen, line the canal banks and tower over the dense inland trees. Nothing smacks of a beach; the trees and emerald grass come right down to the water's edge. Occasionally a terraced, eroded hillside testifies to some of the blasting necessary to create the canal. Several small waterfalls and a few large ones flow into the canal, adding charm to what is already beautiful. While standing in the relative silence of the ship's bow, I could hear birds singing.

Eight U.S. military bases extend across the Canal Zone. An army base specializing in jungle warfare commands the Caribbean entrance. A Marine who has been out in the jungle said a machete is a necessity. He also spoke of panthers, monkeys, and snakes.

We are now pier-side at Rodman Naval Base within sight of the Bridge of the Americas, which is, I suppose, the only thing that actually links the continents. We arrived too late last evening to do much. As usual mail call trumped other activities. After conducting my evening classes, I went to the officers' club where I enjoyed some jolly good fellowship with the ship's commanding officer, a couple of naval pilots, and a staff commander who now regards me as the "Will Rogers of the PACE program." Interesting guys.

Rodman, Panama, August 4, 1991

Prior to leaving for a tour of Panama City yesterday, I walked the edge of the jungle that borders the naval station. In only a few places is it possible to peer more than a few feet past the initial foliage. I paused at one clearing to listen to the chirps, squawks, squeaks, buzzes, and other sounds in the vicinity. A few colorful birds fluttered around. Suddenly, I heard a flapping overhead. Two huge black vultures sat on a limb. Fortunately, they were not directly overhead since these are big birds that do big things! After a few minutes, they flew away to a street lamppost where they sat with their wings fully extended to three feet, looking like the symbol of the old Roman legionnaires. After they left, the chatter in the jungle ceased.

This afternoon, I walked even farther along the jungle's edge, just admiring the countless types of plants. At one point two dozen coatimondis fed on a huge mango tree. When I returned with my camera, the coatimondis had left, but I picked two mangos, the best I have ever eaten. Farther along, cut ants like the ones we have in South Texas had carved out a 150-yard long path by the roadside. Both ends of the trail disappeared into the jungle. Ants were carrying cut foliage in both directions. Strange creatures. Probably, any kind of plant they wanted was within ten feet of their nest.

The tour of Panama City struck me as both highly interesting and a little disturbing. First, the bus drove through an off limits area to military personnel. I wouldn't want to be afoot in that area, day or night. It's a run-down, poverty-stricken, drug-infested slum where much of the fighting took place when U. S. forces ousted Noriega from power. Demolished and gutted buildings still hang on. We stopped in an adjoining area that looked somewhat better. First, there was the 17th century church with two bells salvaged from the original church that the pirate Morgan destroyed when he sacked Panama in the 16th century. The church building had numerous patched bullet holes. Panama's elite use this church for weddings and funerals.

Some vacant land down the street used to be a police station. The Panamanians themselves blew it up when the U.S. toppled the Noriega regime. Later we saw the ruins of this old original town. The Central Hotel stands across the plaza from the church. Even in its dilapidated state it's still in use and retains evidence of what was once a very classy establishment. A large government building and a post office face another side of the plaza. In the opposite direction a block away men with automatic weapons guard the presidential palace.

After viewing the ruins of the original town, we visited the run-down section around the National Theater, the location for operas and ballets. It is somewhat sad to see so many of Panama's national treasures surrounded by decayed real estate that had such obvious fine beginnings. Most of the buildings show French and Spanish influence reminiscent of New Orleans. If Panama could just restore what it once had, it would be a jewel among cities.

The final leg of our trip took us through the new modern area of downtown Panama City. Here, embassies, banks, and other tall buildings compete for the space along the oceanfront. It looks little different from downtown Houston or Dallas.

Along the way we stopped at a couple of restaurants—once to get drinks, once to eat supper. Both restaurants were built on the bohio model. These have thatched roofs made of palm fronds, which are ingeniously woven together to keep out rain, but also look charming. The first restaurant had some macaws and monkeys, one of which was full-grown at about six inches in height. At the other restaurant, I ordered a Panamanian meal of carimola and patacones with sausage. Carimola is made from yucca root combined with ground meat, then breaded and deep-fried. Patacones is fried banana. Both were excellent. So was the friendly service.

This is some more from the small world department. The first time I walked off the pier at the naval base, a voice from a stopped vehicle yelled, "Mr. Lee!" The voice belonged to one of my former students from the USS *Belknap*. He has been stationed here for some time and loves it. He is attached to a small patrol boat unit working with SEALs. His brother is assigned to the same unit. We got in a lot of good visiting over pizza last night.

When I walked into church at Balboa this morning, a man said, "I'm Dale Giess and I know you from somewhere." I thought, "Here we go again." It turned out that he is a good friend of Jim and Sarah Grant of Kenedy, Texas. It's possible that we crossed paths somewhere around San Antonio, we but never could establish a connection.

Malaga, Colombia, August 8, 1991

Our arrival at Malaga, Colombia was a smashing success. The smashing part happened as the ship arrived pier-side without the aid of tugs, and the starboard anchor snagged one of the pier fenders. The fender is constructed of massive I-beams attached to hard cushioning material. We nearly ripped it off the pier. The strong current also caused a minor collision when the USS *Dahlgren* attempted to moor alongside the LST. *Dahlgren* had to anchor offshore.

The successful part was much less embarrassing. The Colombians held receptions for both officers and petty officers. Many dependents of Colombian naval personnel toured our ship, and the Navy band played to an enthusiastic audience. Yesterday, we had another "5K Fun Run." This one started with the first of two long 30-degree inclines. By the time I reached the top, the unusually humid and oppressive air tortured both my lungs and legs, but pride drives a person to do strange things.

Malaga is just a small Colombian naval base about two-years old and still looks new. The Colombians simply carved a site out of virgin jungle to build the base about three miles inside the mouth of a river. The place is accessible only by boat or helicopter. We were cautioned to stay on the roads because of snakes.

We left port this morning under leaden skies with some fog and a cool breeze. Occasionally the skies have opened up. The jungle is pretty from a distance. Near the mouth of the river on the starboard side, vegetation along the water's edge gives way to a dark gray beach lined with shacks in a coconut palm grove. At both ends of the beach, small streams flow into the river. After the second stream, bluffs rise suddenly to confront the ocean, which has pounded out huge caves in the cliffs. On the port side, small islands of dense jungle dot the river from the naval base to the ocean.

We left a crewman in the hospital—suicidal tendencies. The game plan is to get him to Panama—somehow. When he finds out he is stranded in Malaga, Colombia, he may wish he had kept his cool.

Enroute to Manta, Ecuador, August 9, 1991

It was a short night. Since we will cross the equator today, Shellback "festivities" started late yesterday. Shellbacks are people who have crossed the equator. Wogs never have.

First, we had a "beauty contest" on the flight deck. Five guys dressed up like girls and paraded around looking their seductive best to the howls and catcalls of the crew. I was one of the judges. Naturally, we chose the tall, slender "blonde" in the lace panties, white hose, and white pumps.

Later the Wogs ganged up on some of the Shellbacks to inflict

Beauty Contest

Shellback Initiation

Wogs Crawling Down Decks
Note Shellbacks with shillelaghs

some minor mayhem. After "Taps" last night, the Shellbacks strung up some of the Wogs by their bunks and worked them over with their shillelaghs.

At 0445 today everybody hit the deck and initiation of Wogs began in earnest. Mostly, the scene was quite gross. Wogs had to crawl everywhere—up to the signal bridge and then back down five decks to the flight deck. Enroute they were "encouraged" to eat a breakfast of scrambled eggs laced with jalapenos, onions, garlic, hot sauce, etc. without the benefit of eating utensils. Consequently, the eggs ended up in their faces and hair. Some Marines were required to sing the second verse of the "Marine Hymn" while lying on their backs and doing leg lifts. Sailors got to sing "Anchors Aweigh." As they crawled around with their shorts on the outside of their trousers, they were squirted with assorted messy foodstuff. By the time they reached the flight deck, they were already a pitiful sight, but here they got to stick their faces in the holes used to tie down cargo and helicopters and either blow out or suck out the water accumulated there, depending upon the whim of the particular shellback issuing the instruction. Some were placed in stocks and verbally and physically abused. Then came the crawl through a very long tube filled with aged garbage, during which shillelaghs were applied to their backsides. From the garbage tube, they were led, with their teeth gripping a shillelagh, to a watertight box where they were dunked and hit with a water hose. When they came up for air, they were asked, "What are you!" If the answer was anything other than "Shellback," they were sent back through the garbage tube. One guy went through it six times. Low I.Q.? There was more, but this much can be told in polite company. Remarkably, nobody got hurt, and officers, enlisted men, Marines, SEALs, Navy band were all treated alike, even the ship's executive officer who had some difficulty clearing the hot sauce from his eyes. The new Shellbacks celebrated by stripping off their ruined clothing and tossing it overboard. Throughout it all, I just stood around taking pictures, being thankful that I was already a Shellback, and reminding myself that these people really are adults.

Now all the weather decks have been hosed down and the interior passageways cleaned. Late this afternoon the ten-piece Navy band performed during a cookout on the flight deck.

Wogs in Stocks

Wogs going through garbage chutes

The end of a Wog

A new Shellback—an officer

*Marine Shellbacks relishing
their clout*

These men are really good. They play horns as easily as they play guitars and sing, enabling them to have a very wide repertoire. The equatorial weather was perfect. In fact, I am amazed at the weather. I expected constant hot, humid weather in this latitude. Instead, the weather, especially at night, is quite pleasant.

Manta, Ecuador, August 12, 1991

One of the natives told me why the weather is so mild. The Humboldt Current is in collision with the Niños Current. I have known about the Humboldt Current, now known as the Peru Current, since high school geography, but the Niños Current is news to me.

After arriving here early on the tenth, the chaplain and I spent the afternoon searching for churches and getting acquainted with the town. Manta has seen better days. The city is a mixture of a few, new modern buildings and many old, run-down buildings. Some have split bamboo walls, attesting to the moderate year-round temperature. I was surprised to learn that bamboo is so strong. A multi-story building under construction has a crane mounted on top of bamboo scaffolding.

Yesterday, I took a four-hour bus tour of Manta and nearby Montecristi. First, we drove through Manta and saw more of the same that I had seen the day before. Next, we stopped at a coffee processing plant where acres of coffee beans lay spread out on the open-air concrete floors to dry. Obviously, no rain is expected. On the way to Montecristi, we passed what we would call a new public housing project—five hundred homes are under construction. Built side by side like apartments these concrete blockhouses each contains two small bedrooms and sells for 1,000,500 sucres—about $1005.00. They're already sold out to mostly young people. At Montecristi we saw many arts and crafts stores. Three men on a bench saw me open up a sesame candy bar and asked to taste it. They liked it.

An experience last night will reside in my memory forever. As I left the ship alone to walk to town, a young local couple (he is 20, she is 19.) started asking me questions. They spoke no English, but by the time we reached the main gate a mile away, we had exchanged enough information through my poor Spanish for me to be introduced to their friends as their "amigo." We happened to encounter my Spanish-speaking roommate and the commodore's chef, which ended the communication problem. The young couple, Cesar and Flor Marie, invited us to their home; so we piled into a small Russian made cab and took off. They not only insisted on paying for the cab, but also insisted on cooking a meal for us. Protests didn't help.

While Cesar showed us many pictures of his family and friends, Flor Marie prepared a delicious meal of dorado (fish), fried bananas, and stir-fried vegetables. Among the pictures were those of Flor Marie in her graduation cap and gown and Cesar in his military uniform. When boys reach 18, they have to serve a year in the military. Another photo showed Flor Marie at her job in a beauty shop. Cesar works for Pepsi Cola.

When I found out that they were virtually newlyweds, I gave Cesar some money for a wedding present, which surprised and delighted them. Flor Marie playfully presented her cheek for me to kiss. Cesar is outgoing, but Flor Marie is truly effervescent. She is small even by Ecuadorian standards. She stands a little taller than my navel and weighs about 75 pounds.

I have always known that living conditions in third world countries were not very good, but I was not prepared for the stark condition of their home. It is an old building adjoining other old buildings constructed of concrete blocks with a concrete floor. The small living/dining room opens right onto the sidewalk. Furnishings in the room consisted of a home-made table about 30" by 42", three home-made stools with cloths draped over them, a one-burner hot plate on the floor in a corner, and two small Snoopy posters on the walls. One bare electrical cord led to a single light in the ceiling, and another served as an outlet for the hot plate. A homemade ladder rested in a hole in the ceiling that led to a loft where they slept. A small room adjoined the living room. I presume this is a kitchen with a bath next to it. Both of them stood and kept a lively conversation going while the three of us ate. People who have the least are often the most generous.

During the time that we were there, Flor Marie's aunt and mother came by at different times. Some of the pictures indicated that Cesar's and Flor Marie's families have much better living conditions than they do.

After dinner all of us walked to the town square where the Navy band performed from a band shell to an audience that filled the square and the boulevard for a considerable distance. The whole town must have turned out, and the musicians didn't disappoint them.

Before we left to go to the band concert, Cesar and Flor Marie gave each of us a picture of themselves. Mine is inscribed, "Para un amigo muy especial como ud." For a very special friend such as you. Then we exchanged addresses. These kids have not heard the last from me.

This afternoon I went hiking alone. Just as I left the ship, a man and two women in a pickup called to me. Again they didn't speak English. They wanted to visit the ship, but visitation was over yesterday. However, I told them that the ship would be back next Sunday. Then one of the ladies asked for a souvenir. When I said I didn't have anything with me, she said they would be back next Sunday. No doubt! These people love to trade for anything from the U. S.

Next I checked out Bat Beach, a long stretch of fine clean sand about 200 yards wide deriving it name from its shape as seen from the air. At high tide, water encroaches about 100 yards. A bunch of photogenic huts sits well back from the water. As I was walking away, a boy ran up to me, indicating that his camera didn't work, and asked me to fix it. I did. Ecuadorians don't seem to be the least bit inhibited around U. S. citizens. Last night at the concert, a Marine was dancing with six little girls about 6 to 11 years old. All of them obviously were madly in love with him. Today I saw another Marine give a kid $2.00 for shinning his shoes. The boy expected $1.00. He was so thankful that he crossed himself two times.

Leaving the beach, I went through a residential area of nice homes with two-car garages. But the homes quickly gave way to a commercial area. Evidently, no zoning regulations exist here. None of the businesses were open and had steel doors concealing anything behind them. Stopping a man, I asked him in my poor Spanish what time the businesses opened. He smiled and held up three fingers. Since I had an hour and half to go, I joined three band members at a seaside table and spoke the universal word to the waiter—Coca Cola.

These young men are even more fun in private than they are on stage. The time passed quickly and three of us went window-shopping. The drab exteriors of the shops mask a surprisingly vast array of goods. Just about anything that is needed can be bought here. Finally, my two friends went in search of a beer, and I visited the many sidewalk booths operated by Indians from the interior. I bought a few items from llama wool to send home.

Valdivia, Ecuador, August 15, 1991

For three days the Marines have launched the AAVs, recovered them, and then repeated the exercise near this little town. Joint exercises with the Ecuadorians ashore involve the use of live ammunition. Today's exercise brought tragic results. Some of the Ecuadorian's firepower included mortars. Three shells didn't explode, but the Ecuadorians didn't notify our Marines. When the firing stopped, swarms of children descended upon the area to recover the spent brass, which they sell. One of the shells exploded when a seven-year-old boy picked it up, killing him and injuring three other children. A number of our Marines were close by, but none were injured. However, the viscera of one of the children splattered one of the Marines. The host country is supposed to control their civilians, but they often don't, and our troops have no authority over foreign civilians.

Meanwhile, the ship has been engaged in mock sea warfare. For the better part of a day, the ship skulked around Isle de la Plata (Silver Island) with its radar turned off to avoid detection by a "hostile" sub, the USS *Sea Lance*. The island is a barren, flat-topped mountain with just a fringe of vegetation on top. Deep crevices slash the mountain from top to bottom with something white shining on the sharp edges that looks like silver in the sunlight. Hence, the name, Silver Island. Many 18-foot fishing boats with outboard motors crowded the small beach on one side. We have seen these kinds of boats out of sight of land many times. Evidently the seas never suddenly get rough here.

Manta, Ecuador, August 19, 1991

The last time we were in Manta, there were zero liberty incidents. Not this time. Yesterday, one of the men I had tested was wearing a patch on his forehead. When I asked him what happened, he said he had been at the wrong place at the wrong time. The wrong place was the Chicken House. The wrong time was when some liquored up Sailors from the USS *Alwyn* got into an altercation with some of our liquored up guys. It was a black and white thing. Amazingly, the captains of some other American ships were at this place. Our captain immediately made the Chicken House off limits to all personnel.

We had a cookout on the beach yesterday—the usual food. Since it was Sunday, many Ecuadorians showed up—especially children. Some ate the scraps that the Sailors discarded. I couldn't handle that. I wrapped a bun around a meat patty, took my drink, and walked away. I don't think anyone anticipated how our picnic would affect the locals.

When I walked back to the ship, I passed the port authority building located just outside the gate to all the piers. Inside their fence the leaves of a low-spreading tree looks similar to a magnolia. Curious, I asked the two gate guards about the tree. They invited me inside the compound. Using my knife, one of the guards peeled one of the green pods from this tree called almendra. The fruit was red and white stripped. He tasted it and said it was good for the "grippe"— sore throat. Then he broke open the seed and gave me the kernel inside. It's called mani and tastes somewhat like an almond. The trees are grown commercially here. They told me much more, but I did well to understand this much Spanish.

Before the picnic, I got involved in a long conversation with one of the street vendors. His English was as limited as my Spanish; so it was an interesting, learning experience for both of us. I have encountered a lot of friendly people here. If I could spend several weeks here, I am sure I would become proficient in Spanish and be able to function in any country in this hemisphere, except Brazil.

Tomorrow we leave for Peru after some more exercises at sea. I'm not expecting much there. Because of terrorist threats, our movements probably will be tightly controlled. Certainly, we will take no foodstuffs on board because of the cholera threat. The fruits and vegetables from Ecuador have been washed down in chlorinated water before being exposed to the crew.

Today some local water will be brought on board, but it will be subjected to intense treatment and testing. We can make fresh water in port just as we do at sea. The problem is that the pier side water is so polluted that it has to be repeatedly processed into steam to remove all particulates, requiring additional time and fuel. Meanwhile, the crew's demand for water remains the same. For this reason, as soon as we come into port, we usually tie into a shore water supply.

At Sea Southwest of Manta, August 20, 1991

Yesterday, four Marine officers commandeered their official

vehicle and driver to go to Montecristi. I went along to visit a small hat factory. Artisans take about a month to make one straw hat that sells for $80. Made from the paja plant, which produces pale yellow, flat fibers about the width of pencil lead, the hat is so finely woven that it can be rolled into a spiral, stored in a box, and simply shaken out when it is needed for wear. The men bought hats that didn't cost so much, but were still of good quality. One man bought a hat with a brim three-foot in diameter. It's mainly good for posing in silly pictures and dancing around at parties.

Next we visited the shops that I saw the previous week. One of the natives rushed out of a store, calling my name. He was Carlos, the vender I talked to so long the day before. He lives in Montecristi.

Last night a coast guard warrant officer and I went back into the town square where the Navy band staged another concert. They opened the program with an attention-getting Latin rhythm. Then for an hour they combined rock, country & western, jazz, and swing into another brilliant performance. A half-moon combined with a cloudless sky and cool breeze to make a perfect evening. We made one more swing by the booths where the Indians sell their woolen goods. I bought another sweater and a very colorful duffel bag. The bag may come handy for the trip home, and I can always use it for a workout bag.

Callao, Peru, August 23, 1991

After two days of drills and exercises at sea, we arrived here this morning under the same overcast sky that had accompanied us from Manta. Since we are moving into cooler latitudes, a windbreaker feels good on the weather decks. May through November is really winter in this hemisphere, although it doesn't seem so, being this close to the equator. The only signs of winter in Ecuador were the fallen leaves.

When we left Ecuador, we picked up two Peruvian warships to engage in exercises with us. Today, briefings between nations have taken place aboard the various ships. Some of the officers will attend a reception hosted by the Peruvians tonight. Twenty enlisted men will go to an enlisted men's reception. Some of the chiefs are also involved with the Peruvians. The rest of us are spending the night aboard ship—eating pizza and ice cream, playing bingo, and watching all-night movies. We ship out again tomorrow morning, but the crew will have liberty when we return August 31.

That's the magic date for me: Classes will end that day. I have requested a flight home from Lima September 2. I will finish classes earlier than anticipated because the ship's schedule did not interfere as much as I thought it would. This early departure may cost me some mail. We are supposed to receive mail some time tonight and again when we come back here next week. Lost mail will be a good trade-off for going home. However, when I accepted this assignment, I thought I would get to visit all the coastal South American countries, and I am disappointed that the cruise did not work out that way. Perhaps another time, another ship. If we had not spent so much time playing soldier in the Caribbean, I would have gotten my wish. Chile is supposed to be one of the best countries, but I don't want to just ride the ship for an extra week without any work to do.

Ancon, Peru, August 25, 1991

Ancon is a small resort town about a two-hour cruise from Callao. We came here yesterday so that the Marines could launch their AAVs and conduct some field maneuvers with the Peruvians who have a small military base here. The bay here is like a giant "C," and the town sits in the middle of the "C." Low mountains extend from one end of the "C" to the other and are as barren and wind eroded as desert sand. In fact, the terrain looks like desert through the ship's big eyes. Since it is winter here, the beachfront hotels are closed, and only a few modest pleasure boats have anchored offshore from the yacht club. A few nice homes and some apartments overlook the beach. Beyond, are quite a number of hovels thrown together by available scrap materials. Only the market at the fisherman's wharf shows up through the ship's big eyes.

Shortly after 0800 today I mounted the signal bridge and watched what must have been upward of a million birds fly by. They were dark gray and appeared to be sea gulls. They formed a massive black line extending to the horizon against the calm sea. For some twenty minutes they swept by in undulating echelons, flying so close to the sea that their wing tips nearly touched water on each down stroke. The "local" sea gulls have white bodies with wings and tails that are gray with white trailing edges. Yesterday, they plummeted by the dozens into the bay at Callao in search of fish. I watched one bird make seven successive dives before it disappeared out of sight. Today the gulls are not fishing at all.

I have a new roommate—a Peruvian naval lieutenant. He is roommate number three. Roommate number one went to another ship about a week ago. Then a Protestant chaplain spent three nights here. When he left, I thought I would have the room all to myself for the rest of the trip. But when I came in from class yesterday, the Peruvian's gear was in my room. His English is better than my Spanish, but not much. Last night he and some of the ship's officers went back to Callao for a Peruvian reception. They returned at 0230 today with glowing reports about the outstanding food and even more outstanding girls. All my immediate neighbors are Marine officers and SEALs. I always know exactly when the marines return. I think my Peruvian roommate must have been a bit hung over. He slept in until noon. The Marines were not so fortunate. They had to leave with the AAVs about mid-morning.

Salinas, Peru, August 26, 1991

Since last January, I have watched AAVs come and go on amphibious ships. Today I rode on one. Making a beach landing in an AAV with the Marines is a unique experience for a civilian—one that I will always value. A fellow Texan dressed me in full camouflage uniform with helmet. On the way to the beach I rode with the troops in the back of the vehicle. The worst part was waiting our

turn to splash off the ship and having to smell the fumes from the diesel engine. Once underway, the fumes were no problem. With bodies and battle gear tightly squeezed together, we rode in our compartment in complete darkness throughout the trip to the shore. Even though I couldn't see outside, I knew the exact moment the AAV stopped being a boat and became a land vehicle. The AAV is sluggish in water but is quite fast and maneuverable on land. Because we left most of our personnel on the

AAVs going ashore in Peru

The author with Capt. K. J. Leo, USMC (Photo courtesy of Capt. K. J. Leo, USMC)

The author returning to ship (Photo courtesy of Capt. K. J. Leo, USMC)

beach for a three-day exercise, I rode in the Troop Leader's turret on the return trip. It is situated right behind the driver and adjacent to the gunner's turret. The turrets are closed for entry through the surf, but slits in the armor enabled me to see 360 degrees.

After we cleared the surf, all three turrets were opened until we parked the AAV inside the ship. The stern of the ship has a ramp to the tank deck that allows the AAV to climb right out of the ocean. Inside the ship a huge turntable spins the tank around so that it can drive right out of the ship the next time it's needed. All personnel wear life vests, and a boat from the ship escorts the AAVs in case something goes wrong. Even after riding in an AAV and knowing that similar vehicles have been around since WW II, I am still a little surprised that it floats.

For the first time in more than week, we had brilliant sunshine for our landing on Salinas Beach about five miles from the small town of Huacho. Since this area is used only for military operations, nothing has polluted either the beach or the water.

The low inland hills are like a moonscape. Absolutely nothing grows there. Loose, greenish soil makes climbing a slippery endeavor. Only an occasional rock outcropping breaks the smooth surface. In some places the greenish cast turns into a purplish hue. It appears as if a long, hard rain would dissolve the entire mountain range into the ocean. However, that is not likely to happen since the coastline of Peru receives an average of 1.2 inches of rainfall per year. Beyond this low mountain range are fertile valleys that produce plentiful fruits and vegetables. Rain forests are farther inland toward the Andes Mountains.

Peruvian "Moonscape" (Photo courtesy of Capt. K. J. Leo, USMC)

Callao, Peru, August 31, 1991

It's official. My American Airlines flight leaves from Lima at 2323 tomorrow. I plan to get to the airport before noon even though the ticket counter doesn't open until 1900 because the flight is usually overbooked by about 120 people, and too many things can go wrong with a prepaid ticket in a foreign country.

I am supposed to have Navy transportation to Lima, a short drive from here. I hope so because everybody here seems to be armed. Men with automatic weapons are all over the pier. I have been told that anybody is a guerrilla target, not just Norte Americanos.

Today has been hectic. The ship arrived here early today. Late this afternoon I finally got my passport stamped showing my official entry into the country. Now my teaching materials are in the post office and I'm packed and ready to walk off the ship.

Although we have been hanging around Peru for some time, I really haven't seen much of it. Yesterday is the only time I have been ashore except for the day I rode the AAV. We had a joint cookout with the Peruvians on the beach at Ancon where Peru has a military base. After riding on the ship's LCVP to the dock, I took a bus with armed escorts to the base several miles away. The trip was an eye opener. I got a close look at the hovels I mentioned earlier. Never before have I seen such wretched living conditions. The barren land seems as wretched as this section of Ancon, having been strewn with debris of all sorts. Since nothing grows here, I guess the people think they can't hurt the land.

The military base fronted onto the ocean. The breakers rolling in were beautiful against a declining sun, but the beach would pass for a garbage dump. Near the beach, a small museum featured old Peruvian military uniforms and various small arms.

Although the food was a joint enterprise, the ship came up short. We supplied all the patties, wieners, beans, and trimmings. Peruvians supplied some beans and a concoction of potatoes and radishes—both quite tasty. The ship sent about 200 forks ashore. All disappeared. I saw one guard making off with a three-pound can of mustard. Two Catholic shrines grace the premises attesting to the Peruvians devotion to God. But appearances didn't fool any Sailors or Marines. Maybe a benevolent God winked.

The crew has liberty, of sorts, tonight. They can either spend four hours at a shopping mall or spend the evening at a club. That's just enough time for some people to get drunk. The XO got on the intercom to say that he expected zero liberty incidents tonight. That may be wishful thinking, but I pity any man who is foolish enough to get into trouble in this country. I'm staying aboard and watching *Henry V* on a VCR.

Lima, Peru, September 1, 1991

Having arrived at the airport well before departure time, the girl at the check-in desk talked to me off and on. After a while, she asked me to give her my ticket, which she upgraded to first class. When I asked her why she made the change she replied, "Because you've been so nice." So I guess nice guys don't always finish last. However, this was the first time in my life to fly first class, and a huge lady spilled over into my seat all the way to Florida!

Postscript: The USS *Barnstable County* was decommissioned on June 29, 1994 at the Naval Amphibious Base in Little Creek, Virginia and sold to the Spanish Navy.

USS Wasp (Photo courtesy of Elsilrac Enterprises)

USS *Wasp* LHD-1

Rhodes, Greece, October 20, 1991

The two weeks since I left Texas October 6 has been a mixture of excitement, frustration, boredom, and uncertainty. Welcome again to the U. S. Navy Program for Afloat College Education.

Following an overnight stay in the Navy B. O. Q. in Norfolk and the usual briefing for my assignment, I flew out of Norfolk with less than two hours to connect with my trans-Atlantic flight out of JFK airport. I made it to Rome and Istanbul O.K., but my bag didn't. After filing a lost bag report with TWA, I took a Turkish Air flight to Izmir, Turkey, where a helicopter was supposed to transport me to the USS *Wasp* at Saros Bay. No helicopter.

In the meantime, I met the PACE math instructor also assigned to *Wasp*. We checked into the Kordon, a hotel for American military personnel, and notified Norfolk that we were stranded. The next morning, I called TWA in Istanbul about my bag. It had been left in New York but had arrived in Istanbul on a subsequent flight. They promised to send it by the late afternoon Turkish flight. I met the plane. No bag. The Turkish air clerk reflected my disappointment in a strongly worded Telex sent to TWA. Since TWA was closed for the day, I called again the next morning. Before I could say anything, the lady who answered the phone had obviously read the previous night's Telex and offered profuse apologies and promised to have the bag in Izmir by 11:30 a.m. I met the plane. No bag. The Turkish clerk said TWA meant 11:30 p.m. I made my third special trip back to the airport that night only to learn that Turkish Air had logged in my bag at 1:30 p.m.

Meanwhile, my co-worker and I were told to go to Çigli (pronounced Chiglee) Air Base for a helicopter ride to the ship. No helicopter arrived during the two days I was waiting for my bag. Furthermore, no chopper arrived Friday, Saturday, Sunday, or Monday. But every day we dutifully checked out of the hotel, spent the day at Çigli, and then checked back into the hotel at night. The American presence at Çigli is almost negligible. Only two small buildings accommodate the helicopter detachment there. All other buildings formerly used by the U. S. have been abandoned. We spent our time at Çigli in a fly infested bare room with tables and chairs, adjoining a smelly restroom. There wasn't even a vending machine to provide a token lunch. The math instructor spent his time under a tree reading newspapers. I spent a lot of time walking on the tarmac. This situation irritated my new friend more than it irritated me. He carefully and in detail explained to me repeatedly how this experience showed a callous disregard by the Navy and Central Texas College for our welfare. Finally, I told him that I was pretty sharp and understood his sentiment the first time around. He was unimpressed. In fact, each retelling of the complaint gained embellishment, enthusiasm, and a fair amount of imaginative profanity. I felt more than adequately instructed since the words proceeded out of the mouth of a PHD.

On Wednesday, we learned early in the day that we were not going to go to the ship. So we hired a taxi and went to Ephesus, which I visited two and-a-half years ago. Not being constrained by the schedule of a tour group, we took our time and saw much more of the ruins of this ancient city than I did on my last trip. One interesting aspect was a church whose considerable former grandeur was in keeping with the rest of the city. At the front of the auditorium stood the remains of a structure that could hardly have been anything but a baptistery. If so, its presence makes a strong statement about the method of baptism used by early Christians. It is also significant that such a prominent church building could co-exist in a city famous for its great temple of the goddess Diana. When the apostle Paul first tried to introduce Christianity to the Ephesians, the silversmiths

Remains of church at Ephesus

started a riot and the citizens ran him out of town.

We also squeezed in a trip to ancient Smyrna. Only a small part—two or three acres—of this ancient city remain exposed. Modern Izmir has been built over the rest. I have now visited three of the cities of the Seven Churches of Asia mentioned in Revelation. I'm looking forward to visiting the other four. Had I known on any given day that the helicopter was not coming for us, I could have easily made a trip to Cappadocia, one of the most intriguing landforms on earth.

Exactly one week after we arrived in Izmir, we literally caught the last helicopter going from Çigli to the USS *Wasp*. The air detachment closed up the next day and transferred all personnel and equipment elsewhere. I had already called Norfolk and asked for contingent plans for getting us out of Izmir. After six dry runs, I had no confidence in the seventh one.

In spite of the travel mix-up, the stay in Izmir wasn't all that bad. My buddy and I had separate hotel rooms overlooking the waterfront. Because of a six-hour time difference between here and Washington, we saw all but the last two or three episodes of the congressional hearings of the Supreme Court confirmation of Clarence Thomas. We were dismayed that the graphic accusations of Anita Hill were being broadcast across the entire world. Other than sightseeing, the high point of our days was the nightly sampling of Turkish foods in different restaurants. Being very well-read and an interesting conversationalist, my cohort is fairly fluent in French and German and can get by in Danish, Greek, Turkish, Italian, Yugoslavic, and Arabic. Naturally, he ordered all of our meals at the restaurants, thus making an excellent traveling companion.

Upon arriving aboard *Wasp*, we were supposed to share a two-man stateroom. None was available. I am quartered with three Marine captains, all of whom are commanding officers of their respective units. They are courteous, congenial men. All Marines have excessive gear, but being commanding officers, these men have even more. Every conceivable space on the bulkheads and the overhead, stores something—a clutter junkie's paradise. Furthermore, people from their units come into the room at all hours of the day and night, making it impossible for me to get any work done in there. Sometimes I can work in the wardroom or a lounge near the wardroom. One of my students allows me to use one of his computers in the evening.

Wasp is one of the most impressive ships to which I have been assigned since it carries an assortment of helicopters and Harrier jet fighters. However, it also carries LCACs, field artillery pieces, as-

Harrier landing on the USS Wasp

sorted rolling stock, and Sea Sparrow missiles. With 1700 Marines on board, the *Wasp* should be able to cope with political brush fires that are sure to erupt somewhere on the globe in the future.

Seeing Harriers take off and land is a new and interesting experience. Using jets that thrust in all directions, they can take off, land, and hover like a helicopter. Also like a helicopter they can fly sideways and backward. Coming in for a landing, they hover over the port side of the ship's stern and then slip sideways to settle onto the deck. Harriers are usually launched like conventional fighters, but without the aid of a catapult.

Aegean Sea, October 21, 1991

We left Rhodes early today after a delightful four-day stay. Old Town Rhodes, a charming, walled city dates back to the time of the Crusaders. Although some excavation and restoration work still continues, the Italians restored most of the city from about 1912 until WW II when they lost the island to the British who turned it over to the Greeks in 1948. The narrow cobblestone streets wind through dozens of tourist shops flanked by residential sections.

The centerpiece of the city is the Palace of the Great Magisters. Built by the knights in the 14th century, an explosion destroyed it in 1856. When the Italians rebuilt it, they decorated it with mosaics of the Hellenistic, Roman, and Byzantine eras that they brought from the island of Kos. Complementing the palace on three sides, extensive formal gardens surround tropical plants such as oleander and blooming hibiscus. Trees—palm, coniferous, and deciduous—create an atmosphere of privacy and serenity. Visible from the garden a large herd of deer languishes between the moat and palace walls. Both churches and mosques reflect the city's multi-culture developed over centuries of bitter conflict. Cars—and especially motor scooters—whiz through the narrow streets, seemingly oblivious to the pedestrians.

Naturally, I had to check out some of the back streets. Here I enjoyed a Grecian dinner amid the outstanding décor of a restaurant named Akropolis situated in an open courtyard under an orange tree loaded with fruit and surrounded by Grecian statues, fountains, and assorted foliage. Music featuring the bouzooki instrument enhanced the atmosphere. I was the only American diner. Following my meal, Fotis Mahramas, the maitre'd offered me a complimentary glass of ouzo, the national drink of Greece. Clear as water, it is fifty-percent alcohol. The port briefing to the ship's crew specifically warned against imbibing this potent drink. Fotis Mahramas teasingly said I should chug it—that it would make me a big man. Yeah, really. I took one small sip. It tasted like licorice.

New Town Rhodes, a modern Mediterranean city, sits on the northern tip of the island. Modern hotels line the beach, which is a mixture of coarse gravel and coarse, dark sand washed by the cleanest water that I have seen in the Mediterranean, except for the water at Sardinia. Bronze deer, the symbol of Rhodes, atop two posts guard the entrance to the small harbor. Some Rhode Islanders believe these posts were the location of the pillars that supported the Colossus, one of the Seven Wonders of the World, which was completed in 292 BC and destroyed by an earthquake in 225 BC. Others believe Colossus is just a legend.

After strolling by the yacht basin and through the downtown section of new town, I walked from the harbor entrance via the beach around the northern tip of the island. Ending up on a deserted stretch, I settled down with a sack of pistachio nuts watching the sun, bracketed by the rocky coastlines of Rhodes and Turkey sink behind some low clouds on the horizon.

The next day I took a tour to Lindos, a city that still retains much of its seventh century architecture and narrow cobblestone streets. An acropolis under restoration overlooks the town. Although some of the Doric columns that formerly supported the temples date from the fifth century BC, the Crusaders constructed the outer walls when they fortified the city.

The view from the acropolis affords a perfect view of the Harbor of Apostle Paul, a small, circular harbor almost entirely enclosed by sloping cliffs. A sizable bay sweeps across a long sandy beach from the harbor to another part of the island. This is the off-season for tourists; consequently, the beach sported more umbrellas than sun worshipers.

In addition to the classical Grecian ruins of the acropolis, I visited a functioning Byzantine church. A small, one-story structure, it evidently antedates the European cathedrals whose stained glass windows in soaring walls light up the interior. Lavishly painted icons covered the walls of this windowless, dimly lit church. One icon portrayed a saint with the head of a dog. Having been born so good looking that he couldn't keep himself from immorality, he asked Jesus to make him ugly. The methods whereby Christianity can digress from the simple gospel of Jesus seem to be limited only by man's imagination.

The tour included an excellent native meal following which I decided to use my free time to explore the mountainside, which promised some good aerial photos. My meandering took me over the crest of a low rocky mountain where I found a hole in the ground about six feet in diameter and ringed with stones. It had been nearly filled with loose stones. Later, I asked the guide if this were a well from a prior civilization. Surprised by my findings, his interest turned to trying to find out how I got up on the mountain since the whole bay area is fenced in. It was easy. One of my Marine roommates also took this tour. Returning to Old Town Rhodes, we went back to the Restaurant Akropolis where we spent the last of our drachmas on another fine meal. These people make the best baklava I have ever tasted.

The ride back to the ship on the Greek double-decked ferry in the cool, crisp night air ended a satisfying day. The three-quarter moon in a cloudless sky was so bright that only the planets were visible among the stars.

Aegean Sea, October 25, 1991

The ship is in the midst of war games off the northern coast of Crete Island. Two days ago we anchored at Souda Bay for about a day. As usual we are the good guys and are winning. VIP's from other countries keep visiting the ship and expressing their admiration for its capabilities. The ship is at flight quarters during most of the daylight hours; so uninvolved personnel must stay off the weather decks. Occasionally, I climb six levels to the signal bridge to watch the sun rise. Without hearing protection at that position, the jet noise of an incoming Harrier can seriously damage the ears.

Classes are well underway with what appears to be some motivated young men. The Educational Services Officer scheduled classes three hours long. This is a new time schedule for me. So far I have been able to keep the students awake and involved. My last class is scheduled to end December 3. Assuming no change in the ship's schedule, I should fly home from Rota, Spain shortly thereafter.

Valencia, Spain, October 31, 1991

Leaving Rhodes, the ship conducted flight operations as we transited the Mediterranean to Valencia. Yesterday the Harriers flew to Rota, Spain, where they will remain while the ship visits this port and Barcelona. We made the trip under sunny skies and on calm seas.

This ship is so large that no sensation of movement is noticed below the weather decks. During lulls in flight operations, the crew engages in physical training on the flight deck, which is nearly 900 feet long, allowing those of us who jog to have plenty of running room. Physical training on the flight deck takes a little pressure off the ship's well-equipped exercise room, one of the ship's most popular areas.

Being the first person off the ship when we docked today, I quickly found a telephone and called home. A letter from Nita had given me some concern. She assured me that it was not time to hit the eject button.

Valencia is a huge city and I walked all afternoon in the vain hope of finding something interesting. As far as I could tell, it was just "Any City, Europe." I did stumble upon a very beautiful small park with towering trees, trim hedges, and inviting walkways. I shot one picture of a fountain back lighted by the sun through dense foliage. The effect should be interesting. The centerpiece of the park was a stand of the tallest, broadest magnolia trees I have ever seen. However, I wasn't sure they were magnolias because the trunks, being flat and twisted like cypress, were unlike any I have ever seen. I asked a middle-aged gentleman the name of the tree and he said magnolia, which was about the only English word he knew. But it broke the ice. He told me that orange trees grow extensively in the Valencia area and that the climate here is similar to that of Southern California. By the time I understood this and more, we had arrived at his nearby business where he imports packaging materials from Colombia. He showed me around his premises and seemed to be especially proud of his 1930s Bell telephone.

I have found that one of the easiest ways to get to know a foreigner is to show an interest in something unique that is indigenous to the area. If he knows anything about it, an extended conversation usually results.

After hiking some eight to ten miles, I returned to the ship somewhat tired and disappointed and watched the movie *Canine*.

Valencia, Spain, November 2, 1991

You just have to know where to go, and a map surely does help.

A short bus ride took me to a section of Valencia that is replete with architectural masterpieces. Much of it is quite old, but clean and in good repair. The ironwork in New Orleans can't compare with the massive, magnificent ironwork adorning many of the buildings in the historic section of Valencia. Countless "green areas" of walkways, parks, and plazas flourish amid the churches, cathedral, train station, bullring, and commercial establishments. The abundance of apartments and condos intertwined with other buildings makes this part of Valencia very pedestrian friendly. Eighty-four percent of Valencians own their own flats. Thirty thousand dollars will buy a nice one. A half million dollars will buy one of the best available.

A river formerly ran alongside this historic area, which began as a walled city in 130 BC. The river has been diverted around the city, and the former riverbed is now a five-mile stretch of parks, zoo, band and dance pavilions, swimming pool, playgrounds, playing fields, nursery, and a beautiful classical music hall with a large reflecting pool.

This hall for classical music is architecturally modern. Except for the auditorium, glass curving across the top and down the sides encloses the structure. My wanderings also took me by an opera house.

New construction prevails throughout Valencia that shows an obvious concern for restoring and preserving the past. The port area at the main gate has a series of 19th century buildings of unique design in excellent condition. In the middle of the historic section, an archaeological dig has uncovered several civilizations covering more than 2,000 years. The city plans to restore the Roman part. The cleanliness and neatness of this Spanish city of 850,000 compares favorably to the other Mediterranean cities.

Valencia Music Hall

The Iberians first built a city here in 130 BC and gave the name "Iberian Peninsula" to what is now Spain and Portugal. Then came the Romans after which the Muslims took over in the eighth century and stayed 500 years. Modern Valencia still reflects their influence.

Today I went to the castle at the seaside resort city of Peniscola (pronounced Paynyeescola). This castle was the site of the *El Cid* movie of 1954 starring Charlton Heston. El Cid defeated the Muslims in Valencia late in the eleventh century. Although a monument to him stands in the middle of one of the boulevards, Valencians don't like El Cid because he was a mercenary.

The eighty-mile coastal drive to Peniscola took me by several ruins of Muslim mountaintop forts. The tour guide said such forts were widely scattered around Spain. Although the Muslims left some of their culture on Valencia, I haven't seen any mosques. In Rhodes, churches and mosques were almost within rock-throwing distance from each other. A few miles north of Valencia, Sagunto Fort, originally built by the Iberians, has been under restoration for two years and will eventually be opened to the public.

The gentleman who told me that orange trees grow here certainly knew what he was talking about. The trip today down a super highway took me by thousands of acres of orange trees. Because the area produces twenty-three varieties, orange growers harvest the fruit from September to June. The irrigated flat lands between the Mediterranean and the mountains also produce three crops of vegetables each year. Surprisingly, thirty percent of Spain's gross national product comes from rice. Spain, a major producer of furniture, imports much of its wood from the Amazon forests of Brazil. Huge stacks of lumber occupy much of the dock near the ship.

The castle at Peniscola sits on a small peninsula overlooking a small harbor. Although it has been restored and is interesting to see, it ranks somewhere behind Chillon Castle on the Swiss/French border and the one at Palma on the island of Mallorca. Rutted by wagon wheels, the narrow cobblestone street, lined with residences and small shops, winds up to the castle. Here you can buy anything you don't need for your home or person. The castle top affords a commanding view of the long line of hotels fronting on a clean, sandy beach washed by clear, aquamarine water. It's easy to see why people would want to spend their vacations here.

The castle dungeon made a sobering impact on me. As I gazed through the iron grate to the room below, I guess I really understood for the first time the horror of solitary, indefinite confinement in a stone box.

I could only speculate what the castle's sparsely furnished rooms might have looked like when occupied. I liked the clean, simple lines of the few pieces present.

Valencia, Spain, November 5, 1991

Last Sunday I attended one of the most moving concerts I have ever heard. Played in the Valencia Music Hall described above, the music's emotional impact upon me is an experience I would like to sustain forever. The orchestra consisted only of horns and percussion instruments—no strings. The musicians played with unbelievable precision and clarity in a perfect acoustical setting. Fourteen clarinetists made up what is usually the violin section. When the first clarinetist played a solo from Ernst Mohr's "Variation on a Swiss Theme," I didn't see how it could be equaled. But four other soloists followed with similar brilliance. In fact, two flutists played in one-third harmony an intricate solo without the slightest flaw.

The orchestra performed free of charge to a near-capacity crowd. A teacher of history and geography with his two teenage daughters sat next to me. Although he speaks only Spanish, his older daughter, a university student, practiced her English on me, and I practiced my Spanish on her. Her father asked many questions. After the concert, we traded addresses, and they drove me to the center of the historic district where I spent the rest of the day sightseeing and taking pictures. I probably know historic Valencia better than downtown Houston.

Yesterday, I realized how thoroughly I have covered the old city on foot. I took a tour that covered the same territory, but included the entrance into some of the buildings. The city hall, outside the historic section, really stood out. Near the entrance, a large, elegant rectangular room serves as a meeting place for dignitaries. High-backed chairs with red, plush seats line the walls. Overhead, two huge, one ton crystal chandeliers illuminate the entire chamber. An adjacent small museum holds an extensive library of old books and city records dating from the eleventh century, all recorded on microfilm.

Holy Grail?

We also stopped at the town's cathedral. Indiana Jones wasted his time. The Holy Grail is right here in historic Valencia. I took a picture of it. Well, a long explanation suggested that it could be the Holy Grail.

Old gates to Valencia

Another relic struck me as being macabre. The forearm of a man named Vincent who suffered martyrdom by the Romans rests in a glass case. I really like this city, but it seems that churchanity smothers Christianity.

Two gates comprised of two huge towers each are all that remain of the old city's walls. Until fairly recently, one served as a jail. The other, known as Torre De Cuarts, stills bears the marks from cannons and small arms fire made by Napoleon's army.

The tour also took me to the central market where vendors attractively displayed high quality meat, cheese, vegetables, and fruit in clean open air. Thanks to thousands of bats, the town is almost free of flies. Valencians value the bats and refer to them as "flying DDT." In fact, King James I, who conquered Valencia, included on his heraldry not an eagle, but a bat. He is held in high esteem because he established a parliamentary form of government.

El Corte Ingles, the last stop in old town, boasts an exceptionally classy multi-story department store that would fit into any American city.

Valencia, Spain, November 7, 1991

The ship just set the sea and anchor detail. We will be underway by 0745. I guess I'm ready to move on. However, Valencia holds as much attraction to me as Vienna, Austria, and I would like to return "Yet knowing how way leads on to way, I doubted if I should ever come back." But the city will certainly live in my memory and my photos.

Tuesday night, my Marine captain buddy and I took in another program at the Valencia Music Hall. Pianist Mario Monreal, famous throughout Europe, entertained a full house with sonatas from Mozart.

Yesterday, I visited a larger Corte De Ingles across the riverbed from the historic city. It is similar to the Houston Galleria, but much smaller. I had lunch there and attempted to buy a tourist book about Valencia. I found the book in a small shop in a maze of back streets. Being almost out of pesetas, I was able to get the shop owner to accept dollars—no small achievement, since merchants here usually don't accept dollars and he didn't speak a word of English and my Spanish is so limited. After a long walk along the old river, a brief look at the botanical gardens, and a stroll through the museum of natural history, I returned to the ship for my night class.

Almeria, Spain, November 8, 1991

A few days ago, the math instructor and I moved to a two-man stateroom. Although my Marine roommates and I have become good friends, everybody welcomed more spacious quarters. My new roommate has been bunking in a large overflow compartment. Shortly after we came on board, someone stole his backpack containing valuables useful only to him, such as address book and telephone card. The thieves made the mistake of using the telephone card. Now they have a problem with the Navy.

Losing his backpack is not his only concern. Some of his relatives and friends live in Yugoslavia. The Serb's attack on Dubrovnik, located in Croatia, particularly upsets him. Ironically, the beautiful old walled city escaped the clash of armies for a thousand years. I'm glad I got to see it before the shelling took place.

Today we are anchored just off the coastline of all the hotels and apartments that stretch along the beach. The Marines used the three LCACs to transport troops, howitzers, and rolling stock to the beach about two miles from the resort area. I went ashore in an LCAC. It is a hovercraft propelled by two giant fans on the stern. Wearing a phone headset and positioned behind the three men operating the craft, I observed everything that went on. After skimming across the water at 45 knots, the vehicle settled onto the land with no discernible difference in the ride. A Marine lieutenant from the Gulf War told me he had seen an LCAC outrun a Sherman tank doing 60 mph in the desert. After the cargo was offloaded, the LCAC lifted straight up and rotated 180 degrees in preparation for the return trip to the ship. The landing site was the town dump, a good choice considering that the downward jet blast from the LCAC makes a mess of the ground.

I hitched a ride in a HMM V to the resort area to find a telephone to call Norfolk on a school matter. After the phone call, I explored part of Almeria, bought a Spanish newspaper and some film, and had a snack before returning to the LCAC landing site via the long, nearly deserted beach.

Meanwhile, a Marine has invited me to spend some time with the Marines up in the mountains shooting all their small arms. That sounds exciting.

Almeria, Spain, November 10, 1991

Today, my stock with the Marines increased dramatically. They included me in their SPIE rigging. When introduced to the term, I knew the operation involved a helicopter and assumed it had something to do with spying. Quite the contrary! SPIE is an acronym for Special Purpose Insertion and Extraction. That's a fancy term for being yanked from the ground via a long rope attached to a helicopter. The purpose of this operation is to insert or remove troops from an area without landing the helicopter.

First, they dressed me in camouflage fatigues complete with helmet and combat boots. Then I donned a harness similar to that of a parachute, plus a back-up safety rope. Next, rings from these two devices were snapped onto rings on the line from the chopper. Seven Marines and I paired off for the lift-off. My buddy was a Marine captain, one of my former roommates. We were the first two off the ground. Dangling below the chopper at an altitude of about 700 feet, we got an excellent bird's eye tour of the Spanish mountainside. Twice, as we flew over high electrical wires, I thought, "What an unusual way to die."

The author and seven Marines lined up for liftoff

SPIE Rigging. The top pair of figures is the author and a U. S. Marine Captain

Sightseeing Spanish Mountains

Fast roping Marines

Later, the helicopter set us down in reverse order. Then we unsnapped our harnesses and sprinted away from the dust storm created by the downdraft of the aircraft. The ride was exhilarating and unforgettable. Would I do it again? In a heartbeat. Later back at the ship, an officer who learned about the incident said, "Boy, somebody sure put their bars on the line to let a civilian do that!" Grinning, I replied, "They weren't bars; they were oak leaf clusters."

For some time, I watched troops do several "fast roping" exercises from another helicopter. In this operation, the aircraft hovers while men slide down a webbed rope to the ground. A webbed rope plus gloves prevents rope burns to the men's hands. A well-trained squad can evacuate the aircraft in sixty seconds. I wasn't allowed to do this stunt since trainees start on a short rope from a stationary tower.

The SPIE operation better acquainted me with the Spanish terrain. The mountains grow only sparse scrub plants in soil that appears porous and unstable. It's a good place to make western movies. Filmed in this vicinity, two movies starred Clint Eastwood: *The Good, the Bad, the Ugly*, and *For a Few Dollars More*.

Earlier in the day, I took part in a grenade exercise. The only extra gear I had to wear for this evolution was a helmet and a flak jacket. Unlike WW II grenades, these are shaped like baseballs, but have the same shrapnel effect with an effective casualty radius (ECR) of fifteen meters. I had practiced on the grenade range in boot camp many years ago, but this was my first time ever to toss a live grenade.

I also took my first ride on an LCU. The USS *Austin* also carried this type of craft in its well deck. At 0700 the stern ramp from the ship extended to the bow ramp of the LCU while it loaded up Marines for today's activities ashore. Twelve naval personnel operate an LCU.

LCU leaving USS Wasp

The signalman gave me a tour of the pilothouse and crews' quarters. The small, laid-back crew likes this duty. A chief petty officer commands the small craft. Three of these vessels can be joined end to end to form a causeway, thus making it a very effective method of getting men and equipment ashore.

After the SPIE operation, I caught a ride on a HMMV back to the waterfront. With time on my hands before the LCU made its last run to the ship, I decided to see more of Almeria—especially Alcazaba, the old Moorish castle above the town. I checked my progress by asking a man if I were going in the right direction. He indicated a direction that took me through a maze of narrow, twisting, cobblestone streets. Suddenly, I came upon one filled with rundown buildings where some derelict-looking people loitered. The cardinal military rule for being a "hard target" is never to enter an environment that you can't control. This one looked doubtful. I detoured.

Eventually, the castle rose before me and I had no further difficulty reaching it. Arriving a few minutes before it opened, I was the lone visitor. Europeans enter free. Americans enter for 250 pesetas, about $2.50. As usual, the man who sold me the ticket didn't speak English, but his friendliness turned vibrant, when he found out I was from the ship that he could see in the bay. He proudly told me about his Spanish military service and showed me his picture in a military uniform wearing a special citation.

Although the walls of Alcazaba are intact, much of the three compounds composing it lie in ruins, largely from an earthquake in 1522, but also from neglect. Jayman, a Moorish king, embellished the first fort built in the tenth century when he came to power in the eleventh century. Extensive gardens, fairly well kept, beautify this whole section. The second compound served as residences for Moslem kings, suggesting great archaeological value. Restoration work progresses slowly in Alcazaba. New-looking white marble columns formed the focal point of one room, but they have already been permanently scratched with graffiti, a common blight in Spain.

Being all alone in this setting, I felt a bit like being in a time warp. I soaked up all of it. I climbed all of the walls, ambled through gardens of tall trees and flowering shrubs, viewed the ponds and little water canals, strolled through all the musty rooms, observed the rusty cannons in empty ports, and noted the open plazas and ruins characterized by flat, red, jagged bricks. In doing so, I tried to visualize the daily lives of bygone civilizations that lived, loved, and fought here. And I wondered if they knew whether they left anything behind worth knowing. And I also wondered, will I?

Almeria, Spain, November 14, 1991

Yesterday, I left the ship before sunrise to play with the Marines again. The LCU took us to the pier where we boarded five six-wheel drive, five-ton trucks for the trip to the firing range in the mountains. We spent about two hours firing M-16 rifles. First, from 25 meters we fired a series of three single shots at our targets and checked them after each series. Then we moved back about 100 meters from the targets and fired three bullet bursts. It was my first time to shoot an automatic weapon. The M-16 is capable of firing 90 rounds of 5.56mm ammunition a minute. The bullet is only slightly larger than a .22 cal. bullet, but its high velocity causes an air wedge to enter a body right behind the bullet, greatly expanding the wound. Inside the body, the bullet tumbles, ricochets, and ends up most anywhere inside a man. The rifle has virtually no recoil.

After target practice, I caught a ride back to town on a HMMV and did some more sightseeing before catching a "MIKE boat" (a 67-ton landing craft) back to the ship. Almeria has some interesting architecture but can't compare with Valencia. Alcazaba looks pretty at night with its special lighting. I shot some time exposures through my zoom lens from the ship.

Some sad news arrived from the Harrier squadron temporarily located at Rota, Spain. Marine Captain Driscoll crashed on a low altitude-training mission near Seville. His wingman said his aircraft just exploded and went down. A pilot has about five seconds to hit the eject button. He never had a chance.

I have before me a radio message confirming my departure from Jerez Delafrontera (near Rota) at 1000 on December 4 and arrival at Houston Hobby via American Flight 1509 at 1938 the same day.

Alcabaza, Spain

Almeria, Spain, November 15, 1991

Following my class this morning, I rode a RHIB (Rigid Hulled Inflatable Boat) to the pier to do a little shopping. While there, I made my second attempt to reach what appears to be an extension of Alcazaba. It sits on a hill across a small valley from Alcazaba and is connected by a single wall partly in ruins. From the ship, the wall, along with Alcazaba, dominates the Almeria skyline. But as a pedestrian, my destination proved elusive because of tall buildings and twisting streets.

At length, I found myself at the base of the hill crowned by this walled citadel. A large statue—apparently Christ—dominates the center of the front wall. I encountered an elderly woman and a young girl below the entrance steps and asked them the name of the place. The woman said it is Cerro San Cristobal and warned me not to go closer. She seemed to be telling me that it was a hangout for drug dealers. Perhaps that explains why I have seen a profusion of postcards picturing Alcazaba and none picturing Cerro San Cristobal. I swallowed my curiosity and took the woman's advice.

The ride back to the ship on a small utility boat through choppy water drenched my jacket, pants, and shoes.

Almeria, Spain, November 16, 1991

The officer in charge of the well deck invited me to watch the Marines and their equipment being back loaded onto the ship. The well deck is a huge cargo space. A stern ramp can be lowered to permit a boat to enter the ship after it floods the aft section of the well deck.

When I arrived at the control room, the LCU from the USS *Ponce* was already inside the ship. It carried three five-ton trucks. First off was one pulling a howitzer. Next was a truck pulling a water trailer. All three trucks carried Marines. They simply drove off the front ramp of the LCU and up one level to park inside the ship. This was the last trip for the LCU. Last to come aboard were the three LCACs loaded with more equipment. For their entry, the ballast tanks were blown, raising the ship and emptying the well deck of all water.

Meanwhile, flight operations were in progress as were Basic Engineering Casualty Control Exercises (BECCE). This was the third BECCE in four days. The other two were conducted during GQ with lights out.

This has been a working port for both the ship's crew as well as the Marines. As far as I know, I am the only one on the ship to go into town and act like a tourist. These guys are going to be ready for R & R in Barcelona in two days.

Barcelona, Spain, November 22, 1991

We arrived here three days ago under threatening skies and mid-fifties temperature. The ship moored about a mile and a half from the fleet landing graced by a massive statue of Christopher Columbus, the gateway to La Rambla, a street that bisects the city.

Christopher Columbus Monument

A Russian cruise ship occupies the same close-in berth used by the USS *Belknap* when I was here in the summer of 1989.

First, I called Nita and found affairs at home reasonably stable, except for my dad in Missouri. His right leg was amputated just above the knee on November 13. A phone call to his wife Mary revealed that he is recovering well in the hospital and in good spirits.

A brief shower drove me off La Rambla into a produce market. It is not as extensive or quite as neat as the one in Valencia, but still quite remarkable. More varieties of mushrooms were on display that I knew existed. The meat market also offered some items unusual to me: sheep's heads, hogs' heads, and jackrabbits. Considering that Spaniards were the first Europeans in Texas, I wondered if Texas jackrabbits had been imported from Spain.

Barcelona has made significant improvements since I visited

here in 1989. Acres of new sidewalks studded with new lampposts line the streets. Some of the streets have been repaved; others are in the process of being repaved. One street, roughly parallel to La Rambla, has been closed and is being made into a pedestrian way. New construction continues all over the port area. Old buildings have undergone restoration or otherwise have been spruced up. Even graffiti that defaced so many commercial and public buildings has been removed or covered over. Obviously, the city is getting ready for the 1992 Olympics.

More from the small world department. When Kevin Taylor and I were returning to the ship one evening in Valencia, this redheaded girl dashed out of a bar, speaking rapidly in Spanish. She was trying to locate an enlisted man named Adam. She wrote a short message that we gave to the officer in charge of the quarterdeck to pass to Adam when he showed up. I never gave the incident another thought until two days ago.

Walking alone just outside the port gate, I encountered this same girl. She recognized me and again wanted to know how she could find Adam. I told her to check with the quarterdeck, knowing she would not have the credentials to get through the port gate. Leaving her, I took some side streets in a roundabout way to La Rambla. As soon as I stepped onto the pedestrian way of La Rambla, there she was again, determined to find Adam! Valencia is more than 200 miles from Barcelona. Adam must be quite a guy. It's too bad her radar doesn't home in on him the way it does me.

Barcelona, Spain, November 26, 1991

I have crammed a lot of living into the last four days. Friday night seven members of the Barcelona Orchestra performed selections from Telemann, Handel, and Bach at the Ajuntament de Barcelona (city hall). Except for an oboe, all the instruments were stringed. These outstanding musicians played to an appreciative, standing-room-only audience. The performance hall reminded me of the great hall at the Adjuntament in Valencia, except for the presence of crystal chandeliers of typical Spanish-sculpted metal. Rich red and yellow tapestry, the color of Spain's flag, covered the walls.

The next day, I went with a tour group to the country of Andorra. Situated in the Pyrenees Mountains between Spain and France, it's a little larger than Monaco and Liechtenstein. It would easily fit into a West Texas county and has a permanent population of only 50,000. Only 9,000 are citizens of Andorra, and they control all the wealth derived principally from tourism. To obtain citizenship, a person must be a third-generation resident. Although prices there are no better than those in the U. S., they're much cheaper than those in Spain or France. You can buy anything in this tiny place.

Because of the favorable prices and the proximity to ski slopes, the country entertains about 200,000 visitors constantly. Three hundred thousand dollars will buy a small house. Crime is almost non-existent. A small jail confines people guilty of minor offenses. Other offenders are sent either to Spain or France.

The country has no military. It doesn't need one. The people elect a president and 28 representatives from seven small districts. But they also have two princes: the president of France and a Spanish bishop. This arrangement effectively makes the country a protectorate of Spain, France and the Vatican. I suspect that something other than tourism spins the economy of Andorra.

Our tour group began a walking tour of the city after a four-hour ride in the dark on a cloudless morning. Snow on the mountains intensified the sunrise and gave us a temperature of -3 degrees Celsius (27 F) with a lower chill factor. Since everybody in Andorra is Catholic, our first stop was the church. A metal statue of a bishop with his right hand raised in a typical blessing gesture sat outside the entrance. Some joker had placed a cigarette butt between his first and second fingers. This modern building replaced one of ancient vintage that burned in 1972.

Next, we saw their city hall that's largely a museum. In the wintry old days, deep snow prevented representatives from traveling very well; so the city hall had sleeping and eating accommodations for them. These rooms along with their furniture are on display. The beds, no more than 66 inches long, indicated small people. Also on display is the original front door with six separate keyholes. Formerly, there were six districts and one representative from each district had to be present to open the door. A miniature sanctuary sits in front of a painting of the crucifixion of Jesus covering the rear wall of the council chamber. The artist knew the crucifixion story but not the Roman culture. A local official in his breeches, cut-away coat, and plumed top hat stands between Jesus and one of the thieves. The soldier piercing Jesus' side rides a white horse. Andorran trappings adorn both rider and horse.

Not interested in shopping, the main reason people visit Andorra, I spent most of the day walking the city and browsing through stores with Kevin Taylor. We really bolstered the Andorran economy! Kevin bought a scarf for his wife; I bought a small chunk of cheese. In our judgment, the best thing Andorra has going for itself is the crisp, clean mountain air.

The next day, Kevin and I walked about 10 miles in Barcelona, basically following one of the walking tour routes laid out on a city map. We went through the gardens and on up to the old fort on top of Mont Juric (Jewish Mountain), which I had visited in 1989. But Kevin, having never seen the old fort, especially related to the old artillery pieces on display there because he commands a Marine artillery battery. We wound around the mountain to Olympic Village (site of the 1992 Olympics), Spanish Village, and seemingly endless fountains, museums, and gardens. I would like to return to some of the places we saw, but other walking tours also beckon, and time is too limited even to see all of them.

Yesterday, Kevin invited me to take a Physical Fitness Test (PFT) with his company. Surprised, I said, "Kevin, I'm 64 years old. I can't keep up with a bunch of young Marines!" Dismissively, he replied, "I've been watching you work out. You'll do o.k."

Marines are always supposed to be in shape for this test. After some timed stress exercises in the gym, we went outside at sunrise in the cold air to run three miles. After having walked some 25 miles in the two previous days, I wasn't too happy to keep my promise. Nevertheless, I came in well ahead of some of the platoon I ran with. Major Innerst told me today that my "accomplishment" had gone through the Marines like wildfire. Of course, that was Kevin's purpose—using me to motivate his men.

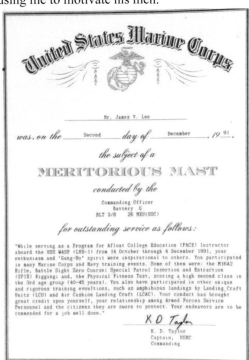

Following PFT, I showered, grabbed a bite of breakfast on the run, and took a tour bus to the Torres Wine distillery and the Cordonui Champagne distillery. Enroute we saw some of the sights in Barcelona and other points of interests. Between the two tasting sessions, we ate a delicious lunch of Spanish cuisine. The ride on the tram through underground tunnels filled with more than 100,000,000 bottles of Champaign impressed me the most. That's a lot of celebrating! The tunnels extend 16 kilometers (about 10 miles) with additional lengthening each year. The family has been making Champaign since 1571, and must have a half a billion dollars in inventory.

Barcelona, November 27, 1991

Kevin Taylor and I took to the streets again today—more than twelve miles of them. We combined three walking tours into one.

First, we went in search of the replica of Columbus' ship Santa Maria. It wasn't in its usual berth. We found it in a shipyard across the harbor undergoing fire damage repairs in order to be ready when the Olympics begin.

Our walks through the city revealed far more construction in progress than I first realized. The town seems in be in a frenzy to look good for the Olympics, but finishing all of the construction by then seems a bit doubtful. Since many of the choice points of interest are closed for renovation, I would like to return to Barcelona in 1993 after all the work is finished and the surplus tourists have gone home.

Our walk through the city today just touched a smattering of things to see and do in this old city. The magnificent architecture just seems endless. Wanting to get an overview of as much as we could, we took time to enter only one building, the Barcelona Cathedral in the central city near the port.

Impressive from the outside with its towering spires, the cathedral is flanked on one side with an enclosed formal garden. Towering palms and evergreens shade a small pond with waterfowl. Around the garden a loggia encloses a series of alcoves with distinctive, painted and sculpted shrines of various people.

Inside, an auditorium seats no more than 500 people on plain benches characteristic of Catholic churches. Almost as much space is devoted to the altar reached by six broad steps on either side of a broad stairway descending to a chamber underneath the altar where lies entombed the patron saint of Barcelona. Two other notables lie in wooden caskets on a wall to the right of the altar. A very broad isle encircles the entire interior of the cathedral. Behind the altar, an elongated semi-circle of ten alcoves holds more painted and sculptured shrines, utilizing much gold overlay.

Behind the seats holding the worshippers, a high wall topped with closely spaced miniature spires encloses a very large choir section with an organ in the middle. This one feature probably sets this cathedral apart from all other cathedrals. Beyond the choir, more alcoves of shrines flank the front door.

Massive, fluted, artistically placed pillars support a Gothic style roof about 80 feet above the floor. Stained glass windows in the upper half of the walls illuminate the interior. Naturally, generous use is made of ironwork and chandeliers. Outside, I took a picture of the cathedral with an old lady surrounded by pigeons in the foreground.

We circumvented, but did not enter the main church of Barcelona, the Cathedral Sagada Familia. Being the tallest structure in Barcelona, and a monument to the city instead of Christianity, the cathedral has a central spire that rises 150 meters. Designed by Antoni Gaudi, the building, which has been under construction since 1883 is so ostentatious that it, as well as other buildings designed by Gaudi, looks like it belongs in an amusement park. Evidently, the word "gaudy" comes from Gaudi.

Cathedral Sagada Familia

Barcelona, November 29, 1991

Kevin Taylor and I had one last fling at Barcelona late yesterday. We spent most of the last of our pesetas on tickets to the Maritime Museum. Models of ships throughout the ages and from all over the world filled the place. Naturally, it contained the three Columbus ships: Nina, Pinta, and Santa Maria, the square-rigger flagship. A full-sized, ornate galley similar to the one used in the movie Ben Hur fascinated me the most. The rowers on the Roman ship were below deck instead of above, a major difference. To pull each one of the long massive oars required the strength of three men.

This port visit exposed me to two other activities I had never experienced before: A Captain's Mast and a Summary Court Marshall. The Mast took place on the flight deck where a large company of Sailors gathered to watch the proceedings against five of their shipmates. I left after the captain resolved the first case. A young man (1) became drunk and disorderly, (2) pulled a switchblade knife (illegal possession) on (3) five other Sailors, including a chief petty officer. The captain hit him with the maximum punishment available to him:

(1) reduction in rate to the lowest rate in the Navy, (2) forfeiture of a half month's pay for two months, (3) confinement to the ship for sixty days (there goes Christmas and New Year's), and (4) mandatory counseling for alcohol abuse. The boy had just gotten off restricted liberty.

The Court Marshall involved a second class petty officer who climbed a grain elevator in Valencia and refused to come down. The ship's captain and executive officer both tried to get him under control only to receive abusive language from him. A less than an honorable discharge from the Navy awaits him when returns to the states via Rota, Spain. It's tragic when people perform badly when so many other people try to help them, but the Navy is just a microcosm of the American society.

The ship is now getting underway for a three-day transit to Rota, my departure point. Visiting Barcelona again has been delightful. My questions and requests for directions have fallen on friendly ears everywhere I have gone. Almost no one speaks English, but when the people see me struggle to communicate in Spanish, their friendliness turns into bemused kindness. I would like to stay in this magnificent city for a long time and just do what I want to do. But my classes are over, except for a final exam tomorrow. So it's time to pack it in.

USS Guadalcanal (Photo courtesy of Elsilrac Enterprises)

USS *Guadalcanal* LPH-7

Off Newfoundland, March 4, 1992

Ever since I boarded this ship on February 25, I have had a very full schedule. I teach seven days a week from 0730 to 2130 with an extended break for lunch and dinner, leaving little time for lesson preparation, grading, sleeping, and exercising. Classes in five different courses are going well, but I always get at least one surprise when I begin a new cruise. This time for the first time, I'm teaching an advanced reading course, but the instructor's material didn't arrive on board the ship.

Thanks to my schedule, I've seen little of the outside world the last nine days. We had two days that were so warm that I slept without cover. But then we hit the fringe of a storm that brought high winds, low visibility, deep ocean swells, and snow showers. Although this ship is more than 600 feet long and carries helicopters, it is surprisingly top-heavy. It rolls like a corkscrew and sometimes scatters men and objects about the deck. Several times, meals have become a jumbled mess of food, men, and broken dishes on the deck. Men seated in armchairs for meals slide from one bulkhead to the other like miniature trains. All of us just take it with good humor. A few meals have been sandwiches served on paper plates.

Naturally, the rolling ship has caused considerable seasickness, which has decimated some of my classes. Fortunately, the instructor has not been included in the decimation.

Ens. Tom Jessen, Educational Services Officer, has been quite helpful. First, he made it a point to see that I came on board to a clean, two-man stateroom with the bed already made up. He had already tested all students and organized the classes. And whatever my needs or that of the other PACE instructor, he promptly saw to it that somebody took care of them. This is my thirteenth deployment on Navy ships, and no ESO has ever performed better. Tom is the oldest ensign in the Navy. He came up through the ranks and was a chief petty officer for several years. In addition, he interrupted his naval service with thirteen years of law enforcement. Some of his very interesting experiences include playing two roles in the TV series War and Remembrance—an officer and a medical corpsman.

Bill Arnesen, the other PACE instructor, teaches math and psychology. He holds a PHD degree in psychology. His beard and somewhat shaggy hair makes him look the part. Being tired of on-campus teaching, he has taught aboard ten ships. He's a soft-spoken, good-natured, easygoing, roommate with a quick wit. Once, when he was not fully prepared for a class two days away, I kidded him about being derelict in his duty. He replied, "I'm just an old derelict—a psycho-derelict."

Lt. Jim Kruse, the navigator, invited me to the bridge to shoot some sun lines with the sextant, but I was buried in enrollment details during the two days we have had sunshine. I probably have spent no more than thirty minutes on the bridge—just a little time to see something besides gray bulkheads and breathe some fresh cold air.

North Atlantic, March 5, 1992

Yesterday, this ship became a part of sizable battle group, in-cluding an aircraft carrier, an LST, two civilian supply ships, and an amphib like the USS *Austin* to which I was assigned a year ago. Also a small Canadian mine sweeper accompanies us, as well as Dutch and German ships. Late in the day, the tanker USS *Neosho*, supplied the ship with fuel, an operation requiring skillful helmsmen on both ships because of rough seas.

Last night, someone deliberately broke a seal on a switch to activate the "A Triple F" system (aqueous fast foaming film) on the hanger deck. This system sprays corrosive foam, which is 95% salt water, to extinguish a class B fire. One-third of the hanger deck re-quired an immediate fresh-water wash down to prevent damage to aircraft and everything else contaminated. Some of the crew worked from 1900 to 2300 to clean up the mess. Capt. Jack Cassidy, nor-mally a pleasant guy, demonstrated considerable displeasure. If the culprit is ever identified, he will be even more displeased. Unlike the civilian court system, military justice aboard ship is swift and firm. For example, as of March 1, all naval personnel who test positive for illegal drugs are automatically out of the Navy, and random testing goes on continuously. Until now, the lowest three pay grades were subjected to some other punishment plus rehabilitation. The theory was that teenage boys deserved a second chance. But no more. Consequently, few make trouble.

About a dozen men, including a former Marine student, from the USS *Wasp* are now attached to this ship. In addition, several *Guadalcanal* crewmen recognized me as the former PACE instructor on the USS *Austin* because we were at Iskendrun, Turkey, at the same time during Operation Provide Comfort last year. I have also encountered Marines who took me ashore in their AAVs in Peru last summer when I was on the USS *Barnstable County*. Seeing so many familiar faces makes me feel less like a stranger and more like one who belongs to the group.

Atlantic Ocean, 50 degrees N. Lat., 24 degrees W. Long. March 7, 1992

Sunrise broke over a fairly smooth ocean with an air temperature of about fifty degrees. Two days of smooth steaming has been a welcome respite from the stormy weather. But the weather people are predicting forty foot swells ahead. Consequently, the ship topped off its fuel tanks this morning during calm seas.

It's decision time for the command of this operation. Originally, we were supposed to skirt the coasts of Iceland and Ireland to reach Norway, but mounting seas ahead have raised the possibility of going through the English Channel.

Last night, Capt. Cassidy startled me with a visit to one of my classes. He just dropped by to lend his support and encouragement. In my thirteen deployments in three years he's the first commanding officer to visit one of my classes. From the first day, he insisted that I call him Jack. Instead of a full uniform, he wears a different color turtleneck every day. The shirts are comfortable, but I suspect he does this to relate to his crew. Ordinance and crash crews wear red; fuel people, purple; aircraft maintenance men, green; flight deck crew, yellow; safety personnel, white; aircraft security, blue; and plane captains who shift aircraft on deck, brown. Showing his sensitivity in other ways, Jack commands a ship with the highest morale.

English Channel, March 9, 1992

We entered the English Channel about noon today. Some of the battle group deployed along the west side of England to brave the heavy seas there. We will meet them in the Norwegian Sea for a NATO exercise before going to Norway.

With the protection of the channel, the ship's movement seems barely perceptible. When we passed the Scilly Islands under overcast skies this morning, the normally lead-gray ocean turned aquamarine. The water must be much shallower here.

Today, I jogged on the flight deck for the first time—nice break from the stationary bike and rowing machine. The fifty-degree air felt colder in shorts and T-shirt with the ship moving at twenty-two knots. But it was a good introduction to the Blue Nose initiation awaiting those of us who have never before crossed the Arctic Circle.

North Sea, March 10, 1992

Tonight, we are dodging oil derricks in the North Sea off Norway, and have transited the English Channel without incident. The ship is beginning to roll again and predictions for rougher weather ahead brought the captain's order to tie down any moveable objects. So it's back onto the bunk with the side rail.

Because of overcast skies, we missed seeing the White Cliffs of Dover today, but tonight a one-quarter moon beautifully bathes the cold ocean under a cloudless sky. It's strange to see the constellation Orion in the southwest.

Norwegian Sea, March 11, 1992

Snow-capped mountains of Norway lie to starboard as we proceed to a rendezvous with the ships that didn't come through the English Channel. Last night's clear sky again turned overcast and pelted the ship with a small amount of hail. Today a 90-knot wind sweeps the flight deck and creates ten to twelve foot swells in a blue-black ocean. With the ship's course in the trough of the swells, we experience rolls of twenty degrees or more. A number of men who got used to a few days of calm are seasick again. Some people just never seem to adapt to the ocean.

Trondheim Fjord, Norway, March 13, 1992

We entered this fjord yesterday about noon and immediately encountered smoother water. The fjord, an "arm of the sea," runs through a narrow, natural channel embraced by a rugged coastline nurturing scattered houses and farms. Last night, we anchored just off Trondheim, a beautiful city of about 40,000 people from which the Vikings launched westward explorations in the tenth century AD. Snow during the night turned the mountainside into picture postcard perfection. Today is a gloriously bad day. After conducting some flight operations, the ship's command attempted to go pierside at

1700, but fifty-knot winds and zero visibility precluded any movement. Someone said it's like being inside an ice cream cone. The inclement weather also prevented the Marine landing scheduled for today. We'll anchor offshore tonight and hope for cooperative weather tomorrow morning.

Trondheim Fjord, March 14, 1992

Moderating winds and good visibility enabled the ship to be moved pierside today. The ship conducted some flight operations, transferring personnel among the various ships anchored offshore. Several reservists have come on board. A lawyer and an accountant are here for two weeks of training before returning to civilian life. The Marines went ashore with their skis and other snow equipment for two days of maneuvers in the mountains. During my break from classes, Bill and I went ashore to look around. Stores close early on Saturday, so we got to see icy streets and interesting architecture. We thawed out with hot drinks in a cozy sidewalk solarium before returning to the ship for our evening classes.

Trondheim, Norway, March 15, 1992

After a day of flight operations in the Trondheim Fjord and a visit by a three-star admiral, the ship moved again to the pier at Trondheim. A short time ago, snow began to fall. A slight breeze gives the snow the appearance of a very dense fog. Visibility is about two hundred yards. Few city lights glow through the whiteout. Some of the crew is working on electronic gear on the ship's superstructure. Others form a human chain to pass provisions from trucks to ship. Snow more than an inch deep has already turned the helicopters on the flight deck into surrealistic machines. From the comfort of the Flag Bridge where I have visibility of about 330 degrees, the night is enchanting. But the men working outside only experience wet, miserable weather. I feel for the Marines in four-man tents somewhere in the mountains.

Malagen Fjord, Norway, March 18, 1992

Tonight we are anchored in this beautiful fjord about fifteen miles from Tromso, Norway. Surrounding snow-covered mountains glistening under a full moon behind a wisp of clouds have created a gorgeous night. Splotches of black-mountain terrain and trees contrast starkly against the predominantly white landscape.

Yesterday, we warm-blooded types underwent the dreaded Blue Nose initiation. That's all it was—dreaded. The ceremony consisted

Above the Arctic Circle

Arctic Ocean

of painting each man's nose with blue cake icing as he went through the chow line. Everybody looked ridiculous, but it surely beats being hosed down with salt water on the flight deck while wearing nothing but underwear, which is the initiation event on some ships.

We crossed the Arctic Circle at 0244 yesterday enroute to another Marine landing in northern Norway. After we pulled out of Trondheim Fjord into the Atlantic, two reserve officers on the Flag Bridge engaged me in conversation. Both were gamely trying to be sociable without throwing up. They were two of several reservists from Pensacola, Florida, that came on board at Trondheim. All that they are going to see during their two weeks of annual duty is some Norwegian fjord and the rough Atlantic.

The ship has been very busy with flight operations the last few days. The choppers have moved reservists who flew over from the states to various ships in the battle group. In addition, a number of NATO military personnel with their strange uniforms and insignia are on board. Ships have conducted mock battle with each other. Yesterday the ship splashed two enemy aircraft, but got hit by the third one, causing fire and flooding. The crew got quite a workout during GQ. It's all designed to keep the fleet sharp. I used to watch these same kinds of exercises when I was on board the aircraft carrier *John F. Kennedy* and wondered when such expertise would ever be needed. *JFK* was on the "point of the spear" in the Persian Gulf, and some of the F-14 and A-6 pilots were men with whom I had brief associations. Now, I watch young, ski-laden Marines airlifted to snow-covered mountains and wonder when they will ever be called upon to fight under such conditions.

Malselvfjorden Fjord, March 23, 1992

The ship has been anchored here for two days while the Marines have been deployed ashore in battle maneuvers where they learned some valuable lessons from the Norwegians about combat in snow-covered mountains. Meanwhile, the ship conducts daily flight operations and other training exercises within the ship.

Two days ago, a call came from one of the smaller ships in the area for an emergency pick-up of a seaman who had been severely burned when a steam pipe broke. An airborne *Guadalcanal* chopper responded within seconds. They airlifted the man to Tromso where he was initially treated and then sent to an air base in Germany. Without the quick response, the man would have died. Constant drills aboard ships seem to cover every conceivable contingency. In spite of being surrounded by huge quantities of explosive fuel and ammunition, personnel on the ship probably are safer than they would be on a Houston freeway.

For safety and environmental reasons, cigarette smoking aboard naval vessels is rapidly becoming banned. No one can smoke in a workspace on this ship unless everybody who works there agrees. The Navy is also cracking down on alcohol abuse. A guy who gets two DWIs is automatically out of the Navy with a less then honorable discharge. Furthermore, no recruit with a DWI or illegal drug offense will be accepted into the Navy.

Matthew Hudgins, a naval reservist from Pensacola, is on board for two weeks. He is an engineer with the Naval Education and Training Program Management Support Activity. His organization is two or three bureaucratic levels above the PACE program. It's a think tank that's already working on the problem of educational deficiencies of recruits ten years from now. That's a sad commentary on the American school system. The organization is currently monitoring sixth graders to see what educational gaps exist when they graduate from high school so they can be dealt with when the Navy receives them.

My own educational environment improved considerably yesterday. The staff of PHIBRON 4 left the ship, and I now have the use of their dining/lounge area. It has a spacious long table that will accommodate all my students in each class. Besides, it is right next to my stateroom. So I no longer have to go to the other end of the ship and down three decks to reach my classroom.

Malselvfjorden Fjord, March 24, 1992

My stateroom is right under the flight deck. This morning, I awoke to the sound of snow being scraped off the flight deck. Flight quarters was called at 0530 but canceled after the deck had been cleared of snow three times. Finally, the captain just invited the crew topside to enjoy the snow. Some of the men built a huge snow woman on the bow, evoking witticisms about frigidity. Christmas songs on the 1MC enhanced the festive mood.

By mid-afternoon, the snowstorm subsided and quite a number of reservists flew off the ship to return to Pensacola. But the ground troops had to operate without Marine close air support due to poor visibility in the mountains. Some of the troops were supposed to have been backloaded today but they are still stuck in the snow. We had one near tragedy. This afternoon the ship dispatched the Navy's largest helicopter to retrieve a British helicopter off a mountain peak that almost crashed. The pilot of the craft didn't discern the mountain peak from the falling snow until the last instant. He pulled up abruptly and pancaked against the mountainside. Although no one was hurt, damage to the chopper rendered it inoperable.

The ship went to General Quarters from 0730 to 1030 today. I went back to bed. Today is the first day in a month that I have slept eight hours in a twenty-four hour period. That's the difference between feeling good and feeling terrific.

During GQ, eight separate drills were carried out to deal with simulated fire, flooding, and battle damage. The teams achieved near-perfect scores for their performances.

English Channel, March 29, 1992

Today my students and I got sent back below decks for our classes. One of the ship's officers came by my class yesterday afternoon. Seeing the carpet badly in need of vacuuming, he angrily informed us that we could no longer hold class there. My students were not responsible for the dirty carpet. Marine officers use the space at night to watch television. Furthermore, a fire party yesterday got the entire area filthy when they responded to a smoking transformer. The officer blew a beautiful opportunity to display professionalism and fair play in front of his men. He made no attempt to get the facts.

Ironically, he provided a perfect example for the lesson in logical fallacies that I had under discussion when he entered the room. In blaming my students for someone else's action, he illustrated a classic case of post hoc ergo propter hoc. Later, when Bill Arnesen and I were discussing the incident, I observed that people often have two reasons for their behavior or decisions: the real reason and the one that sounds good. I suggested that the real reason might be that the officer couldn't bear to see enlisted men using officers' facilities—especially staff officers' facilities. Bill retorted typically, "Yeah, he probably has a staff infection."

We left the Norwegian Sea amid brilliant sunshine with intermittent snow flurries. I got a few shots of some spectacular coastline. For three days, rough water, exacerbated by following seas, returned the ship to its corkscrew rolls—some as much as thirty-one degrees. For a ship this size, that's a lot of roll. When we transited the North Sea yesterday, I shouldn't have been surprised to see a large oil refinery in the ocean. Since the North Sea is full of oil wells, it only makes sense to have a refinery close by. After we entered the passage between England and southern Norway, calmer seas and sunshine brought a bunch of us back onto the flight deck for jogging. Today, we had hoped to see the famous Dover Cliffs. But again, the weather didn't cooperate. I was in class anyway.

Plymouth, England, April 1, 1992

We arrived in this beautiful city two days ago, and I still haven't seen much of it. I intend to remedy that situation tomorrow. The entry into the harbor whetted my wanderlust appetite. Ships approach the city through a long, narrow S-curve channel marked by buoys. The channel winds it way through underwater obstructions placed in the harbor to prevent German submarines from entering the port in World War II. A BBC TV cameraman joined me on a high perch on the signal bridge during the hour-long trip into port. He indicated key points of interest and told me a bit about himself. He was four-years-old when WWII broke out, and he lived about fifty miles from London near a U. S. Army Air Corps installation right across a rose garden from the quarters that housed Glen Miller and his band.

Upon arrival Monday evening, I went to a local pub along with about dozen Sailors and Marines to play skittles. When I signed up for the event, I had no idea what the game was or where it would be played. The evening turned out to be fun and relaxing. Before we left for the pub, shipboard personnel were warned that if they over indulged, the Britons would consider them persona non grata. I managed the evening with two non-alcoholic drinks and three games of skittles.

The game is similar to bowling, but played on a shorter, narrower alley. Nine pins are set up in the shape of a diamond, the broad side of which faces the player who uses a ball somewhat larger and heavier than a softball. A player gets three tosses at the pins, which are the same size on both ends and bulge in the middle. Spectators lining the rail boisterously cheer the teams. Eleven Americans squared off against eleven Britons and we won all three games. I started off poorly but took down all pins with one ball in the last game. At a late hour I hiked back to the ship. Most of the other men hung around until closing time just relaxing and talking to the friendly natives who gratuitously sent some of them back to the ship in taxis.

Yesterday, a tour bus took me to Warwick Castle and Stratford-on-Avon in central England. Because of the travel time, I didn't get to spend as much time as I wanted to at either place.

Construction of Warwick began two years after the Norman Conquest in 1066 with completion in the fourteenth century when it became a major fort. The Castle now serves as a museum. But from the beginning of its construction in 1066, it played key roles in the various English wars fought over several centuries. On display in Warwick is a device formerly used throughout Europe that caused even the most hardened criminals to break down. Immobilized in a suit of iron straps, the victim was hung outdoors without water or food and subjected to heat, cold, rain, insects, birds or passer-by tormentors until he died. The United States Constitution prohibits cruel and unusual punishment. Likely, this was the type of punishment the country's founders had in mind.

Warwick Castle

Warwick Castle Scene

After its military significance declined, noblemen who occupied Warwick refurbished the living quarters to reflect their lavish tastes. Since it was actually lived in until about a dozen years ago, it's still in superb condition, including much of the original furniture, tapestry, and carpeting. Wax figures of real people occupy all the rooms depicting a weekend party in 1898.

Of course, Shakespeare made Stratford-on-Avon famous by being born there. This old house is still in good condition, and no efforts have been made to conceal the small but necessary restoration work. Relatives of Shakespeare lived in the house for two centuries before it became a commercial building. When P. T. Barnum tried to move the house to the U. S., Charles Dickens initiated a move to keep it in England and turn it into the shrine that it is today.

Shakespeare actually lived most of his life in a cottage owned by his wife Anne Hathaway. Architecture of both houses reflects the times. Wood lathing and plaster finished the walls of solid heavy timbers caulked with a mixture of clay, and horsehair. Thatched reed covered the roof of the Hathaway house. I was told that this type of roof could last seven centuries. Both houses are quite picturesque. To see all there is to see relating to Shakespeare would require several days, and I only had a few hours.

Coincidentally, a news article and editorial reported in yesterday's edition of The Times that a woman named Lillian Schwartz, a consultant to AT&T Laboratories in New Jersey, did some computer matching of facial features of a photograph always thought to be that of Shakespeare. She says the computer shows the face to be that of Queen Elizabeth I, minus a mustache. The editorial writer opined, "It is now left to the feminist literary fanatics to carry the argument to its

Shakespeare's House

Anne Hathaway's House

logical conclusion. Why would Shakespeare's friends illustrate the First Folio with a coded portrait of Elizabeth in male dress and mustache except to convey the cryptic message that she wrote the works inside? No woman much less a queen, could admit to writing for the disreputable theatre. If Elizabeth I did not write Shakespeare, she missed the opportunity of her life." It is refreshing to read something controversial besides American political dirt.

Another interesting fact about Shakespeare is that he was 46-years-old the year that scholars published the King James Bible. The 46th word from the beginning of Psalm 46 is "shake." The 46th word from the end of Psalm 46 is "spear." Interesting, but coincidental.

Today, I got another good look at the English countryside as well as several villages—particularly Truro and Penzance— when I went through Cornwall on the way to Lands End, the very tip of the southwestern coast of England. The beautiful drive through Cornwall, with its hedges, streams, and rolling hills, delighted me. Light rain fell intermittently from overcast skies, softening the view. Some fifty miles from Lands End a string of low mountains parallel the road. Denuded and semi-razed, these mountains have furnished tin ore for centuries. Small, abandoned smelters sprinkle the region.

During the last two hundred years, many ships have gone aground on the rocks and shoals between Lands End and the Isles of Scilly. An oil tanker, the most recent one grounded, had to be set afire to clean up the mess. Some say that in the old days, the Cornish people caused many shipwrecks on their rocky coast by misplacement of lights on the shore. They would then steal the wrecked ship's cargo and strip it of anything valuable and praise God for delivering this bounty into their hands.

England, with its lush hills, valleys, and moors is a beautiful country. Sheep and cattle graze on cross-fenced emerald meadows amid manicured hedgerows fed by running streams. Looking quaintly interesting, some older houses share common walls. Newer homes have open spaces. Although some of the newest are acres of look-alike houses, all retain a certain distinctiveness compared to American dwellings. I would love to stay here for a long, long time.

Plymouth, England, April 2, 1992

I began this day with a three-mile walk to Plymouth Dome located next to the lighthouse on the waterfront. This extraordinary two-story structure houses an audio-visual presentation in a series of rooms depicting the history of Plymouth from the sixteenth century until the present. Through it and the many miles I walked in the city, I gained an expanded understanding of and appreciation for the achievements of its citizens, such as Francis Drake and Captain Cook, and the inextricable link of Plymouth to the United States.

On January 1, 1944, the American army took over 30,000 acres of South Devon about twenty miles east of Plymouth, moving three thousand people from farms and villages to provide a training ground and staging area for the assault on Utah Beach, France, on D-Day, June 6, 1944. British Author Leslie Thomas wrote a novel entitled the *Magic Army* recounting those five months. Although the characters are fictional, Thomas seems to be historically accurate. The book is a bit bawdy—as military stories often are—but also funny, poignant, and sad. Since I had seen the area, the book especially interested me.

Nazi bombs mostly obliterated downtown Plymouth in WWII. Consequently, a master plan to rebuild the city created broad avenues, parks, pedestrian ways, and a sense of order and beauty. During WWII, the citizens demonstrated their indomitable spirit by dancing amid the rubble with American GIs between bombing attacks. When I entered the town's largest department store today, a medley of Glen Miller's songs greeted me from the store's P.A. system. Britons still remember this popular American bandleader of WWII. They still express their thanks to American Sailors and Marines for America's help during those trying days. Shopkeepers, the barber, sales clerks, and people I met on the street—all treated me with cordiality. After a twelve-mile hike through Dartmoor tomorrow, I will reluctantly leave this city with fond hopes for a return visit.

Off Scilly Islands, April 4, 1992

Yesterday, a forty-year-old Englishman took two naval officers, three Marine enlisted men, and me on a twelve-mile hike through Dartmoor. Having traveled some distance from the ship bathed in early morning sunlight, I arrived at an overcast moor chilled by a stiff breeze. I wasn't quite prepared for what I saw or what I felt. Seeing the guide in waterproof boots, I questioned whether my Reeboks

The author hiking across Dartmoor

Dartmoor Stream

were equal to the challenge ahead. Proffering a walking stick, he said that they would be adequate if I stepped cautiously. He also offered me a knitted cap that I gratefully accepted.

Beyond being wet, the moor wasn't anything like I had imagined. First, it covered an immense area of rolling hills so desolate that the guide carried a compass. A sudden fog can hopelessly disorient a hiker. Underneath the shallow soil, peat prevents rainwater from soaking deeply into the land. Hence, water runs through the grass into rivulets that become swift-flowing, pollution-free streams.

Although covered in grass, heather, and other vegetation, rocks also strew the landscape, which, along with hard clumps of grass, allow few level places to set foot. There are unlimited ways to sprain or break an ankle. Fortunately, I completed the hike with sound ankles and dry socks. Some years ago, the guide was not so lucky. He snapped an ankle six miles from his car.

Although the day started off bitterly cold, we weren't the only idiots facing the icy wind across wet ground. We encountered other hikers—some in groups, some in twos. Walking the moor seems to be a popular, year-round pastime. Part of the interest in walking the moor is proving that you've been there.

To that end, hikers must use a map and compass to locate ink stamps with special markings hidden at various places across the moor. By stamping a sheet of paper, the hiker proves his presence at that location. The guide said the moor appears especially beautiful in the spring when the vegetation turns green, and purple bell-shaped blooms emerge on the heather.

The walking stick proved to be a valuable tool for balance, ease of walking, and very useful for testing the ground. Once, water that

Images hidden throughout Dartmoor

appeared to be about an inch deep swallowed more than two feet of the stick. Who knows what lies in some of the bogs? The guide said that an American fighter plane from WWII had surfaced in one of them. Apparently, it went straight in and remained there for nearly five decades.

Foxes, badgers, skylarks, a few deer, and other wild life inhabit the moor. Although domestic animals, Dartmoor ponies (somewhat larger than Shetlands), and Scottish black-face sheep run wild. Because the sheep are never sheared, their wool eventually rots and drops off, but they keep the moor evenly grazed like a lush pasture. Their commercial value vests in the lambs slaughtered for their meat. Various farmers on the moor own the sheep and identity them with blue markings. The moor is a national park, but people who lived here before it was designated a park, retain ownership of their portions.

Stands of fir trees planted after WWII occupy some of the moor. When they are eventually harvested, oak and other trees indigenous to the region will replace them. However, no one plans to expand the forests. Some indigenous trees that originally grew on the moor have become extinct.

Dispersed across the moor, ruins of rock shepherds' houses intermingle with centuries-old rock fences and a Stone Age burial ground. Grassed-over shell holes testify to the moor's prior use as an artillery range.

Walking an English moor gave me an exhilarating and unique experience, but after six hours of wandering over hills, along brooks, and across fences through biting cold, I welcomed a rocking chair by the fireplace, fish and chips, and apple cider at a country pub.

Azores Islands, April 8, 1992

We passed through these Portuguese islands early today, having turned south two days ago to avoid rough seas. Two crewmen flew off the ship on emergency leave to the Navy/Air Force base on one of the islands for further transfer home. Off our starboard quarter, the islands no longer provide shelter. Consequently, the ship is pitching fifteen degrees into mounting seas. Predictably, vomitus maximus afflicts some of the crew, including the doctor. Some of the men just couldn't handle the luxury of four days in port and three days of calm seas. Since leaving Plymouth, everybody just wants to go home. I'm ready too. Except for four days in Plymouth, it has been a grueling schedule with more than the usual slow-learning students. But one student in Basic English will forever occupy a special place in my memory. It's a self-paced course requiring each student to take a test when he completes a module. If he fails it, he studies some more and takes a second test. Well, this guy busted his first test and was vocally upset about it. Finally, I admonished, "Well, you don't have to flagellate yourself over it." Then I kind of grinned and asked, "Do you know what that word means?"

Drawing himself up with great indignation he replied, "Mr. Lee! I know more than you think I do! Of course, I know what it means, and I'm not going to fart myself to death!"

It took a while to get the class back under control. All Sailors are well acquainted with the word "flatulence," but this young man missed the nuance.

Midway between Norfolk and Azores Islands, April 12, 1992

Today the crew received its first shipboard holiday since leaving the United States. Many men sunbathed on the flight deck on a calm sea under a sunny sky. Others jogged and did calisthenics. Having finished both basic skills classes yesterday, I had five extra hours of free time. I used some of it to close out the paperwork on the two completed classes, a considerable relief.

But the biggest sense of peace and freedom came from standing on the very tip of the forward part of the flight deck and just succumbing to the elements. From that position, I sense no sights, sounds, or feelings, except the rushing wind, blue sky, and blue water whose four-foot swells give the ship a slight gentle roll. Tonight a three-quarter moon in a cloudless sky outshines all but a few of the brightest stars and planets, reminding me of one of the reasons I like to go down to the sea in ships.

The ship's crew did a small amount of work today. We played leapfrog with the four other ships in our battle group. In this operation, the ships line up in single file, and the last ship passes the other four at close range. The junior officers on the bridge receive training in ship handling that's especially useful in refueling operations. The signalmen also got several hours of training in flag hoisting.

When we passed the other ships, raunchy-looking Sailors and Marines in assorted military and civilian attire lined the port side of our flight deck. Rather than standing at attention, the usual military courtesy, they did a series of "grandstand waves" from one end of the ship to the other to the raucous sound of rock music. Then an announcement came over the 1MC that the flight deck was open for dancing. But no one did.

While all this was going on, a sailboat appeared a considerable distance off the port beam. We were about 900 miles from Norfolk,

900 miles from the Azores Islands, and 900 miles from Bermuda. I hope the little guy makes it to wherever he is going.

About 500 miles from Morehead City, NC, April 13, 1992

Last night, Bill and I received some rare recognition. Every night, one of the ship's three chaplains says a prayer over the 1MC just before *Taps*. In his prayer last night, he thanked God for the "two civilian instructors on board." I'm afraid we received it a bit irreverently, for at that precise moment, a Marine captain passed by the open door to our stateroom and became a one-man cheering section. Consumed with laughter, we didn't hear the rest of the prayer.

Preceding the prayer each night on the 1MC, the ship's commanding officer reviews the accomplishments of the day and tells the personnel involved now great they are. Once, the chaplain, in his prayer immediately following, told God how great the captain is. After dinner last night, the department heads did some spoofs and skits. A Marine colonel referred to that incident as "major sucking up."

The entire crew spent yesterday cleaning the ship—field day they call it. After a thorough cleaning, the old ship doesn't look too bad. And it is an old ship. It was new back in the sixties in the early days of the space program when its sister ship, the USS *Iwo Jima*, plucked astronauts out of the Pacific after a splash down. (Note: The ship was decommissioned on August 31, 1994, and sunk as a target in the Virginia Capes area on May 19, 2005.)

USS Harry E. Yarnell

USS *Harry E. Yarnell* CG-17

North Atlantic, June 28, 1992

After four consecutive amphibious ships, I'm back on a sleek guided missile cruiser. Although it was commissioned in 1963, it's in surprisingly good condition. In fact, it's probably the cleanest and best-looking ship to which I have been assigned. I share a two-man stateroom, which is convenient to every facility I need.

As usual, I got a schedule change. I was told originally that the ship was going to South America. Instead, it is going to the Baltic Sea to be the flagship for a NATO exercise. Having already been to South America, I welcome the change.

Also as usual, a glitch turned up in my class assignments. I was scheduled to teach basic English and basic reading (four-week courses) concurrently with two college classes (eight-week courses) followed by basic math and another basic English course. I received twice the amount of some material for basic reading and none of some other material necessary for the class. By the time the radio messages to and from NETSCLANT authorized basic math to replace basic reading, I had lost four teaching days for that course. This has the effect of extending my deployment four days unless I can make up the lost days when the other classes are not in session. The missing basic reading material should reach me at Portsmouth, England.

For a change, the ship has a female on board, a very young LTJG. She and her husband are both naval reservists. It seemed odd to see a male officer standing on the pier at Norfolk waving goodbye to a female officer on the ship. She will be on active duty for only two weeks. Then she will fly back to the states from Den Helder, Netherlands. But she will never forget these two weeks. Yesterday, she was the victim of a very old Navy gag. The people on the bridge conspired to make her the lookout for the "mail buoy." There she was with her binoculars wearing her bright orange kapok life jacket on the very point of the bow with sound-powered phones to the bridge to receive her instructions. A black buoy would indicate regular mail, an orange buoy registered mail. The bridge personnel had planned a series of course changes to throw spray over the bow and thus drench her, but before the course changes could be executed, the XO took pity on the lass and told her it was a joke. In the meantime, dozens of people, including me, took her picture. The teasing carried over to breakfast today with considerable levity. She took it all with good humor

There are endless methods to initiate a newcomer to shipboard life. Typically, they are sent on errands to get "fifty feet of chow line," a set of "sonar bearings," a "shorted fuse," or a "fallopian tube." One of the best happened to a guy on another ship. He was sent to the engine room to get a "BT Punch." He ended up on the receiving end of the fist of a Boiler Technician. He asked for it three times before the message penetrated his brain.

The weather has been almost picture perfect—brilliant sunshine, four to twelve foot ocean swells, and a cool breeze. This ship with its narrow hull just slices the water with a gentle pitch and roll. During some of my free time, I just sit on the foc's'le and enjoy the ride. Standing at the rail all the way forward, I am overwhelmed by the immense, primeval power of the ocean tossing about this lonely little speck of a plaything we call a ship.

Yesterday, we took on fuel at Ponta Delgata on San Miguel Island in the Portuguese Azores. I went ashore and inquired about a phone that I could use to call home. No phone was on the pier, but one of the dockworkers offered to take me into town to a phone. But with the ship due to leave in less than two hours, I ruefully declined.

This morning the ship underwent a high-speed run—31 knots. Periodically all naval ships undergo such a test to be sure they can function at top speed in case of an emergency. I was on the fantail watching the twenty-foot "rooster tail" kicked up by the ship's screws when something suddenly sent white smoke up the stack and then shut down the engines. We were dead in the water for about an hour but are now back up to cruising speed.

The crew was supposed to have a steel beach picnic on the fantail late this afternoon. However, our beautiful weather suddenly turned overcast with light rain and 4000-yard visibility. We ate food that was already prepared, but used the wardroom and mess deck as usual. Food on this ship has been some of the best Navy food I have had. In addition, much of it is low calorie.

Jogging around the main deck is possible but not too enjoyable because of all the obstructions. So I daily burn off at least 500 calories during 30 minutes on the stair-climbing machine. The ship has a small but well-equipped exercise room, including free weights and a universal machine. Since we have no Marines on board and few naval personnel are very gung ho for exercise, I've had no problem using the facility whenever I want it.

English Channel, July 6, 1992

I slept more than ten hours last night—a most unusual occurrence for me. After four days of hard sightseeing extending beyond midnight, I needed it.

Upon arrival at Den Helder at 2200 last Thursday, I immediately went ashore to a snack bar and used a five dollar bill to buy a cup of hot chocolate and apple pie in order to get change in Dutch guilders—a necessary coin to operate the pay phone for a call to the States. After the second attempt, Nita came on the line. She had just arrived home. Midnight in Den Helder is 1700 in Texas. We discussed plans for her to meet me in London at the end of this assignment. It's too soon to know.

The next day at a travel agency, I picked up a three-day train pass for unlimited travel in Holland for about $48.00 and then had a one-day trip to Belgium and Luxembourg tacked on at a discount. This information is easy to come by, but some of the crew didn't get the word. A two-man pass for three days of unlimited travel is only $60.00, and since the crew must travel in pairs, they paid almost that much for a round trip to Amsterdam.

After purchasing the train tickets, I used the rest of the day to see Den Helder. Getting around town is easy since everybody speaks English, a mandatory subject in school.

The houses are small, neat, and always landscaped. If the Dutch have ten square feet of land available, they will plant a garden. Most of the houses in the city share common walls like apartments. Doors usually open right onto the sidewalk. Out in the suburbs, houses have more open space, but are still small by American standards.

Den Helder Suburbia

Everybody, including elderly people, ride bicycles as a practical means of transportation. Streets and sidewalks are laid out to accommodate cyclists. Consequently, pedestrians must be wary of speeding bicycles. In the countryside, park and ride lots have boxes in which to lock bicycles. But Holland also has enough cars to create quite a traffic jam around Amsterdam on weekends. Japanese cars are noticeably in short supply. European-made cars predominate.

A bus ride took me within a fifteen-minute walk to a beach about seven miles south of the city. Taking the "fietspad" (some Dutch words are easy to translate), I entered a long grotto-like growth of trees and brush. Wild roses and honeysuckle scented the air. This footpath led to the backside of one of Holland's famous dikes. This part of the dike was a high, nature-made dune lined with bike and Moped trails.

Few people were on the beach itself, the day being windy and a bit chilly in spite of the bright sun. Small children made sand castles; some ventured into the water. I decided to walk back to town. Soon the beach turned into five-sided or six-sided stones mortared with tar and sloping upward from the water line. Above this band of stones is a very wide expanse of asphalt. Although still sloping upward, it levels off enough for bikes and cars to travel on the dike. Above the asphalt, grass covers the rest of the dike, which flattens on the top to a width of about 25 feet. The dike looks be at least two hundred yards wide at the base. People use the dike for recreation. I encountered several bikers, strollers, and horseback riders. One kid was doing figure eights with his kite. Two more were trying to keep theirs in the air.

The next day, I caught the 0610 train to Belgium and Luxembourg. I was immediately impressed with the beauty of Holland's countryside. The rich, flat fields of Holland produce a wide variety of vegetables, some grain, and hay—all interspersed with a blaze of commercially grown flowers.

Cattle and sheep fill many meadows. I had to talk to more than one native and eventually visit the Zuider Zee Museum to understand

Commercially-grown flowers

the function of all the canals that lace the fields and cities. Dairy products, vegetables, and flowers are major exports. Since the Dutch are the world's most experienced dike builders, they also export dike and hydraulics technology. Phillips electronics is here, and of course, Royal Dutch Shell. I was surprised to learn that North Holland has enough natural gas to export. Gasoline at the pump costs 1.8 guilders a liter—about $4.10 a gallon, a little more in Belgium. The government intentionally keeps the price of gasoline high to discourage auto driving and to subsidize public transportation.

The flat lands of Holland give way to hills and forests in Belgium, which are reminiscent of parts of Arkansas. Luxembourg is so small that you can travel through it in about the time it takes to say the word. At first look, it's uninspiring. I caught the next train out. So did a lady and her daughter who had planned to spend the night there.

Returning to Belgium, I stopped for dinner at the Sheraton Hotel in Brussels. Not wanting to end up with useless change in Belgium money, I chose the Sheraton in order to use my Visa card. They even provided me with a copy of the Wall Street Journal, the first real news I have had since leaving the states.

As the train slowly pulled into Brussels, my attention was drawn to the first run-down buildings I had seen on the trip. They appeared to be storage places for scantily clad mannequins—until some of them moved. Then I realized I was looking at one of the town's red light districts. Sex shops and the like surround the train station in Brussels. You have to go at least two blocks to get back to civilization. But in Amsterdam, the red lights are not just over a door. The walls of multi-storied buildings for an entire block are lighted up Las Vegas style with red neon.

When the train left Amsterdam, two young boys from the ship sat near me, telling me about their evening there. One bared his chest to reveal writing from a felt marker. How it got there is immoral, quite original, and almost unbelievable. Indeed, the spirit gravitates to that which it secretly admires and reveals itself in overt action.

Arriving in Den Helder at midnight, I welcomed the two-mile hike from the train station to the ship after spending so much time riding. At the ship, the quarterdeck watch told me that food and drink were being served in the wardroom. I opened the door, took one look, and backed out as an enlisted man was delivering another case of beer. Obviously, the Americans and their Canadian visitors from the ship next to us had been toasting each other for some time. I went to the mess deck for scrambled eggs, ham, biscuits and gravy, and fruit.

After a few hours sleep, I left the next day with Lt. Brian Riley.

Near The Hague, we spent several hours at the Floriade, a stunning 175-acre tract covered in flowers, horticulture exhibits, and other landscaping. A serious devotee could spend a week there. Rock Wool had a very interesting exhibit showing how Holland is using Grodan, a product made from molten rock, to raise vegetables free of disease and insects in green houses. Already, green houses cover enough of Holland to create a noticeable glare to air travelers. It seems that this process could make a considerable amount of conventional growth obsolete.

Returning to The Hague, we bought a city map and did a walking tour of downtown. Enroute, we saw most of the government buildings, including the queen's "working palace" and its nearby gardens. At length, we found a park where we ate our sandwiches and fed the birds. Afterwards, we had hot chocolate at a sidewalk cafe. The Hague seemed to be deader than downtown Houston at night, so Brian suggested that we go to Amsterdam. Being Irish, he wanted to visit a particular bar featuring live music. He wasn't sure where it was, and we must have walked six miles before we found it. We found it packed with people and cigarette smoke and didn't even go in. Amsterdam had plenty of other nightlife, none of which interested us. By one of the major city canals, we ate the last of our food and took the train back to Den Helder. Brian is not accustomed to so much walking and fell asleep right away. The walk from the train station to the ship woke him up enough to put away a kiwi milk shake at a late night snack bar. This deployment is going to be a long six-month deployment for Brian. He got married just before the ship left Norfolk.

Yesterday, I went to the Zuider Zee museum alone. Original houses and shops have been moved (sometimes brick by brick) from various parts of Holland to form a typical 18th and 19th century village. Some of the houses actually date back to the 1700s. Here, I learned that the peninsula on which Den Helder sits was at one time far inland. Ten thousand years ago, the Netherlands extended past the Dogger Bank in the North Sea. The sea rose because of warming climate that melted the polar ice caps. The sea has continued to rise during the last few thousand years by about two feet every hundred years. Hence, global warming is not exactly a recent phenomenon. By 900 AD, the land near and around Den Helder was just a bunch of islands and inland lakes. In the 11th and 12th centuries, the population began to get serious about building dikes. Eventually, a long dike closed off the North Sea to form the Zuider Zee, now an inland, fresh water lake.

Dutch windmill

Since so much of the land is below sea level at various depths, it's subject to flooding because evaporation does not eliminate all of the rainfall.

To deal with the problem, huge windmills were developed to pump water from lower canals to canals at a higher level, or into the sea itself. The wind turned a wheel that was geared to an Archimedean screw that lifted the water into a sluice connected to a higher canal. The screw I saw at the museum was about four feet in diameter and about 16 feet long. Of course, the mills could have been in various sizes depending upon the volume of water to be moved. Small metal mills dot the landscape now, but mechanized equipment is used for big projects. Fascinated by this whole aspect of Holland, I bought a book on the history and development of the Zuider Zee.

Today, under clear skies I am again transiting the English Channel. For the fourth time, I will not see Dover Cliffs because we are too far out in the channel.

This afternoon, I saw my first "sail by." Now that the USS *Yarnell* is on location and we have the admiral and his staff on board, two other ships are going home—the British ship *Exeter* and the Canadian ship, *Skeena*. When Exeter overtook us, her decks were crowded with personnel performing every bit of nonsense they could think of. Some danced in a chorus line; some had a static display of Stonehenge; others dressed themselves in a variety of costumes. Messages written on sheets draped over some of the super structure. A pirate flag hung from the barrel of the five-inch gun. The crew sprayed their fire hoses at us. Our deck gang sprayed back, but since we were downwind, none of the water hit the other ships, and most of it drenched the men on *Yarnell*. *Skeena* passed by performing the same kind of nonsense. Their helicopter cut across our bow with a crewman holding a Canadian flag while being suspended on a cable below the aircraft. Then the helicopter scooped a huge bucket of water from the ocean and dumped it on *Yarnell*. There was much more. I missed a lot because so much happened simultaneously. It's amazing how much juvenile activity you can get away with if you wear a military uniform!

Portsmouth, England, July 11, 1992

This is my fifth day in Portsmouth and it seems that I just arrived. Since the ship will be here 13 days, I simply must get some teaching done in this port, because the other five port visits in the Baltic Sea will be four- and five-day visits—just enough time for all the crew to get an adequate amount of time ashore. From a tourist standpoint, this is the cruise of a lifetime, and I'm extremely fortunate to be on it. From a working standpoint, the cruise is a challenge. Some of my students have missed classes because both the meeting times and locations of the classes have been altered this week to accommodate other activities. Navy brass come and go. Visitors come and go. I made myself scarce when eighteen thousand people toured the ship in one day at Den Helder. Formal dinners, complete with candelabra and mess men in formal uniforms, have graced the wardroom. The ship has constantly undergone spit and polish, causing some to recall

Roofless church

the old Navy axiom, "Shoot, it may; shine, it must."

On the first afternoon in port, Lt. Brian Riley, one of my two Educational Service Officers, and I took a fast walking tour of the seaside encompassing Old Portsmouth.

Among the sights were the remains of an old fort near the naval yard, a roofless church (still used) that was fire bombed in WW II, an indoor water slide, and several lawn bowling courts full of players. At one point, we ate fish and chips on the beach and watched a hover-craft ferry passengers to and from the Isle of Wight. The hovercraft, the first in the world, has been in use since the late 1950s. The Navy LCAC is the military version of such a vessel.

Portsmouth has an important history of involvement with the British Navy both in training men and in repairing ships. A number of museums here bear that out. In fact, docked nearby are the HMS *Warrior* and HMS *Victory*, square-rigged battleships turned into mu-seums. Both are magnificent vessels. Built in 1860, *Warrior* is iron clad and steam assisted, but *Victory*, which pre-dates it, reeks with romance, and I would love to sail on such a ship. Another old sailing ship the *Mary Rose*, sunk for many years and partially restored, oc-cupies its own special building because of its fragile condition.

The central city has a shopping "precinct," our version of a two-story mall.

Transportation here affords no deals like the one I got in Holland. A twelve-hour round trip to Scotland costs $400.00 by train. But for twice that amount, you can spend a week in Scotland or England with a tour group, and that includes hotels, breakfast and dinner. But tak-ing off a week is out of the question. So is the eight hundred bucks.

Portsmouth lacks some of the beauty and charm of Plymouth. However, numerous stretches of flowerbeds adorn the parks at sea-side and elsewhere. In addition, Victoria Park's huge, stately trees mute the city's traffic noise. Walkways wind through a formal land-scape of perennials, shrubs, and rose gardens, one of which is set in large, concentric circles.

Situated in the center of the park is an aviary with seemingly every colorful, exotic bird in the world. A large pen of rabbits, guinea pigs, and similar species adjoin the aviary.

Yesterday I realized a long-held dream. I went to Stonehenge, that 5,000-year-old mysterious ring of massive stones on the Salis-bury Plain. Much of Stonehenge will always remain a mystery. But some of the known facts are absolutely astonishing. First, some of the stones weighing upwards of 50 tons came from the Preslie Moun-tains about 240 miles distant. Second, mortise-and-tenon joints held the lintels in place on the uprights. Then vertical tongue-and-groove

Stonehenge

joints locked the lintels of the outer circle end-to-end. Nowhere outside of the Mediterranean were these building techniques used in Europe at that time, and the workmen at Stonehenge accomplished this feat with stone hammers, some the size of footballs. The stones line up with both the mid-summer and mid-winter sunrises. Stonehenge was a place of Neolithic worship and burial.

Later in the day, I spent four-and-a-half hours in Bath, a city chartered in 1590 by Queen Elizabeth I. However, because of the natural hot springs, the Romans built a spa and a temple to Minera around 60 A.D. Throughout the centuries, people have been drawn to Bath in order to drink and to bathe in the water. Because some evidence of the Roman presence still exists, a sizable open space has been set aside for archaeological exploration.

The thermal water also attracted English royalty and other notables. I washed down a sandwich brought from the ship with a drink at the Saracens Head, one of the eateries frequented by Charles Dickens.

The town not only has its share of cathedrals, but also other

Homes modeled after the Roman Coliseum

buildings, both public and private, of architectural interest. One group of homes consists of four quadrants in a circle modeled after the coliseum in Rome. The structures are three-stories tall. The front of each level has its own distinctive columns—Doric, Ionian, and Corinthian.

One of the many rivers in Britain named Avon runs under Pulteney Bridge, which is reminiscent of the bridge I saw over the Arno River in Florence, Italy, albeit smaller.

This tour also took me through an area used by the British army. For several miles, the bus was stuck behind a column of slow-moving armored personnel carriers. In the process, we passed a village built on a German model that is used by NATO troops to train for street fighting.

While I was eating a baked potato at a country pub about an hour from the end of the tour, the bus driver joined me at the table. Talk turned to the Lock Ness Monster. From that time until we returned to the ship, he told me more than a dozen tales of strange, mysterious, and unexplainable phenomena in Britain. Prior to reaching the pub, we had passed a road sign proclaiming "Dead Maid's Hill." He said that a young woman was killed there in the late 1920s or early 1930s, and that she frequently appeared by the roadside where she was killed. Many people have seen her. He claims to have seen her four times.

In Culloden Moor at North Inverness, Scotland, on a still night, people can sometimes hear the clash of ancient armies.

In Bedgellert (translated Gellerts Grave), North Wales is a human cemetery where Gellert, a dog, is buried. Bees, flies, insects, and birds flit outside the walls of the cemetery. Inside the cemetery, nothing lives except the plants in the ground.

Overlooking Portsmouth is a sort of an amphitheater where General Montgomery addressed his troops just prior to the Normandy invasion on June 6, 1944. The driver said he had been there on a still day and clearly heard and understood Montgomery talking to his army. After listening for about five minutes, he decided to leave, and as soon as he moved, the voice stopped.

There were more stories. We passed through what used to be the king's forest where other strange phenomena occurred. The driver referred me to a book *Mysteries of the Forest* by Michael Holien. It's and old book, and I may not be able to find it, but I intend to try.

Serious efforts are underway to re-establish the old forest, which British shipbuilding denuded in the last century. A major problem is finding some of the species of trees that were indigenous to the original forest.

Since no classes are scheduled for Saturdays or Sundays in port, I chose today to borrow a shipmate's bike for an outing on the Isle of Wight. Big mistake. First, the day was overcast, but so has been every other day in this port, so I didn't expect rain. Second, the bike is a racer fully loaded for all contingencies—lights, bell, speedometer, saddlebags, tire pump, and water bottle. Lacking a metric Allen wrench to raise the seat, I asked a gentleman at the departure point for the Isle of Wight the location of a bicycle shop. He was a British naval officer and insisted that we put the bike into his car so he could drive me to the bike shop some distance away. As we loaded the bike, the valve stem on the front tire somehow got knocked askance. Instant flat, ruined tube. Cost to replace—$9.00. Two Allen wrenches—$2.00. Round trip ticket on the ferry to Wight was another $11.20. Upon arrival at the island, I went to the tourist bureau for maps and information. Shortly afterward, rain began to fall. After I waited out the rain in the shelter of the train station for an hour, one of the locals told me the rain likely would continue all day. I caught the next ferry out—$22.20 sadder and wiser. Back at the ship, I took out my frustration in a long workout in the exercise room.

Portsmouth, England, July 13, 1992

Dawn arrived with clear skies and brilliant sunshine yesterday. Even so, comfort required a sweater. I took an early morning train to Chichester to attend church. My luck from the previous day held. No buses run on Sunday to the church about four miles from the train station. A taxi driver told me (a) the round trip cost was $20.00 and (b) the address I had was a residence.

One of the locals assured me that there was nothing to do in Chichester—especially on Sunday on a nippy day in July. Cathedral bells suggested I might as well take in an English church service. After a ten-minute walk, I found the place locked. They had an 0800 service and a late afternoon service. I admired the church's seven-centuries-old architecture for a while and returned to the train station and observed a "car boot" underway in the parking lot. A car boot is a flea market operated out of peoples' cars.

The same chap who told me there was nothing to do in Chichester said the remains of a Roman palace had been excavated in Fishbourne, the first town on the way back to Portsmouth. I spent several hours there. A modern building covers part of the foundation walls and mosaic floors of the palace, which was destroyed by fire in 280 AD. Outside, a formal garden with boxed, double-row hedges characteristic of Roman landscaping closely duplicates the original. Artifacts found by archaeologists piece together a story of military occupation, seafarers, domestic life, and pomp befitting someone who must have been at least as important as a Roman senator. The probable occupant during its prime was Tiberius Claudius Cogidubnus, a local king. Construction at the site started as early as 43 AD. Since 1805, people have noticed evidence of this ancient civilization, but it remained for a workman who dug up a mass of ancient rubble while cutting a water-main trench in 1961 to initiate serious efforts to protect and explore the site.

Arriving back in Portsmouth, I still had time to mingle with the people along the expansive parks adjoining the waterfront. Several games of soccer occupied much of the space. So did cricket and kite flying. Along the pebble beach itself an amusement arcade, gambling house, carnival, sea world, and museums did a brisk business. I chose the D-day Museum and stayed until it closed. A unique feature there is a mural of embroidery depicting the landing of American, British, and Canadian forces on Normandy June 6, 1944. The mural covers the entire outer wall of a large rotunda. Walkmans guide visitors through the scenes. The place closed before I could see all the other exhibits. I always come away from such a place with a renewed appreciation for my heritage. Just the picture of the horse-mounted cavalry of Poland waiting to meet the German Panzer tanks in 1939 is at once sad, poignant, and absurd.

Portsmouth, England, July 16, 1992

My classes have been canceled for today. The ship is participating in a Navy-wide stand-down to deal with the problem of sexual harassment. I guess that's a good idea. However, treating another human being, regardless of sex, with respect and courtesy seems to me to be a fundamental, natural social skill. I think some people just don't put into practice what they inherently know to be proper conduct. Consequently, this all-day session isn't likely to tell anyone anything he doesn't already know. The message probably will be, "Shape up or ship out."

Certainly, some attitudes among Sailors need changing. As an English instructor, I try to play a small role in that effort. One of the first things I tell a new class is this: "If you want to write well, you must speak well because you tend to write the way you speak. Therefore, to write effective, expressive prose the first thing you need to do is eliminate from your vocabulary all profanity because those are generic words so common in our society that they have lost their shock effect. If you speak well, you can function in any level of society; otherwise, you will deliberately handicap yourself. One of my objectives is to change the way you think, and if you are willing to do that, you will have improved speech that will influence your writing." Some men accept this point of view and actually change. When one of my students, a chief petty officer, cut out the profanity, he later told me that his men no longer felt threatened, were more cooperative, and more willing to offer constructive suggestions for work improvement. But I heard another chief, a non-student, use the F word four times in one sentence—as a noun, verb, adjective, and adverb. That may be creative cussing, but he didn't communicate any information. He was just throwing a juvenile fit.

The Tailhook affair that triggered today's stand-down seems to have two viewpoints among Navy personnel with whom I have discussed it. Some think the men involved should have really been "hammered." Being discharged from the Navy isn't sufficient punishment, according to them. They should have to serve prison time before being discharged.

Others don't condone what happened, but point out that this type of conduct has been going on ever since airplanes started landing on ships. Women know in advance what to expect at these parties and don't have to accept the invitation. Some women go for the express purpose of trying to bag a pilot. Military personnel are not supposed to enter any environment that they cannot control. And if they do, they must accept the responsibility for their own actions. A woman who shows up drunk at a Tailhook party has little to complain about.

I suppose there is merit in both points of view. But what Americans don't see in popular news sources is another side of the sexual issue. Sizable numbers of women serve on larger ships such as tenders. More than one source has told me that some women try to score with as many men as some of the men do with the women. But for the foreseeable future, the benefit of doubt will go to the women, and some male Sailors are apt to have anxiety problems because a vindictive woman can easily cost him his career. No civil law prevails here, but rather the Uniform Code of Military Justice. All Navy personnel will be made to clearly understand that sexual harassment is an intolerable act that the Navy is dead set on eliminating.

I read the July 13 issue of U. S. News and World Report that chronicles all the Navy's mistakes of the last decade. Essentially, the Navy is just a microcosm of America. Both the Navy and America still manage to function at a fairly high performance level in spite of the problems. And neither this stand-down nor the November election will be a watershed event.

My travels today took me to four museums.

The first was the birthplace of Charles Dickens. It's a rather modest-looking house now, but a picture hanging inside shows it

Home of Charles Dickens

when it had bay windows, was vine-covered, and fronted with a colonnaded porch having a Roman roof. A death certificate hangs over the couch on which Dickens passed away. He died of apoplexy on June 12, 1870 at age 58. He left explicit instructions forbidding any monument to be raised in his honor. None has been. He and his wife separated in 1858. The next year he published two of his best works, *Great Expectations* and *A Tale of Two Cities*. I guess "it was the best of times and the worst of times."

None of the museums required a great deal of time to see. The City Museum and Art Gallery depicted the history of Portsmouth, but didn't go into too much detail. A group of young students were taking notes as they observed the exhibits.

Seaside Castle is an old fort first built by Henry VIII as a defense against the French. Periodically updated over 400 years, it became a museum in 1960. Having seen so many old forts, I don't need much time to see them any more.

The last museum on my itinerary was the Natural History Museum. I could have spent hours there. It's the only such museum having a walk-in, live butterfly display that I have ever seen. The museum focused on British animals, birds, fish, and plants. It also had a decent display of the solar system and another one showing the cycles of the ice ages.

Portsmouth, England, July 18, 1992

When I arrived in Portsmouth, the ship's command changed my classes to end at 1600. Following classes yesterday, Brian Riley said, "I've got a car. Let's go to Stratford-on-Avon to see a Shakespeare play." I didn't think we could be there in time for the 1930 perfor-mance, but thought the attempt would beat staying on board the ship all evening. We might have made it on time if we hadn't taken some wrong turns because of confusing British road signs.

Brian rented a little red car that was smaller than a Ford Fiesta. Even though he drove at high speed, many vehicles (including a mo-torcycle) passed us. As my apprehension grew, the Shakespeare play lost its appeal. In fact, I apologized to the Lord for placing one of his servants in such a perilous situation and earnestly implored his help for a healthy return to Portsmouth.

Seeing that we couldn't make it to Stratford-on-Avon on time, we decided to stop in Oxford. The plays there also started at 1930. We arrived at 1950. After driving around town a while, we strolled through part of the Oxford University campus. On a great expanse of lawn, a theater group presented an open-air production of Shake-speare's *A Midsummer Night's Dream*. We arrived too late for it also.

When the campus closed up, we settled down in an upstairs cafe for pizza and some good conversation. Brian is a graduate of Notre Dame, very smart, and a good conversationalist. Even though we are a generation apart, we have similar interests and enjoy each other's company.

For the return trip, he wanted to go through Reading. I protested because our map showed no road numbers going from Reading to Portsmouth, and I said we would just get lost. He assured me that we could just head south and not get lost. But we did. In fact, we almost ended up in London! Driving a car with right-side steering on left-sided roads was a new experience for Brian. More hours of hold-your-breath driving and missed turns ensued. We finally arrived back in Portsmouth at 0200. Toward the end of the trip Brian got tired and sleepy, but I stayed very alert. I rolled out of bed at 0600, and after a full day of activity, I am still alert. Since I didn't drive, it wasn't a white-knuckle trip, but I won't have to exercise my abs for several days. Tomorrow I go to London—with a professional driver.

Today was my last chance to finish my sight seeing around Ports-mouth. After spending quite some time in the Royal Navy Museum, I became overwhelmed with the realization that the British Navy has fought nearly every country on every continent on every ocean dur-ing the last 400 years. In the process, they devastated their human and natural resources. And what do they have to show for it? Sadly, the U. S. has fallen into the same pattern. There must be a better way. If only our diplomatic corps was as good as our military.

I have been in over 30 countries and several islands, and every-where I go, I see monuments raised to military leaders and fallen heroes. Why not the peacemakers, the statesmen, the scholars, the innovators, the captains of industry? O course, some of them are recognized and even venerated, but they pale in number compared to the violent ones.

Leaving the museum, I sought solace in an ancient cathedral. People milled around outside. The open door revealed others standing in the rear of the auditorium. I thought I was mingling with other tourists until I looked at the altar. A wedding was in progress.

Out on the street, a horse and carriage awaited the bride and groom. The black carriage was a perfectly restored 1873 bow fronted brougham. The horse was a Welsh Section D Cob, a magnificent stallion. A friendly, uniformed man and a uniformed young girl awaited the couple.

The British people are genuinely friendly and courteous. Upon my leaving the church, an incident reminded me that I have seen no panhandlers here.

A young man politely approached me saying, "Excuse me, sir. Could you spare fifty pence?"

"Yes," I replied. "What do you want it for?"

He said, "To play cricket."

I watched him trot off to the nearby cricket field with my blessing.

The HMS *Victory*, a museum, sits in a permanent dry-dock about 200 yards from *Yarnell*. I have admired this old square-rigged battleship ever since my arrival here and was glad to take a look inside. This was the flagship of the diminutive Lord Nelson, who fatally received a musket shot while winning a decisive battle against the Spanish and French fleets at Trafalgar in 1805. The ship, carrying 104 guns and crew of 850 men was already an old ship, having been commissioned in 1765. Victory, is still a fully commissioned ship— the oldest commissioned ship in the world. The vessel requires constant maintenance, but 30-40 percent of the wood pre-dates 1765.

I didn't bother to tour the other two battleships, the *Warrior* and the *Mary Rose*, which is mostly rotted away, having been under water for more than 400 years. The French sunk her in Portsmouth Harbor while Henry VIII watched from the fort now known as Seaside Castle. The four-masted pride of the British fleet went down with 700 people on board. Fewer than 40 survived. Unaccountably, the French then withdrew. The attack prompted Henry VIII to greatly expand the Portsmouth defenses.

Portsmouth, England, July 20, 1992

My London trip took me to the usual tourist attractions: Changing of the guard at Buckingham Palace, Westminster Abbey, St. Paul's Cathedral, Tower of London, Big Ben, Houses of Parliament, Trafalgar Square, and the National Gallery. Six hours of continuous walking gave me just a quick overview of some of London's most famous landmarks. London could hold my interest for a long time.

Thousands of tourists witnessed the colorful changing of guards. Thick crowds also swarmed Westminster Abbey. Even in this place, statues of military commanders rank alongside churchmen. At St. Paul's Cathedral, a worship service included some antiphonal A Capella music enriched by the church's acoustics. At Trafalgar Square, a huge assembly with loud speakers and banners denounced the presence of Turkish soldiers in Cyprus. All kinds of groups with some kind of issue to publicize commonly use the square. A statue of Lord Nelson, atop a tall slim monument, looks down upon the scene. So do thousands of pigeons in the late afternoon, presenting a certain hazard to the participants. On a street overlooking the square, sits the National Gallery where I viewed some sixteenth-century paintings.

Shipboard life is turning back to all business. The boilers were re-lighted today, shifting electrical power from shore to the ship's generators. Tomorrow morning we get underway for seventeen days. The crew had one last fling this afternoon—barbecued ribs, beer, and soft drinks on the pier. Crewmen from the other NATO ships attended. The Germans brought some good food—unidentified, but good. Some of the men ashore this evening are overindulging in pubs.

I got one last look at an old British ship this afternoon, the HMS *Minerva*. Undergoing restoration, it's docked next to HMS *Victory*. It should be open to the public in 1994. The ship has a shallow draft, which enabled it to enter rivers with its six-inch guns for close-in shelling. She supported the unsuccessful World War I Gallipoli Campaign where the allies engaged the Germans and Turks in bitter trench warfare in an attempt to break through to Constantinople, meet up with the Russians, and take pressure off the Franco/German front. The unwieldy, ill-designed ship was a presage to the failure of the campaign itself. But she helped oversee the successful withdrawal of allied troops from Gallipoli in 1916. She is one of the few remaining ships in the world built in World War I. Departing, I contributed the last of my British money to her restoration fund.

Having returned to my ship after visiting HMS *Minerva*, I was standing at the rail of the main deck reading *Minerva*'s history and was vaguely aware that some people were boarding the ship at the quarter deck. A few minutes later a pair of hands suddenly covered my eyes. I turned to face an attractive young British woman accompanied by two British naval officers. Without hesitating, she planted a firm kiss on my lips! Then she just smiled and walked away with her two British naval escorts. It all happened so fast that I didn't even get a chance to pucker up! Later, I learned that she is part of a committee to welcome NATO ships to Portsmouth. I thought, "What a friendly country!" I never saw her again and remain pleasantly puzzled.

Off Land's End, England, July 25, 1992

We spent 13 days in port under mostly overcast skies. It feels good to again see 360 degrees of blue water, blue sky, and brilliant sunshine where low swells from a cool breeze gives the ship a gentle roll.

The crew's intensive training coordinates with several other NATO ships: British, Canadian, German, Spanish, Portuguese and Dutch. Crewmen from some of those ships train on *Yarnell*, and some of our crewmen are scattered throughout the flotilla. They come back with interesting stories of differences between the ships. The uncleanness of the Canadian ship's engine room amazed one of our engineers. The men who work there must remove their shoes before entering another part of the ship. Such a condition is unthinkable on an American ship. Oil and dirt are conducive to fire, and nothing short of battle damage is more serious than a fire in the "main space." Another radical difference is the availability of beer on the German ship.

Most of the men get very little sleep because of almost round-the-clock drills of one type or the other. One perceptive, weary officer acknowledged that this could be a normal routine under battle conditions. And that, of course, is what they train for.

In that respect, all the men are taking a keen interest in the state of affairs in Yugoslavia and Iraq. They speculate about a naval response and whether this ship will be a part of it.

One of my shipmates mistook me for a deep thinker and laid some heavy reading on me. Joseph Campbell, having spent a lifetime devoted to mythology, has written several books, including this tome—*Myths to Live By*. I suspect that Mr. Campbell has his feet firmly planted in mid-air. He dismisses all religions, including Christianity, as myths having form but no substance and useful only to the primitive societies from which they originated. But now that men have dug up a lot of bones and astronauts have left their footprints on the moon, it is clearly evident that each man himself is the center of the universe, and having sprung forth from the earth without the aid of any god, is mutually linked together by "Mind At Large." In consequence, he says man has imparted some of his intelligence to the animals and plants. God, in whatever form He exists, is probably somewhere having Himself a good laugh.

English Channel, July 31, 1992

After my last class tonight, I walked out onto the weather deck to greet the prettiest sight I have seen in a long while. The sun sets late in this latitude, but it had already dipped below the horizon, tinting gold crests on blue wavelets in an almost calm sea. A thick haze that has hovered over us all day diffused the horizon into a wide powder-blue band topped by one of fuchsia that blended into near white before disappearing into the dark blue sky.

I completed two basic skills courses this week—English and math. Forty percent of the English students and seventy percent of the math students are now ready for college level work. All made progress, but absenteeism hurt some of them. I have started a new class in each subject and also added a basic skills reading course, the one that ends at 2200. That puts me in the classroom eight hours a day—four hours without a break—seven days a week. The crew continues its heavy training schedule. A tanker refueled the ship three times in a twelve-hour period. The ship didn't need the fuel. Rather, the crew needs the skills to refuel under different sea-states any hour of the day or night.

Today, the tanker brought us fifty-two sacks of mail. Nita remembered me with letters and Sanka coffee. Getting mail from the oiler put the crew through a different evolution. The mail came across via a line connecting the two ships. We also exchanged some men, using the same technique.

We are through playing war games off the southwest coast of England and are now heading back up the English Channel for Baltic Operations (Baltops) in the Baltic Sea.

Fredrikhavn, Denmark, August 2, 1992

The ship anchored here about noon today to take on supplies and to "dump and pump"—unload our garbage and sewage. No trash can be dumped into the Baltic Sea. Getting through Skagerrak Strait and Kattegat Strait presented an interesting navigation exercise for the quartermasters. The English Channel and North Sea blessed us with very calm water but cursed us with overcast skies and haze, which again obscured Dover Cliffs. It seems strange to wear a windbreaker in August. Two Norwegians aboard told me that the weather is unseasonably cool. They usually wear T-shirts and shorts this time of the year.

Although the crew is very busy launching small boats, handling supplies, and ferrying NATO dignitaries back and forth, they were supposed to have a steel beach picnic. It was moved inside because of a refueling operation. All this activity caused my classes to be canceled today. I needed a day anyway to get caught up on my paper work, correspondence, and sleep.

Last night several men faced a number of charges at Captain's Mast. Today the ship is sending them home to be discharged from the Navy. I don't know the charges, but I do know that some men deliberately get caught with drugs in order to get out of the Navy. This type of discharge is neither honorable nor dishonorable, but it could haunt such men in the future. The defense cutback is putting a strain on military personnel. More than fifty of the crew are first class petty officers, and most of them are not likely to ever make chief. That's more than ten percent of the crew and far more than that needed for a ship this size. But with other ships being taken out of service, the men have to be assigned somewhere. Some accept incentive packages to leave the Navy. One man with ten years service received a separation payment of $45,000 but no retirement, no medical benefits. One first class petty officer with thirteen years of service told me that he is not interested in early separation. Rather, he wants to get in his twenty years with all the perks that go with normal military retirement.

Baltic Sea, Off Poland, August 3, 1992

We weighed anchor about midnight and began transiting Kattegat Strait and Great Belt, which required alert navigation on the part of the bridge personnel today. The flat coastlines of Danish Islands to starboard and Sweden to port seemed to squeeze all the channel traffic into a tight mass. Ferry boats, barges, and small boats constantly cut through our single-file convoy at right angles, requiring critical course and speed changes. The flatness of the land combined with the haze and overcast skies revealed little to see, even through the ship's big eyes.

Approaching Tallinn, Estonia, August 6, 1992

The time is 0715 and the sea and anchor detail has been set for entering port in this former Soviet province. The USS *Yarnell* is the second American warship to visit this city since 1922. I suppose this is what journalists like to call an epoch-making event. Until we have our port brief, I really won't know much about what awaits us except for a community relations project on Sunday. The chaplain has some kind of party lined up for disadvantaged children. More than seventy Sailors have already signed up without knowing any details. It seems that American military personnel and foreign kids have always related well to each other. Naturally, my classes have been suspended for this four-day visit. Yesterday morning's class fell victim to a GQ drill. A refueling operation devastated last night's classes. The Educational Services Officer has sent a message to NETSCELANT canceling the courses that were supposed to start after I leave. This ship's schedule is just not conducive to PACE courses. That's unfortunate for the crew. I personally spent three hours collating the entire test scores accumulated over the past year. There are enough prospective students to fill every level of math course through the second semester of college, plus business and/or psychology. That would be a full load for a follow-on instructor, but it isn't going to happen. The class interruptions are going to back up my departure from the ship by three to four weeks. That's donated time to the Navy. On the positive side, I continue to get free room and board, plus visits to some exciting ports.

The Baltic Sea has been good to us. We have had a very smooth ride, albeit under mostly cloudy skies. In addition, I saw my first perfect rainbow yesterday. Using a smooth white cloud as a background, the rainbow extended from horizon to horizon. Beautiful. Two evenings earlier, I saw another simultaneous sunset and moonrise. The two heavenly bodies were only 80 degrees apart. For the Norwegians on board, that's normal, but for me, that's quite unusual.

Tallinn, Estonia, August 6, 1992

Petty Officer RM3 Randy Sherrod and I teamed up for an excursion ashore after the port brief. Sailors must wear their uniforms in this port, and they certainly do attract attention—a lot of smiles, stares, and salutes. It's really an ego trip for the young Sailors, for I saw more pretty girls in the first two hours here than I did in two weeks at Portsmouth. I suspect that they were imported for the benefit of personnel from all the NATO ships. Nearly, all of them are fair-skinned, blue-eyed blondes. Ethnically, they are related to the Finnish people.

Tallinn is more affluent than I expected; however, it lags far behind any western democracy. Stores have a fair selection of merchandise, but they don't have much of it. I don't know whether this is due to lack of capital or lack of need.

Estonia is a small country, having something in excess of 1.5 million people. Nearly half live in Tallinn. Tall towers, huge gates, and segments of massive walls indicate the presence of an ancient walled town in Tallinn near the docks. In a large square in the center of old town, about 1,000 people thronged around a band playing western style music from a raised platform. Surrounding the platform commercial buildings and spired churches exude a unique charm but also show signs of fifty years of neglect.

I got quite a bit of unsolicited information from a gentleman who stopped Randy and me just to talk. The Soviets took over the country in 1938. At that time, the Soviets forced thousands of Estonians to move to the Soviet Union, while sending 100,000 Russians to Estonia. Now, Yeltsin has issued an appeal for all Russians to return to Russia. The Estonians would like to see that happen, but the Russians in Estonia don't like Yeltsin and don't want to return. In the meantime, Estonians want their language to be the official language. On an ominous note, the man warned us not to travel alone in the city at night. He spoke of a Russian Mafia that robs and beats people with no opposition from the Russian police, which still has ties to the KGB. Estonia has a police force comprised of Estonians, but it is not very powerful, and the policemen I saw were very young. Next month, the Estonians will elect representatives to run the country that is already a member of the United Nations. Also, they have coined new money, the kroon, which has a current exchange rate of about eleven kroons to one dollar. Prices vary widely. An open-faced sandwich with apple juice costs twenty-five cents, a post card more than four times that much. But a stamp to the U.S. is about twenty cents. It was eighty cents in Holland. A can of Vidal Sassoon hair spray costs five dollars.

Randy had been giving me a hard time about being a Texan. Before this man left us, he asked me where I was from. When I told him, his face lit up and he said, "That's a very famous place and very large." I said, "Randy, tell him where you are from."

He said, "North Carolina." The man looked puzzled and said, "That presents a problem." Randy tried to explain where North Carolina is and much to his chagrin, the man said, "That's somewhere between Texas and New York." He couldn't have said it better if I had set him up.

Because of the ship's deep draft and the harbor's shallow depth, we are anchored some distance from the fleet landing. Consequently, the ship's motorboats are used to transport personnel to and from the shore. Among those of us who returned late this afternoon was a young, drunken, glassy-eyed seaman who needed the help of two of his buddies to get him back to fleet landing. He spent the trip in a rocking, pitching boat all doubled up with his face in a plastic bag. Some people just have all of the fun.

Tallinn, Estonia, August 7, 1992

Chaplain Bruce Boyle approached me at breakfast to see if I wanted to take a trip around Estonia today. The opportunity had just materialized, and I grabbed it. The twelve-hour trip covered about 200 miles of western and southwestern Estonia via a brand new bus with all the amenities. The tour guide spoke flawless English.

Leaving Tallinn, we passed numerous factories that help characterize Tallinn as an industrial center. Then we passed a long residential section of substantial homes on spacious lots. All had been neglected. In the 1940s, the Soviets summarily claimed the residences for the state and sent the occupants to Siberia. Now, the Estonians are tracing the records to ascertain the true owners and restore the property to them or their heirs.

Our first stop was Haapsula, a city of 15,000. On the way, we passed through a sparsely populated area of extensive forests, fields, and peat bogs. Estonia is forty percent forests, twenty percent bogs, thirty-five percent arable lands, and the rest is urban. Because of the plentiful trees, Tallinn operates a sizeable paper factory, which is a major polluter that the Estonians want to eliminate. The problem is that paper is exported to the Ukraine in exchange for much needed grain and sugar.

The countryside is beautiful and raises some wheat, barley and enough cattle to export dairy products. The dairy herds are mostly the Friesian breed obtained from Holland many years ago. Since the 1970s, Estonia's farmers have been some of the country's most prosperous citizens, and collective farms are changing into private ownership and private coops as old land titles are searched. Truck farming occupies much of the farmers' effort, thus adding to their independence as well as increasing their income.

Haapsula used to attract tourists because of its spa. Many Scandinavians came here to bathe in the mineral waters. Some Estonians use thermal energy to heat their residences. However, Haapsula is a shell of what it was before the Soviets occupied the country. And the "Kruschev high rises" in the middle of the town only detract. My visit to two stores disclosed the economic calamity of communism like nothing else I have been exposed to. On the second floor of a department store, all the goods were clustered in two small areas, leaving rows and rows of shelves completely empty. Nearby at a small grocery store, people queued up for something that was in short supply. I have read about and seen pictures depicting such a scene, but the impact of witnessing the event is hard for me to describe. I guess it is a mixture of sorrow and anger.

I bought an excellent loaf of bread for 1.5 kroon—13 cents. But even this small amount is expensive for retirees whose income is 200 kroon per month, about $18.00. Bread used to be cheaper under the Soviet system—so cheap that it was more economical for farmers to feed bread to their livestock than wheat.

While I was walking around, a cute little blue-eyed blonde about twelve years old kept finding ways to cross my path. She always smiled and waved. Evidently, she wanted to talk to me but was shy. Finally, I tried to initiate a conversation. She spoke practically no English. About all we could do were smile and admire each other. I took her picture. Her name is Laura.

I ended up in Parnu for lunch and a four-hour visit. The city, sitting on the Baltic Sea, has a long, beautiful beach of fine sand. The tour guide said it was the only beach where ladies could sun bathe nude. Because of a stiff, chill wind, the beach was nearly deserted. A sign warned that the water was polluted, but the tour guide didn't know why.

Parnu, like most other Estonian towns, has a basis for beauty

Polluted Baltic Sea beach

and charm. I saw three 19th century churches, unique because of wood construction. Inside one of them, a pipe organ in the balcony and a very large chandelier dominated a T-shaped auditorium of fine acoustics where a wedding was about to take place. Generally, the churches in Estonia are Lutheran. The buildings with the "Dairy Queen" domes are Russian Orthodox.

A cathedral in Tallinn originally was Catholic, then Lutheran, now Baptist. Many Parnu buildings still in use date from the 18th century. Nearly all of them need paint. Maintenance is a slow process because of a paint shortage. The Soviet paint was of such poor quality that it only stayed on a building for a short time. Even with shortages, the Estonians have made remarkable progress during their eleven months of independence.

The shops here also had very limited merchandize. I saw meat

Russian Orthodox Church

for sale in only one store, and it was not something I would buy.

A park in the center of the city featured a beautiful statue of Lydia Koidula, an Estonian poetess still held in very high esteem. The statue overlooks a reflecting pool surrounded by a blaze of roses, zinnias, and various other flowers.

The roads of Estonia are mostly two-lane but capable of carrying traffic at high speed. We met few cars and no trucks. Most of the cars are Ladas or some other Soviet model. The tour guide said that these cars, while cheaper than others, are not good quality and that parts were hard to get now that the Soviet Union has been fragmented. Almost no Japanese cars can be found here.

One of the American Sailors marred the trip by drinking too much alcohol and vomiting on himself and the bus. When we got back to Tallinn, the tour guide detained him and told me she was going to make him pay for cleaning up the mess. The new bus didn't even have 1500 miles on it. The Estonians don't have very many things that are really nice, and I was quite embarrassed. Late that night, an incident in town marred the whole port visit. What happened depends upon who is talking, but as best as I can piece the story together, here are the essentials. Some Russians, presumably mafia types, without warning started hitting NATO Sailors in a bar. It turned into quite a melee. The injuries to the Sailors were relatively

Statue of Lydia Koidula, Estonian Poetess

minor—bruised ribs, black eyes, busted noses—that sort of thing. An Estonian told me that the fracas could have been staged to try to discredit the conduct of NATO Sailors, thus discouraging more NATO port visits. An incident earlier in the evening made the newspapers. Four British Sailors from HMS *Andromeda* got into a fight with each other, and one was knocked through the biggest plate glass window in the biggest store in town. When the owner tried to break up the fracas, the Sailors turned on him. The police came and nabbed two of the men while the other two ran away. After being turned over to their own ship's command, the Sailors returned to offer an apology and pay 4,000 kroon, about $350. The Sailors must have been British soccer fans.

Tallinn, Estonia, August 9, 1992

Yesterday, an all-day trip took me east to Narva, a city of 80,000 across the river from the Russian city of Ivangorod. Two ancient forts face each other across the border, one flying the Estonian flag of white, black, and blue, the other the Russian flag of white, blue, and red. In the town's center, stands the one remaining statue of Lenin in the former Soviet Union.

Narva, completely destroyed in WWII, has been rebuilt, but not to pre-war standards, according to the tour guide. The usual Soviet high-rise residences dominate the skyline. Sent to Estonia in the 1940s, Russians comprise 95 percent of the population. While Estonians disdain such compact living, Russians prefer it.

Heavily damaged in WWII, the old fort has been restored and is now used as a museum and for civic functions. The Danes built the initial structure in 1277. Then in the 14th and 15th centuries, the Swedes enlarged it and extended fortifications along the river. Because of ongoing disputes with the Germans, Sweden built 216 such forts. All but one have been destroyed. Chalk up another monumental waste of human and natural resources to the military-industrial

Russian apartments

complex, which derives its impetus from people who hate each other.

Narva is again caught in a border dispute. Estonia's border extended well beyond the river before the Russians took the country in 1938. When Estonia declared its independence in August 1991, it reclaimed territory up to the river. Since the relocated Russians make up nearly all of the populace and everyone there speaks Russian, Yeltsin, at the urging of hard liners in the Russian parliament, is claiming the city for Russia.

There are very dangerous forces at work here. Recently, Vladmir Zirinovski of the Russian Democratic Party made a speech to the citizens across the river in which he demanded the return of all former Soviet provinces, including Estonia. His view of the new Russia also includes the conquest of Finland and neighboring countries. While the common people in Russia favorably receive such talk, the Estonians are understandably quite alarmed. Zirinovski's oratory appeals to Russian masses much as Hitler's did in the 1930s. Estonians are pinning their hopes for a peaceful existence on Yeltsin, knowing full well that a sizeable segment of their own country, such as Narva, would side with Zirinovski if he, or somebody like him, came to power in Russia. Estonians view the 45,000 Russian troops in their country as occupation forces and want them out immediately. Russia is saying 1994. Estonians want the western democracies to tie any aid to Russia to the removal of Russian troops from their country. Yeltsin seems to favor this idea, but can't be too accommodating because of Russian hard liners who might depose him.

Next month, the Estonians will elect a parliament of 101 representatives who will then choose a president with restricted powers. Only Estonians and Russians who were in the country prior to 1938 will be able to vote. That excludes 600,000 Russians who can apply for citizenship to take effect in one year, if approved. Naturally, the immigrant Russians don't like this idea. But the Estonians contend that Soviet citizenship has been abolished everywhere; and now that Estonia is a free country, it has the right to determine the citizenship status of non-Estonians.

Obviously, Estonians are eager to get their political message across to westerners. They point out that the Estonian language and culture are 5,000 years old. For most of that time, they have been dominated by outside forces. They have a keen appreciation for their recently gained freedom and are willing to endure whatever current economic hardships necessary to maintain it. When the Soviets occupied Estonia in 1938, the citizens in unified protest joined hands for 723 kilometers, about 433 miles. That's more than half the distance from El Paso to Texarkana.

West of Narva some 25 miles sits Sillamae on the Baltic Sea. Before the break up of the Soviet Union, this town was so secret that no one except its inhabitants could go near there. No outsiders even knew the population of the town. All factories are now abandoned, but the Russian population is still there. I asked the tour guide how the people survived without jobs. She surmised that they might receive support directly from Moscow. When I asked why the people still lived there, she just shrugged and said, "Waiting for the next coup attempt?"

We drove through some of the residential areas. Crumbling bricks and flaked paint characterize the high rises of recent vintage set among unkempt grounds. Structures built during the Stalin era display attempts at elegance with such devices as faux columns under windows. Across from the town hall, a small, reasonably well-kept park surrounds a large bronze statue of a muscular worker holding up two rings that appear to be a nuclear symbol. Just outside the park, holes in a large obelisk indicate where job performance formerly received recognition. Children in Narva ganged around Sailors in uniform, as do children everywhere. But not here. The children peeped behind curtains in their houses and kept their distance. Evidently, they, too, had been taught to avoid outsiders. The Estonians, with a native population half that of Houston really have their work cut out for themselves.

Leaving Sillamae and its ominous atmosphere, we drove through much of Lahemaa National Park. At a large park building at Altja, gracious Estonians awaited us for lunch prepared by the local women. The main dish consisted of small chunks of meat, potatoes, cabbage, carrots, and rutabagas. Side dishes included rye bread with jam, thin filets of marinated fish, diced beets, diced cheese, cucumbers, and tomatoes. During the meal, a whimsical middle-aged gentleman entertained us with music on an antique accordion. He accompanied some of the music by singing songs that were definitely country and a bit bawdy, according to an interpreter sitting beside me.

After lunch, we had a picture taking session with the locals and spent some more time driving through Lahemaa National Park. We stopped at a cluster of buildings that were originally a German manor. Situated on a small lake within its own park, the manor is undergoing restoration. Here, Sailors bought just about all the souvenir shop's merchandize. I bought an LP record of birdcalls for 1.5 kroon—thirteen cents.

This afternoon, I spent time walking around Tallinn just seeing some of the town's attractions that I missed the first day I was here. I tried to find something in an antique shop worth taking home. Despite favorable prices on many items here, I found nothing.

Aarhus, Denmark, August 14, 1992

It's a pleasure just to walk the streets and admire the Danish architecture. This is a clean, prosperous-looking city of bustling people. Bicycles being about as popular as cars protect bicycle trails parallel to many of the streets filled with new cars from Europe, Asia, and the United States. Aarhus is an expensive town for Americans. Here are some randomly noted prices: Hamburger $4.40, Danish roll $1.25, Coke from a machine $1.20, postcard stamp to the U. S. $1.00 (the highest I have found in Europe), Levis 501 $90.00, Kawasaki 750 motorcycle $14,000, the smallest Nissan car $24,000, a gallon of unleaded gasoline $3.75.

My early morning hike took me past some of Aarhus's statues and sculpture. Christian X, mounted on a horse, naturally, is the grandfather of Margrethe, the current queen of Denmark. He was king during the Nazi occupation and used to ride his horse through the streets of Copenhagen. In front of the city hall sits a most unusual bronze sculpture, a big sow with a litter of pigs. I'm not sure what it is supposed to represent—something about Denmark's prosperity. Pork is one of Denmark's exports. The Danes themselves don't seem to know much about their sculpture. In front of the fine arts museum stands a large, black granny knot. The artist probably meant it for something else, but it's a knot a Sailor would never tie. Then there were these nude bronze figures by the tourist office. Water spilled over two bodies. One is a devilish-looking young man, apparently a sea god, whose feet are fish tails and whose curly hair is arranged to appear as two horns. He is attempting to persuade a beautiful young woman to join him. This is something out of the Hans Christian Anderson stories.

At the tourist office, I bought a bus ticket for about $6.30 that enabled me to have unlimited bus travel for 24 hours. Included was a three-hour guided tour of the city and a trip through Old Town. On an ala carte basis each of these two excursions would have cost $6.30. And after these events, I still had free travel around the city. Evidently, no one else on the ship figured this out even though the information is clearly stated in a booklet brought on board from the tourist office. Even if they did figure it out, most men couldn't take advantage of it. They have to work until at least 1500. By the time they get ashore, everything is closed except, bars, discos, and snack shops. It's no wonder that some young men spend their time overseas getting drunk and eating Big Macs.

Stops on the city tour included one at the Aarhus Cathedral.

The original was built in 1201, destroyed by fire a few years later, and then rebuilt to its present immense size. Originally Catholic, the church became Lutheran during the protestant reformation in the 16th century. A special box for the queen sits directly in front of the pulpit. The Catholic paintings depicting scenes such as purgatory have been white washed, but some of the scenes clearly show through the over-painting. The ornate Catholic altar remains in its original state as a reminder of the excesses that the Lutherans wish to avoid. Behind the altar, a solitary stained glass window decorates the building. All others are clear glass.

Old Town followed the same concept as the one at the Zuider Zee Museum in Holland. Buildings of all sorts had been dismantled piece by piece and reconstructed to form a Danish village as it appeared two or three hundred years ago. Typically Danish, many of the buildings have high-pitched roofs over walls of massive horizontal and vertical beams with bricks filling in the open spaces between the beams. Some of the bricks are laid in intricate patterns. The buildings vary in color from dark red to brown and yellow. Cobblestone streets wind through the village and over the bridge of a simulated river.

The city tour also took me through the Aarhus University cam-

Danish Old Town

pus. During WWII, the Nazi Gestapo used one of the buildings as their headquarters. The Danes sent this information to the British RAF who destroyed the building with a surgical strike. A new building replaced the one destroyed.

About 14,000 students attend here. In Denmark, students in "superior" schools (including trade schools) receive from the government 2500 kroners (about $450) per month. This is not a loan and students don't have to be poor to receive it. Sounds incredible, but that's what the tour guide said. This may help to explain in part why the country has a 52% income tax rate plus a 14% value added tax.

We stopped briefly at a war memorial at the edge of a forest just below the queen's summer palace. The white stone walls of the round memorial contain the names of Denmark's military personnel who fell in WWI and WWII. Embedded in the walls, four large bas relief sculptures convey themes ranging from men going off to war to men returning home.

After the guided tour, I took another bus to the southern outskirts of town to see The Museum of Prehistory at Moesgaard. This museum traces the development of the Danish people from about 8,000 B.C. to the present. One section of the museum contains the skeletons and artifacts from an ancient village found by scuba divers way out in the Baltic Sea. What could have caused the flooding of such an immense land area? This museum has one of the bodies found in a peat bog in 1952. The bog effectively tanned the skin. This particular man died by having his throat cut. Skeletal remains indicate that Danish people have changed very little in appearance in 10,000 years.

This museum sits inside the same forest overlooked by the queen's palace. From the museum, I hiked two kilometers through the forest to the beach. Beech trees forty to sixty meters high obliterated the sky. The only sounds were my footsteps and the ripple of a brook leading to the sea. Breaking out of the forest, I came upon a penned-up pony not much taller than a Great Dane dog. He wanted to be petted. I accommodated him.

The nearly deserted beach of gray sand and pebbles stretched far

Danish pony

toward the city. A few hundred yards away, a concession stand on a bluff overlooked some paddleboats looking like a row of mechanical lobster claws. Here, I bought some ice cream and relaxed on a park bench to contemplate the low, sculpted clouds hanging over the sea.

On the horizon, rain showers fell on the Helgenaes Peninsula. The return bus trip took me through more miles of the forest.

Aarhus, Denmark, August 16, 1992

"Leg godt." Danish for "play well." Americans know it as Lego. At Belund, lies Legoland, which I visited yesterday. Contrary to my expectations, I am impressed. Countless millions of Lego blocks make up scale models of just about anything man-made or found in nature. Authentic-looking trains connect entire villages. Boats cruise lakes and go through a drawbridge stopping traffic on highways. Another boat goes through the locks of a canal. There's an entire airport, a jungle full of animals, the Capitol at Washington, the Statue of Liberty (1.4 million pieces), Mt. Rushmore, the Taj Mahal, European castles, and much, much more. The electronics that make the trains run, trucks drive, ships sail, canal locks open and close are as

Legoland village

Legoland airport

Legoland Mt. Rushmore

Legoland Statue of Liberty

impressive as the Lego structures. The park is full of rides and shows similar to the one at Six Flags Over Texas.

Inside a long building, kids experience hands-on creativity with Lego blocks. Also inside, is Titania's Palace, the world's largest miniature palace completely furnished. Nearby a large collection of dolls and antique wind-up toys impress children and adults alike.

The hour-and-a-half one-way drive took me through rolling hills that look a lot like southern Missouri. Trees and meadows mostly make up the countryside, which the Danes take good care of. The cities through which I passed look as clean and well kept as Aarhus.

Today, Otto and Ketty Baake, a local retired couple, invited me to lunch in their home and later drove me around the environs of Aarhus. They couldn't have been more gracious. In Holland, I learned to like smoked herring. In the Baake home, I learned to like pickled herring, which was just the beginning of a most excellent Danish meal. Ketty formerly worked for a travel agency. Otto formerly taught apprentices how to use metal lathes and other such machines. Now he spends some of his time gardening. His house, including each room, as well as the front yard and back yard, looks like something out of Home and Garden magazine.

When they brought me back to the ship, I gave them a tour of the vessel, which impressed them as much as they and their home impressed me.

Prior to my meeting with the Baakes, I went to church at the 800-year-old Aarhus Cathedral. I didn't understand the language, but I still found the different rituals and customs interesting. Even though the building is huge, it needs no P.A. system, for a speaker can be heard easily anywhere in the building.

I soaked up as much as I could as fast as I could during these few days in Denmark. Tomorrow, it's back to sea and back to teaching.

Skagerrak Strait, August 20, 1992

The crew just bolted to general quarters—again. The ship took imaginary bomb hits and the forward part of the ship is imaginarily flooding. I guess we were due. Yesterday, we came under attack from sixty-eight imaginary airplanes. Our missiles bagged all of them. That's the function of a guided missile cruiser. Fore and aft, we carry three different types of missiles of various ranges plus torpedoes at port, starboard, and amidships. This is a fighting machine to be reckoned with. It can take out planes, subs, or other ships. When we are not in port, the crew conducts round-the-clock training exercises.

They may need the skills sooner than expected. Uncertainty about our schedule has hung over the ship for the last few weeks. In two days, we will enjoy liberty in Stockholm, Sweden for a few days. After that, the ship may go straight to the Adriatic Sea as a show of force against the Serbs in Yugoslavia. Not even the admiral of this NATO force knows whether the ship will continue on its original mission, or suddenly be diverted. Civilians in NATO are making such decisions—or wallowing in indecision. Naturally, today's GQ interrupted one of my classes. Regardless of interruptions, I intend to wind up my teaching no later than September 2—twelve days from now. In the Navy, that's known as getting "short." So in three days, I will be a "single digit midget." But I haven't a clue as to my date of departure from the ship—or the country.

Stockholm, Sweden, August 25, 1992

Reveille at 0500 yesterday aroused me in time to see some

spectacular scenery as the ship left the Baltic Sea to transit a very long channel leading to Stockholm. Clusters of islands continuously flanked the ship through the successive turns, requiring careful navigation. For at some points, land came within 100 feet of snaring the ship on either side. Before channel markers existed, ships could possibly wander aimlessly among the 22,000 islands that make up this archipelago.

These small islands appear to be no more than 150 yards from waterline to the treetops. Having no sandy beaches, they appear to be just cooled lava sprouting trees comprising the full spectrum of green. Under a solid blanket of tufted clouds, the grayish, lavender, lichen-encrusted rocks exudes an air of charm, mystery, and foreboding as if an old Viking sea rover lurking in a cove would suddenly descend upon his hapless prey. But by contrast, the only swans I have ever seen outside a zoo or other protected environment, paddled peacefully near the shores of some of the islands.

By the time we reached Stockholm, the sun, thinning the cloud layer, cast a diffused glow over a beautiful, clean city that tastefully blends the ancient with the new. The city sprawls over fourteen islands connected by fifty bridges. We are anchored practically downtown—anchored because the pier is too short to accommodate this ship. Four other NATO ships are pierside. We are a two-minute boat-ride away.

When I called Nita today, she asked me to try to find some Swedish Christmas cards and decorations. A local Navy lady directed me to two department stores featuring "reasonable prices." After I discovered that neither store had any Christmas merchandise available, I tried to find something else to take home. It was a depressing experience. American dollars buy about half as many Swedish kronas as they did in 1984, even less value here than in other European countries I have visited: Levi 501 jeans, $115; Snicker candy bar, $1.40; Wall Street Journal, $2.30; a Big Mac, Coke, fries, $8.00; a beer $7.00.

That last item ought to keep our crew out of pubs. However, all these NATO ships carry beer (some also have hard liquor) for special occasions—namely port visits. The first night in a new port, the NATO force has a ritual called Force Breakfast from 1000 to 0200. Last night was such a night. Besides the food, the booze flowed freely. The Canadians have a concoction called "Moose Juice." Here's how they make it: Three liters of milk, 3 liters of vanilla ice cream, 3 teaspoons vanilla, 12 ounces Kaluha, 12 ounces brandy, 40 ounces dark rum, and four cups of crushed ice. They mix half the stuff, stir for five minutes, then add the other half and stir for five more minutes. Supposedly, it makes 40 eight-ounce servings. They say it tastes like ice cream. Having seen some of the "moose toddlers," I don't intend to find out. Item: The ship's Plan Of The Day for August 24 reads in part, "Some studies have suggested that moderate drinking is linked to lower risks for heart attacks. However, drinking is also linked to higher risk for high blood pressure and hemorrhage stroke." Item: The August 25 P.O.D. reads in part, "In a study of flight performance, pilots were given enough alcohol to produce a BAC of at least .10, then observed 14 hours after their last drink when they had an undetectable BAC. They showed decreases in precision and accuracy on all variables tested." Early today, the ship conducted a random urine test for drugs. It seems the Navy, by its actions, is sending mixed signals on alcohol compared to other drugs.

Early today, I watched the city wake up by walking extensively. Like other Baltic cities, Stockholm's streets provide protected lanes for bicyclists who have the right of way over pedestrians. Large numbers of cycling commuters match the speed of the cars. Only the cafes and tobacco shops open early. Most stores open about 1000. The elegant stores remind me of what downtown U.S.A. used to look like before shopping malls took over. On the lawn next to the opera house, a small mob of people faced a woman directing them in Tai Chi. Anybody could join in regardless of their attire. Nearby, a checkerboard about 10 feet square held large chess pieces. Later in the day, I returned to watch a game of chess. So did a lot of other people.

Outdoor chess game

Back at fleet landing, I boarded a bus for a one-hour tour of the central city. A very gracious elderly tour lady cut short some of her explanations because of some very discourteous British Sailors. These guys constantly made what they thought were hilarious comments, drowning out what the woman was trying to say. Exasperated, I finally directed a comment to them that quieted them down. They mistook me for a naval officer, and I didn't bother to correct them. The Swedes provided the tour, including lunch, at no cost, and I was appalled that people could be such boorish guests in a foreign country.

I have been stuck on a bus before with rowdy British Sailors, and it all begins to add up. This incident sheds a whole new light on the bar brawl in Estonia. It was the Brits, being well lubricated with alcohol, who probably got obnoxious, making the Russians resentful. Then the fight spread to all the Sailors in the bar. I later learned that one of my students was suddenly confronted with five angry Russians. He had a camera just like mine—a heavy, metal-cased Pentax 1000. Wrapping the shoulder strap around his hand, he started swinging at heads and put several Russians down to stay before the strap broke. After smashing two tables on some others, he and his buddies had room to get away. This muscular kid with a wedge-shaped torso has impressed me with his workouts in the ship's gym, and even though he is quiet and unassuming, he is no stranger to violence. Any nightmares the Russians may have about the brawl probably include a black face filled with rage.

To me, the most interesting part of today's tour was the visit to the city hall, which sits on Lake Malaren, the city's only fresh water lake, which is separated from the sea by the town's only lock. The Nobel Peace Prize presentation takes place in the great hall here each year. Nineteen million mosaic tiles, most of which are gilded in 23 carat gold, cover the walls of this huge room. A wide marble staircase descends from this room to one below that can be used for concerts or receptions. The pipe organ in this room has 10,500 pipes, making it the largest pipe organ in Sweden.

The impressive council meeting room seats 101 representatives, 45 of whom are women. The roof closely replicates an old Viking hall roof, an upside down ship. But no one knows for sure what a Viking hall looked like.

Atop the spire on the city hall sits three gold crowns like the ones decorating the heraldry of Sweden and Cologne, Germany. The heraldry dates back quite a number of centuries to the time when the Swedes and Germans battled each other for all the Baltic countries. So nobody knows for sure their significance either. But the Swedes have decided they are symbolic of the Three Wise Men.

In response to my question, one of the Swedish naval liaison ladies set me straight about the "peaceful" swans I saw as we passed through the archipelago. They are quite prolific around the islands. She said that they were very aggressive after the young ones hatch out. Twice she has been forced to flee from attacking male swans. According to her, a blow from their powerful wings can break a person's leg. I need to check out that statement.

North Sea, August 31, 1992

The "cruise of a lifetime" has been aborted. The ship has been ordered to proceed directly to the coast of Yugoslavia. Evidently, the U. N. is contemplating a show of force against the Serbs. I will miss visiting Kiel, Germany and a planned trip to Berlin via Poland. Also missing from my agenda will be Aalborg, Denmark.

Of course, this puts the crew's future port visits in limbo. They won't return to Norfolk until Christmas. In the meantime, the prospect of cruising in a circle in the Adriatic Sea thrills no one.

It has been a good cruise filled with hard work and hard play. Even so, I have found time to stay physically fit and read four books plus more than a dozen from the Bible. Besides the book on myths, I read *Flight of the Intruder*, *The Good Times*, and the *Zuider Zee Project*. *Good Times* is a fascinating account of the years from 1947 to 1963 during which Russell Baker rose from a police reporter with the Baltimore Sun to editorial columnist with the New York Times. *The Zuider Zee Project* is a quasi-technical treatise on dike building and land reclamation in Holland. The book details the methods used to drain the seawater from hundreds of square miles on the North Sea coast. Holland's land use is inspiring. It takes about 20 years from the time salt water is drained from the land until it is ready for agricultural use. The types of soil determines whether the land is used for agriculture, forests, recreation, or wild life habitats. The Dutch plan entire cities, taking into account industrial zones for employment opportunities. The U. S. could learn a great deal from them about land management.

We left Stockholm Friday under cold, overcast skies. Three out of four days there started out that way, but turned somewhat sunny as the days wore on. Even so, and with stratospheric prices, the general consensus of the crew is that Stockholm is the best port they have ever visited. Some dream about returning and taking their wives. But of course, most of us, for a variety of reasons, won't pass this way again. This is one reason I endured a cold, gray day topside during a three-hour transit through the archipelago between Stockholm and the Baltic Sea. Houses from mansions to cottages cover the islands within sight. Some have only one house because they are so small. All are beautiful.

As usual, I played as hard as ingenuity and physical endurance permitted. But I just scratched the surface of things to do, things to see, and places to go. And the people immediately won our hearts. Their friendliness and sense of humor seems so American. Except for the accent, they would pass for Americans since most speak English fluently.

Judging from their buildings, Sweden is a rich country. Some buildings may be centuries old, but they are well built, architecturally interesting, and in good repair.

Likewise, all the cars are in good shape. Naturally, Volvos dominate the streets, the rest being mostly German makes. Sweden enforces a unique safety law. Cars must have either wiper blades or jets on their headlights to keep them clean. And motorists in all Scandinavian countries must drive with their lights on.

As usual, the older parts of the city held the most interest for me. Strolling through Old Town, I passed several musicians hoping for a contribution from shoppers. A young girl flutist appeared to be the most cultured, and contrasted sharply with the rhythmic group from the Caribbean. A talented guitarist also offered his cassettes for sale. A quaint lady played a small organ in front of Ahlen's Department Store. But clearly, the combo from Ecuador was having the most fun.

Obviously, people from many countries visit Stockholm. In fact, so many come from Russia and Estonia looking for jobs that they are beginning to concern some of the town's citizens. Stockholm is beginning to experience some of the same alien problems that the U. S. has had with Mexico and South America for decades.

For once, I happened to be in the right place at the right time and got some pictures denied the rest of the crew. Three new ambassadors arrived in town to present their credentials to the king. A procession of elegant horse-drawn carriages passed in front of the parliament building on their way to pick up these personages. Later, I got a shot of them leaving the king's working palace.

The palace contains a large Lutheran cathedral open to all people, not just the royal family. Although Lutheranism is the state religion, other sects enjoy freedom of religious expression. A trip to *Vasa* Museum highlighted my last day ashore. Built in 1628, the warship *Vasa* sank ignominiously on its maiden voyage before clear-

Procession of Ambassadors

ing the Stockholm harbor. As soon as the wind filled her sails for the first time, the top-heavy ship just heeled over and went down. All but about 25 people escaped. At the inquest to determine the cause for this disaster, no one received blame. It seems that the ultimate responsibility for the design of the ship rested with the king. During the building stage, he ordered the ship altered to have two gun decks instead of just one. His reason? The king of Denmark had a two-gun-deck battleship. As further testimony to the king's vanity, ornate sculpture decorates the ship—especially the stern portion. It's hazardous even for royalty to try to keep up with the Joneses.

Settling upright, the ship's masts extended far above the water as mute testimony to the king's folly. Consequently, all masts were severed below the water line. Otherwise, the ship lay completely intact until raised in 1961. Except for the part buried in the mud, worms destroyed the HMS *Mary Rose* in England. *Vasa* escaped that fate because the worms can't survive in the brackish water of Stockholm's harbor. Cargo, eating utensils—even a flask of rum—were found in the ship. It is reported that the 300-year-old rum was quite tasty.

The ship rests on a pontoon slipped beneath it after it was raised. Then it was towed to its present location where a specially constructed building houses it. Here, the critically controlled temperature and humidity continues the drying process. The ship, plus all the exhibits, could easily occupy a full day for someone whose interests include ships and history. Unfortunately, I didn't have that much time to spend there.

It is now 0830, August 31, 1992. My classes are finished. All reports are completed. All teaching materials are in the post office for return to Central Texas College. As soon as my clothes come

Vasa

back from the laundry, I will pack and be ready at 0700 tomorrow to transfer to a tugboat that will take me ashore at Portland, England for a flight back to the states.

Postscript: The USS *Yarnell* was decommissioned on October 29, 1993 and subsequently sold to Northern Metal, New York City for scrapping.

USS Belknap

USS *Belknap* CG-26

Gaeta, Italy, January 24, 1993

The call came from Dan Page, the PACE Coordinator in Norfolk, instructing me to leave Houston on Sunday morning of January 17 for arrival in Norfolk that afternoon. Earlier he had informed me that he was having difficulty finding a PACE instructor for the USS *Belknap*. Having had a positive experience four years earlier on the ship, I readily accepted the assignment.

At Norfolk, I received the usual briefing, ID, and travel orders to be issued Monday morning so that I could catch a flight that afternoon to meet the USS *Belknap* at Lisbon, Portugal on Tuesday. Since I expected to have free time Sunday evening, I called John Sigler and set up a dinner date with him and his wife Gail in Norfolk. John was the captain of *Belknap* the last time I served aboard that ship. He is now a retired two-star rear admiral. Although I was excited about seeing him again, it was not to be. The naval base closed Monday the 15th for Martin Luther King's birthday, so Norfolk sent all my documents ahead of time, and I took a flight from Houston to Lisbon by way of Dallas and Madrid, Spain. With several hours between planes at Dallas, I had a nice visit with Gail who met me at the airport.

I arrived on time, and for a change, so did my luggage! Unfortunately, *Belknap* left port the day before my arrival. Because of tensions in Iraq and Bosnia, the ship cut short its Lisbon visit and canceled the scheduled port calls to Rota, Spain, and Gibraltar. After spending a night in a Lisbon hotel, I flew to Rome and arrived in Gaeta via a rental car one day before *Belknap*. With time on my hands Wednesday evening, I started walking the streets of Gaeta to reacquaint myself with its environs. I ended up spending an hour and a half with Mike and Rosa Cuoco, the Italian couple I met here in 1989. They were as gracious as ever. Mike is a retired teacher who has gone to considerable length to create a bridge of understanding between the local Italians and the American military personnel and their dependents. He's very desirous of making young Italians aware of the vital role that Americans played in ridding Italy of Nazism in World War II. When he speaks of Monte Cassino and all those American crosses at Anzio, he chokes up. The GIs saved his life.

A few weeks ago he and Rosa hosted President George H.W. Bush's Secretary of Defense Dick Chaney and his wife. Mr. Chaney was here doing archaeological research at Monte Cassino. Capt. Walt Doran the present captain of *Belknap* was military advisor to then Vice President Bush. He is being promoted to admiral and transferred to a new assignment next month.

I noticed quite a number of interesting sites that I missed the last time I was here. Gaeta was once a walled city. Some of the old stone walls still stand with fragments of facades in reticulated patterns used by the Romans. For the first time, I noticed the old Roman baths just off the fleet landing. It's easy to overlook them because of litter and vegetation. The old arches next to fleet landing have been restored since I was here. But the large building across the street still appears to have the same scaffolding with no progress made in four years. Piccalo Alley still bears the marks of war. However, most of the rubble has been removed. It's obvious that the walls of some buildings were once common walls to structures now non-existent. One end of Piccalo Alley is being resurfaced with gray stones. This has the happy effect of curtailing motorcyclists who used to whiz down this pedestrian way.

The people seem friendlier than they did when I was last here. Of course, it is quite likely that I'm the one who has changed. I'm more at ease with foreigners than I was four years and thirty countries ago.

Gaeta, Italy, February 7, 1993

My class materials did not arrive until Friday night. Since we are scheduling no classes on weekends, I've simply lost a week from a business standpoint. But that's fairly normal for this job.

The past two weeks have consisted of long days and short nights. Based on information from Norfolk, I expected my classes to be organized so I could begin teaching the next day after my arrival. Not only did I not have any teaching materials on board, but also the only list of prospective students was the one I brought from the states. In addition, the Educational Services Officer, through whom I am supposed to channel all my activity, was not even designated until I came on board. Then he spent three days in Naples during his first week getting briefed on how to do his job. Upon his return, he spent four days teaching some kind of class ashore. Consequently, I organized the classes by test scores from the sheets I brought with me from Norfolk and worked through the command master chief to locate a suitable space for classes. And strangely, the XO made it a point of telling me he likes to make life difficult for teachers, which may explain why the PACE coordinator in Norfolk picked me as a last resort to find an instructor for the ship.

Classes are now up to speed and running smoothly. I will soon be giving placement tests to other prospective students who will need the four-week basic math and English courses as soon as the current classes end about February 23. I am in the classroom from 0700 to 1915 with a 45-minute break for lunch and one and one-half hours for dinner. Ten-plus hours in the classroom in addition to preparation time at night makes a very full day, but I'm free Saturday and Sunday.

For the first few weeks of this assignment, the USS *Belknap* is staying in Gaeta. In fact, the USS *Puget Sound*, a tender, is alongside doing several million dollars of renovation to *Belknap*. The caustic fumes from work on the ship were so heavy in my berthing area that I was transferred to quarters on *Puget Sound*. *Belknap*'s wardroom is being refurbished, so I also get my meals on the tender.

Yesterday, I teamed up with Jeff Pickhardt and Charlie Nausbaum, two chief petty officers from *Puget Sound*, and took a train to Rome. We revisited the Coliseum and some of the other sites I had seen four years ago. This time, we added St. Peter's Cathedral and the Sistine Chapel in the Vatican. The paintings in the Sistine Chapel have been restored at great time and expense. Our walking tour also took us by Trevi Fountain and the Pantheon, perhaps the

Pantheon

Castel S. Angelo on the Tiber River in Rome

best-preserved building from the Roman Empire. Located in Plaza Della Rotunda, it was founded by Agrippa in 27 BC, later rebuilt by Hadrian, and consecrated as a church in 606. Rafael and some Italian kings are buried there.

Not far from the Vatican, the Castel S. Angelo sits on the bank of the Tiber River. Hadrian built it in 139 AD as a burial place for the imperial family and their successors. Later converted into a fortress, it now houses a collection of paintings and arms.

Jeff and Charlie are both super guys, and we really enjoyed seeing the sights together. At the train station in Rome, we were met by the usual pack of Gypsies trying to steal everything on our persons. Swarms of little kids tried to stick their hands into our pockets. The best defense was to put all objects in our front pockets, cover them with our hands, and then get away as quickly as possible. All three of us have had experience with people like this, and they got nowhere with us. But as soon as we boarded the subway to the Vatican, a man tried to pick Jeff's pocket! He didn't succeed either.

Gaeta, Italy, February 14, 1993

Yesterday, I took the train to Herculaneum, an ancient seaside city near Naples that Mt. Vesuvius buried under fifty feet of mud when it erupted and also destroyed Pompeii in 79 A. D. Although the hardened mud has made excavation very difficult, it left Herculaneum and its furnishings better preserved than Pompeii. Thus, the city has been very useful to scholars in reconstructing the lifestyle of the early Romans.

Hercules founded Herculaneum about 500 B.C., but it came to real prominence and riches under the Romans beginning about 90 BC. The city is much smaller than Pompeii, having had a population of about 5,000, and can be toured fairly easily in an afternoon. During most of my time there, I had the city all to myself.

Herculaneum

Herculaneum residence

Interior of Herculaneum residence

Herculaneum residence

I don't know why more visitors were not there. Many of the buildings are still intact, and it is easy to identify the residences, public buildings, baths, and various shops. Unlike other Roman cities that used marble and granite extensively, Herculaneum is constructed of bricks and overlaid with plaster that is at least two to three inches thick and then painted, with red seeming to be a preferred color. Mosaic tiled floors adorn all the buildings, and columns are everywhere—residences, public building, and sidewalks. Some of the columns are plastered smooth while other are fluted and capped with Corinthian capitals—even the rectangular ones. Herculaneum was a very classy city.

When I see something like Herculaneum and Pompeii, I wonder whether the people there were so corrupt that God buried them, or whether they just had the misfortune to be at the wrong place at the wrong time. As I moved about the city, I tried to picture the daily lives of its people. They must have been rather small. Most of the doors were about eye-height to me. With the absence of other visitors, the silence of the city filled me with a funereal feeling and a keen awareness of my own mortality.

Gaeta, Italy, February 15, 1993

Since the ship had a holiday routine yesterday, I returned to Naples to take a 40-minute hydrofoil ride to the Isle of Capri. I have wanted to see this mountainous island since I was in grade school. It's beautiful, quaint, and definitely Mediterranean in every aspect. A narrow road winds up the mountain from the ferry landing to the town of Capri, affording a continuous panoramic view of the town, mountainside, and shoreline. The town's streets are almost too narrow for any vehicular traffic. Sidewalks that wind around, through, and under buildings are so narrow in places that if two people meet, one must turn sideways. Even so, Capri is a get-away spot for people with plenty of money to spend at expensive hotels and upscale shops. I would love to return to Capri in its peak season. Since this is the off-season, many of the shops, as well as the hotels, are closed. Some are undergoing renovation. In addition, the cable car to the top of the mountain won't be operational until the tourist season starts—a major disappointment for me.

But my biggest disappointment was twisting and spraining my right ankle and bruising and skinning my left leg and left hand from a fall in an isolated part of the island. Because there was no traffic and walking was almost impossible, this was the beginning of an eight-hour ordeal of walking followed by bus, boat, taxi, and train rides back to the ship. Some day the incident will become just another unimportant saga.

Gaeta, Italy, February 20, 1993

With the aid of an elastic wrap, my ankle seemed sufficiently improved for my return to Rome today for another look at the ancient ruins scattered around the central city. Hitching a ride with Dirk Blanchard, duty driver for the admiral's staff, I arrived at the coliseum early enough to get inside. The floor of the coliseum has been destroyed, but the rooms and tunnels, which supported the floor, are considerably intact. A young man from New Zealand and I took turns taking "I-was-here" pictures.

The ruins of Roman Forum are adjacent to the Coliseum. I spent most of the rest of the day here. The ruins still reveal a city that was magnificent in its prime. I enjoyed the time spent here even though a strong, cold wind blasted a bright sunny day. Not having had lunch, I warmed up over hot Italian vegetables and cappuccino before taking the night train back to Gaeta.

My basic skills classes will end next week. For one of my students, classes ended a week ago when he brought a loaded .357 pistol aboard the ship. He is on his way out the Navy via the brig with a less than honorable discharge. Another Sailor, not a student, had two days left on his enlistment and was due for an honorable discharge. After drinking too much "celebration," he arrived at the ship one night belligerent and violent—even threatening the officers who were trying to help him. One hour after appearing at captain's mast the next day, he was off the ship and on his way to the states with a less than honorable discharge.

As usual, my students as a group are above average in attitude, which makes for a rewarding teaching experience, especially those in basic skills classes. One old salt, whose family lives in Gaeta, beams with pride as he tells me how he is now able to help his little daughter with her math homework. One of my students got into a rather funny misunderstanding with his young son one night when he was ashore. Both father and son were quietly reading when the son asked, "Dad, what's a seaman?" His father thought he said semen and launched into a rather detailed explanation of human sexuality. The son just looked bewildered and didn't say anything. But after a short time, he asked, "Well, Dad, what's a petty officer?" Another man, not too long out of high school, gamely struggles to overcome his deficiencies in both English and math. His divorced parents went separate ways, leaving him and his brother alone. He hasn't seen either parent in more than three years. Poignant stories of crews of naval vessels could fill a lot of books.

Gaeta, Italy, February 26, 1993

Today, Demetrius Carter, one of my college students, and I went to Naples. He wanted to do some shopping at the Navy Exchange on the NATO base, and I wanted to see the museum housing many artifacts from Pompeii and Herculaneum. Cornelius has been on *Belknap* only nine months but already speaks Italian fluently, having learned Spanish formerly.

At the museum, an Italian man became our uninvited guide. I started to dismiss him, knowing he would want money for his "services." However, thinking he might be useful, I changed my mind. I should have followed my first impulse. He proved to be nearly useless and then made a sour face when I paid him what we thought his ten-minute "tour" was worth. I doubled the amount and he again made a sour face. When he continued his sour face routine after I had tripled the money, I instructed Demtrius to tell him the Italian equivalent of "get lost." The guy was just another beggar. We then toured the museum at our leisure. Although I enjoyed the museum, I was disappointed because the Pompeii exhibit that came to Houston a few years ago was nearly as complete.

Later, at the Navy Exchange, Demetrius made his purchases, and we both got haircuts. As we were leaving the exchange, a light mist began to fall, so we asked a cab driver about taking us the few blocks back to the train station. Thinking he had us at a disadvantage, he demanded $10. We just laughed and walked off. A block or so later, a friendly Italian businessman picked us up and took us to the train station.

On the train, we encountered our third con artist for the day. Some guy walked into the car and dropped a junk trinket on each passenger. Nobody bought anything. It was just another form of begging. Often, a young man or woman will board a train at one end and beg this way through the entire train before disembarking at another station. I suggested to Demetrius that he write a classification essay about Italian beggars. Demetrius is a straight "A" black student and delightful traveling companion. Completely at ease with his race, he regaled me with black racial jokes for much of the train ride back to Formia.

Gaeta, Italy, February 28, 1993

Demetrius and some of his buddies went to Rome, and I tagged along for one more chance to see some more of the ancient city. First, we went back to the Vatican. This time, I went underground to see the tombs of the popes. I have been told that marble stripped from the coliseum and other ancient structures became building material for St. Peter's Cathedral.

Vatican

Leaving the Vatican catacombs, we went to one of three other ancient burial sites. At one time, about 500,000 bodies occupied this three-level city of the dead. Extending more than 15 miles, the catacomb passageways could cause the unguided visitor to become hopelessly lost. Rooms along the passageways held the bodies of entire families. In the absence of rooms, recesses in the walls from ceiling to floor held people of all sizes. The actual remains of people have long since been removed, except for a few bones under glass to provide a macabre tourist attraction. I don't know what I expected, but after several minutes, the sameness of the place made it seem rather uninteresting.

With remembrances of Ben Hur, I had wanted to see the old Roman Circus, the site of chariot races. Our bus took us right by it. It is now just a poorly kept grassy park, not even worth a bus stop.

Coliseum

Spanish steps

Since Demetrius' buddies hadn't seen the Coliseum, we stopped there for a while and also strolled past the Roman Forum before going to the Spanish Steps. These very broad steps rise about forty yards above a fountain in the middle of a large plaza to a huge church at the top. Leading away from the steps, a broad street divides a long line of upscale shops. Evidently, this is where the pretty people hang out because young folks jammed the Spanish Steps and filled the streets as well.

Some time before we took the night train back to Gaeta, I lost my gloves. I don't know whether they fell out of my pocket or whether they were stolen while I was in a crowd. Their monetary value wasn't very much, but it saddened me to lose them. They were the last gift I ever received from my mother.

Last week, I gave more placement tests for prospective students. My first four basic skills classes ended February 23. Since the ESO failed to order new cycle numbers, I'm still awaiting approval from NETSCELANT to start four new classes; consequently, this week appears to be wasted.

In the meantime, with nothing but my college night class to teach, I hiked to Formia today to try to do a little shopping and just get away from the ship. As I stepped onto the pier, a crisp, cloudless day greeted me. Walking along the seawall in Gaeta, I noticed the fresh snowfall on the mountains overlooking Formia, creating a "Kodak Moment." Later, I left the roadway, preferring a long stretch of beach at Formia. Here, the early morning breakers drowned all human noise. Mist from the breakers hung low over the beach like ground fog, softening Formia's shoreline. Sheltered from the cold wind, and warmed by the sun, I left fresh tracks in the smooth, brown sand since the tide was going out. About five miles after leaving the ship, I settled down with a newspaper, a cup of cappuccino, and a croissant at a waterfront sidewalk cafe. Simple pleasures are often the best.

After doing hours of window-shopping, which netted one purchase for my son Kerry and his wife Liz, I retraced my steps to Gaeta. Along the Formia beach, I selected an assortment of fresh seashells for a lady in Beeville, Texas, who collects them.

Gaeta, Italy, March 4, 1993

Early this morning, I hiked back to Formia, or rather the other side of Formia. Anyway, it was a long walk. I have taken to walking as much as I can because my right ankle, injured more than two weeks ago on Capri, still precludes jogging.

Today's objective was the market held every Thursday. It's really just an open-air department store with booths arranged in a grid pattern. Judging from the size of the crowd, merchandise here must be considerably cheaper than in the local stores. I settled for a pair of lined leather gloves for less than seven dollars and lunched on calzonni, an Italian turnover made from pizza dough and stuffed with cheese, before returning to the ship.

Gaeta, Italy, March 18, 1993

Yesterday, I took a bus to the town of Cassino, the site of a costly, bitter battle in WWII. The major attraction here is the rebuilt Abbey Monte Cassino and the nearby WWII cemetery for Polish soldiers atop a mountain overlooking Cassino. At the insistence of New Zealanders who fought alongside Americans, Monte Cassino was needlessly bombed into rubble. Because of Monte Cassino's religious and art significance, neither the Germans nor the Americans had been willing to destroy the structure. Thanks to American tax dollars funneled through the Italian government, Monte Cassino—although smaller—now rivals the grandeur of St. Peters Cathedral in Rome. A

Monte Cassino

great deal of American foreign aid has gone to similar projects, such as "old towns" scattered around Europe.

The trip was a minor fiasco. Arriving in Cassino about 1100, I expected to take a bus up to Monte Cassino right away. The next bus didn't leave until 1500! So for the next four hours, I made the best of the situation by walking the streets of Cassino and seeing as much of the city as I could. It was mostly just another Italian town.

At lunchtime, I attempted to enter a restaurant, but the door was locked. However, the proprietor and his wife were having lunch and opened the door for me. I thought they were just getting ready to open up for the day. They were most gracious in allowing me to be their only customer since they were really closed for the day. They were eating the specialty of the house, and that's what I ordered—tronchetti, a delicious assortment of unidentifiable ingredients wrapped in pasta in a long roll and served in slices. The proprietor said it was his own recipe and not to be found anywhere else.

At the appointed time, I was at the bus stop for the trip up the mountain. After a 30-minute wait, I thought it best to take the 1530 bus back to Gaeta and see Monte Cassino another time because it was getting so late. However, the bus to Monte Cassino showed up first and the driver said he would bring me back down the mountain in time to catch the 1730 bus to Gaeta. Everything went according to plan until the 1730 bus to Gaeta failed to show up. The 1530 bus had been the last bus to Gaeta for the day. The person who gave me the bus schedule failed to tell me the buses didn't run after 1530 on Sunday!

So I checked out the train schedules. The only way to get to Gaeta by train was via Rome. This meant traveling two long legs of an isosceles triangle instead of the short base. This plan had several faults. First, I had enough lire for the ticket to Rome, but had no assurance of being able to convert dollars into lire for the ticket from Rome to the Formia train station near Gaeta. Second, I didn't know when I would be able to get out of Rome but knew the trip would put me into Formia too late to catch the last bus to Gaeta. This would mean about a two-hour walk in the middle of a cold night. I went to plan C.

With the help of an English-speaking Italian, I negotiated a taxi ride to Gaeta for $47.00—about $45.00 more than the bus ticket I already held. Although I fumed about the situation all the way to Gaeta, rationalization eventually took over. Many tourists spend thousands of dollars to go from the United States to Italy to see such sights as Monte Cassino. Considering that I got paid to come here, a $47.00 error isn't all that bad. Besides, I cashed in my return bus ticket and cut my loss to $45.00.

Gaeta, Italy, March 12, 1993

I started four new basic skills classes this week, so I am back in the classroom for 12 hours a day with a break for lunch and dinner. The command master chief helped me shape up the classes. He is second only to the X.O. in authority and he spelled out attendance requirements to the new students in varied and colorful detail. Consequently, the students have responded even more enthusiastically than usual. Now the CMC has gone to the States for a month, leaving no one to enforce his rhetoric. The lieutenant who claimed to be the Educational Services Officer when I first came on board quit after two days. The chief petty officer who replaced him was fired for incompetence. The CMC turned over the duties to a first class petty officer whom I have seen only one time. When I was on *Belknap* four years ago, both captains gave me the run of the ship, and I was blessed with the friendship and cooperation of the officers—especially the staff officers. During the last four years, *Belknap* has had a one- hundred-percent turnover in personnel, and it really shows.

Mediterranean Sea, March 18, 1993

The ship finally got underway yesterday, having been in port in Gaeta longer than anyone on the ship can remember. The ship will make no port calls, but rather spend some time in the Adriatic Sea monitoring the events in Bosnia. The scheduled visits to Israel and Egypt have been canceled, much to my chagrin. Port calls to Portugal, Spain, and Gibraltar had already been aborted. This is my second time to go to sea without making port calls. I have tried to offset this disappointment by soaking up as much of Italy as I can.

The ship is now carrying a helicopter. Therefore, four pilots have moved into my berthing space that was already crowded. However, they are good-natured and congenial. Flight operations, GQ drills, and other events are decimating my classes.

Off Sicily, March 19, 1993

The GQ alarm sounded at the beginning of my 1430 math class. A little earlier, snow-capped Mt. Etna slid by our starboard beam. As we transited Messina Strait, a small amount of steam rose from the crater framed by a clear blue sky over a calm ocean. For a change, the weather decks require only shirts.

Evidently, the crew will practice GQ every day, further eroding class attendance. Since we are at sea anyway, I'll use as much as I can of Saturdays and Sundays to make up the time.

Ionian Sea, March 20, 1993

For those of us not jaded by too much time at sea, an ocean sunrise often treats us to fleeting glimpses of heavenly artistry unmatched by any captured on canvass. At 0530 today, such a sunrise fanned out clouds in a thirty-degree angle from the point where the sun was about to appear. A grayish blue cloudbank on the horizon spread into streaks of pink, amber, and powder blue from the vertex of the triangle toward the northern sky. Just south of the apex, a thin isolated wisp of pink clouds lightly veiled the silver sliver of a late-rising moon. The kaleidoscopic scene vanished in just a few minutes. By noon, low-lying fog cut visibility to a half mile, requiring periodic blasts on the ship's whistle. But by mid-day, brilliant sunshine had overcome the fog and dazzled the eyes. Leaving Messina Strait yesterday afternoon and transiting the Ionian Sea last night, we arrived on station this morning. The USS *Belknap* now has full responsibility for all NATO air traffic dealing with the relief efforts for the civil war in Bosnia.

Adriatic Sea, March 27, 1993

For several days, the ship has plowed a triangle about 25 miles from Bar, Yugoslavia. Weather has been mixed. Some days have been clear and sunny, others overcast with low visibility. Seas have ranged from smooth to sufficiently choppy to cause some of my students to become seasick. My classroom is the most conducive to seasickness of all the locations on the ship. A former sonar compartment and situated all the way forward at the waterline, it undergoes the most rolling and pitching.

Today, the ship will turn over the command of the operation to the USS *R. K. Turner*, another cruiser, which just arrived from Norfolk. Considering the short time on station, I wonder why *Belknap* relieved *Wainwright* instead of *Turner*. A good guess is that the ship needed some sea time to sharpen the crew's skills after such a long stay in port, as well as an opportunity to check out the systems that were repaired in port. Of course, *Belknap* is the Sixth Fleet flagship, and it may have been politically expedient to have some direct involvement in the Bosnia turmoil.

The aircraft carrier *Roosevelt* just replaced the USS *John F. Kennedy*, which is heading for Norfolk. Sadly, the USS *Roosevelt* has already lost a surveillance aircraft with its full crew. No one seems to know the cause of the accident yet. The plane is a twin-engine, early warning craft easily identified by the radar dome on its top.

The ship took on fuel from the USS *Milwaukee* from 0730 to 0830 today. A cold wind whipped across the decks under an overcast sky. The sea is choppy. Even so, the refueling crew prefers these conditions to the refueling operation four days ago. Then, they took on provisions before refueling. The whole six-hour operation was carried out in the dark and finished about 0100 the next morning. Some of my students didn't show up for class the next day, and the ones who did had difficulty staying awake. For dinner, the next evening, Capt. Moeller joined the crew on the mess deck for lobster and prime ribs. Later, the men were given all the ice cream and toppings that they could eat. This is just one of the ways a captain can show his appreciation for a job well done. The men respond well to this captain who has only been in command a few weeks. The crew can set battle stations in five minutes, which may be a *Belknap* record. Because we are where we are, that time is abetted by the ship's staying at "condition three"—one level below battle stations.

Following the early morning refueling, the ship set a course for Gaeta that will take us out of the Adriatic into the Ionian Sea where weather conditions that are already a challenge for the helicopter crew are expected to deteriorate even more. The present helicopter is larger than the one the ship carried four years ago. It covers so much of the flight deck that there is almost no margin for error.

Gaeta, Italy, March 31, 1993

My college class is over. Tomorrow I will give the final test to my basic skills students. I have a prepaid airline ticket back to the states waiting for me in Rome, and I am scheduled to leave here via the ship's car and duty driver on April 2 at 0800. In the meantime, I made one more trip to Formia with Demetrius Carter to buy some more Italian candy to take home. Arivederci Italy!

USS Mobile Bay (Photo courtesy of Elsilrac Enterprises)

USS *Mobile Bay* CG-53

Arabian Sea, February 13, 1994

The seven days since I left Texas has been a full week. After Nita retired from Exxon Coal and Minerals last August, we returned to our permanent home just west of Kenedy, Texas. At least, I thought it was permanent. During the last ten years, Nita had become "citified" and no longer wanted to live on a thirty-four acre hill with a great view in a two-story house that I built to her specifications. So we sold the place and moved to the chic little village of Salado in central Texas. We had barely plunked down our belongings in a brand new house when I got a call from San Diego requesting my presence on a ship in Bahrain. I scooted a bunch of our stuff to one side of the garage, kissed Nita goodbye, and took off for San Diego.

After briefing me for my new assignment, the San Diego office routed me to Bahrain via New York. Somewhere over the middle of the United States, the airline captain gave the passengers a jarring bulletin. JFK Airport was weathered in; so were Washington and Chicago. So we headed for Dallas—150 miles from where I started!

At DFW Airport, I quickly retrieved my luggage and checked other flights that would get me to Bahrain at the appointed time. Luftansa had a flight leaving immediately for Frankfurt that would connect with another flight to Bahrain. As I was making a hurried call to San Diego to relate the change in planes, the ticket agent was urging me to get off the phone and board the plane. As soon as I boarded the plane with my entire luggage in hand, the steward closed the door, and the plane backed away from the terminal.

It was a case of hurry up and wait with a four-hour layover at Frankfurt. I had a valentine that I had intended to mail to Nita from New York. But now I needed German postage. The clerk watched me peel off the American stamp and affix the German stamp. When I handed him the letter, he looked at it disgustedly and said, "You Americans! You're the only ones who don't put the name of your country on your mail. I guess you think the United States is the center of the universe."

Having endured surly clerks in airports and train stations across Europe, I was ready for this one and terminated the conversation with this bit of impudence in my best Texan drawl. "Sir, that letter is goin to Texas. And I reckon that most of us Texans do think that *Texas is* the center of the universe."

My arrival at the Bahrain Airport was a good omen. Having never been in Arab territory before, I didn't quite know what to expect. A man named Hamza was supposed to meet my flight from Frankfurt. He did and whisked me right past customs without my passport being checked! As we were about to leave the terminal, a tall young man asked, "Are you James Lee?" He is the Educational Service Officer for *Mobile Bay* and had a car waiting to take me to the ship, which left port the next morning. Unfortunately, I did not get to visit Bahrain at all.

I am berthed in the captain's in-port cabin. It's a two-room suite with a private bath, desk, conference table, TV, radio, and three phones. I even have an indicator by my bed that gives the ship's course and speed. Besides, a chief petty officer has loaned me his personal laptop computer. Since all the officers gave me a sincere welcome aboard, the food is excellent, and, for a change, I have a bonafide classroom with all necessary facilities, it doesn't get any better than this for a PACE instructor.

Today was supposed to be a day to give placement tests for students and otherwise just kick back, but some unexpected excitement turned up.

This seven-year-old Aegis class cruiser to which I am assigned is part of a battle group of several ships, including the aircraft carrier USS *Independence* and the USS *Bunker Hill*, another Aegis class cruiser. This morning we were making our approach between an oiler and a supply ship to receive replenishment from both sides of the ship. I was on the bridge enjoying some good-natured idle banter with the XO when all three generators malfunctioned, causing the ship to lose all electrical power. The good news is that the accident did not occur twenty minutes later when, without power or steering, we would have been hooked up with fuel hoses to the oiler. The Navy has contingency plans for everything, but an emergency breakaway under that condition could have been extremely dangerous. We were dead in the water for about two hours while the engineers located and corrected problem.

Yesterday, a similar problem befell *Bunker Hill*, and for a while, it appeared that she would have to be towed. However, the carrier supplied the necessary parts, and she is proceeding under her own power today. Two of her helicopter pilots spent the night on our ship. One of the pilots slept on the couch in my suite.

It took two days to get out of the Persian Gulf, through the Straits of Hormuz, and through the Gulf of Oman. Hormuz looked like huge barren rocks stretched across the ocean. Somewhere in the straits, some Iranian boats blasted through the battle formation. Although small and relatively ineffective against warships, the mentality of the men who man them is never taken for granted. They have been known to stretch cables across the strait and let the forward motion of the victimized ship pull their small boats alongside the stern of the ship. Using grappling hooks, they then board the ship, take over the crew, and plunder its cargo. Of course, this activity is carried out in the dark. Once, they fruitlessly snared an American submarine this way.

Today, we are about ninety miles from the Laccadive Islands off the West Coast of India. The sea has been remarkably smooth. Yesterday, the sun rose in a cloudless sky over a glassy sea, casting a brilliant gold beam across the dark blue water. An ever-so-pale lavender haze rimmed the horizon. It's a very peaceful Sunday out here. Some of the men are sun bathing.

Indian Ocean, February 15, 1994

We have passed within about fifty miles of Cape Comorin on the southern tip of India and have swung around to the south of Sri Lanka. The sea continues to be extremely smooth. It is quite unusual for a top-heavy cruiser to ride as steady as an aircraft carrier for such a long time. We will enjoy it while we can. The South China Sea will be different. When the ship headed straight into the sunrise this morning, the sun glistening on the sea's tiny wavelets created what appeared to be more than a dozen strobe lights alternately flashing on the horizon. In nearly five years at sea, I have never before seen anything like it. For a while I just stood transfixed on the port bridge wing; before turning my attention to the flying fish for a long time.

I have been too busy organizing classes to watch much marine life. Yesterday, I did see a large school of porpoises. And for years, I have heard about the poisonous sea snakes that abound in the Indian Ocean, but so far, I have not seen any. The captain says that they stay mostly in shallow water. That's not a happy thought for swimmers since the snakes are reputed to be aggressive.

Part of the ship's electrical system crashed again last night. Some areas of the ship have been blacked out, causing some heads and water to be secured, and spaces to be under emergency lights only. For a while today, my suite had the only functioning toilet for all the officers. The men in the electrical division worked all night last night trying to fix the problem. After two hours of sleep, they were back on the job. For noon chow we had a steel beach picnic on the fantail because the kitchens were without power. This morning I got good and sweaty in the exercise room only to return to my room to find my fresh water turned off, but it was back on within an hour. The electricians have all systems up and running again. Since the malfunction affected everybody, this incident has provided very valuable training for the entire crew.

Indian Ocean, February 17, 1994

One of the generators failed again last night, causing me to abort my last class because some of my students were part of the repair detail. The lights in my stateroom came back on about 0500. There must be a bunch of tired, sleepy, frustrated men on board today. Since the "glitch" still has not been isolated, some of the ship's drills have been canceled in order to concentrate on the electrical problem. The helicopter cannot be launched because there is no assurance the ship would be able to recover it without proper electrical power. Meanwhile, because of the uncertainty of consistent air conditioning, the men are now authorized to wear white T-shirts and shorts. The captain says that if the problem is not fully corrected in the next forty-eight hours, our port visit to Manila will be canceled and we will head for repair facilities in Singapore where the technicians can rely on shore power while tracing the fault in the ship's system.

Classes are going well, albeit with not as many students as I was supposed to have. The sophomore literature class is full, but the freshman composition class has sixteen instead of twenty, and the pre-college writing class has five instead of ten. The literature class textbook is a 2,000-page tome. There is no way these students can digest all that in six weeks of class time. Consequently, I have assigned sections of it to each man who thoroughly reads his part and then gives a condensed report to the rest of the class. The students are responding very well. The Bible heavily influenced much of the early American literature under discussion, and I am surprised and saddened that so many young men are totally ignorant of the contents of the Bible. In the words of Cicero, "To be ignorant of what occurred before you were born is to remain always a child." Quo Vadis, America?

Bay of Bengal, February 18, 1994

The captain returned from a conference on the aircraft carrier at noon today. The ship's electrical problem must be corrected in port. Consequently, we are scheduled to arrive in Singapore on February 22. As a result, either the port visit to Manila or Hong Kong will be canceled, thus allowing the ship to return to its homeport in Yokosuka, Japan on schedule. Some of the crew are sending radio messages to their wives and girl friends who were supposed to meet them in these ports.

The weather continues to be outstanding. Yesterday, we did encounter some small white caps, but today the ocean is devoid of waves—just long, low, gentle swells. Following a day of brilliant sunshine, the night has a moon designed for cruise ships.

Bay of Bengal, February 19, 1994

It's official. Starting February 22, the ship will spend seven days in Singapore and then go to Hong Kong, bypassing Manila. This suits me. I have been to the Philippines. However, I was really looking forward to going to Corregidor where men a scant decade older than my generation made their last stand before the fall of the Philippines to the Japanese in WWII. But I have always wanted to go to Singapore, which should also afford some side trips into Malaysia. In addition, from Hong Kong I should be able to visit Mainland China.

Bay of Bengal, February 20, 1994

The ship has been involved in some anti-submarine warfare exercises for the last few days. Hence, we are still in the Bay of Bengal. Although today is Sunday, work for some of the crew started at 0600 because of a vertrep. They did relax with a "smoker" on the helicopter deck this afternoon. A smoker is an old Navy tradition of staging boxing matches. The only reward for the winners is bragging rights. I didn't watch the fights since I rate boxing as a sport on the same level as bull fighting. I guess it gives the young men an opportunity to work off some energy and frustrations. But I spent the time in the exercise room keeping my own body in shape.

Nobody really smokes at a smoker. Smoking is one of the vices on which the Navy is moving toward zero tolerance just as it did on drugs. The only two places that men can smoke on this ship are the fantail and the starboard break, a small sheltered area up forward on the main deck. The Navy is getting tough on alcohol too. An infraction under the influence of alcohol no longer gets a mere slap on the wrist. Obesity is also becoming intolerable. The fatties on this ship are required to work out every day. If overweight Sailors fail their physical readiness test twice, they are on their way out of the Navy, regardless of rate or years of service.

Andaman Sea, February 21, 1994

For the last day or two the ship has been undergoing training exercises of various sorts. Last night we passed by the Nicobar Islands off Indonesia and are now heading into the Strait of Malacca, probably the most dangerous body of water in the world. Two conditions combine to make it so: The strait is very narrow and it is one of the most heavily traveled shipping lanes anywhere. Collisions are frequent. Just yesterday, the USS *White Plains*, one of the ships in our battle group, picked up two people from a burning vessel. Another hazard faced by some merchant ships is piracy. That seems unbelievable in this century, but pirates from small, fast boats out of some island in Indonesia can easily board an unarmed ship in these waters where maneuvering is restricted. After robbing the ship, the pirates may just leave the crew tied up and allow the ship to run aground or to collide with another vessel.

The imminent transiting of this strait plus the unfound glitch in our electrical system prompted the captain to cancel all unnecessary shipboard activity today and conduct a safety stand down. Although Navy bulletins frequently report accidents about naval personnel, I personally have known firsthand of very few over the years. It's a tribute to the constant attention to safety that more men are not injured because the ways to get hurt on a warship are unlimited. As I have stated earlier, projections protrude everywhere from the bulkheads, decks, and overheads, making it easy to trip, stab, scrape, slice, or bruise. Of course, ladders invite falls. And it only takes one careless man to cause an electrical fire or galley fire. Then, too, the whole ship is a combination fuel tank and ammunition dump. These are just some of the hazards. Now we are entering a strait where we have to watch out for all the travelers of the world who may not be so safety conscious.

Singapore, February 28, 1994

The ship has been in port for a week and I have packed in a short lifetime of activity. By the time the ship was pierside on Tuesday, there was really no time to go out on the town. Down at the mess deck, money had to be exchanged, brochures distributed, and hotel and tour information dispensed. Then the XO had the usual port brief, which included some sobering rules.

Possession of drugs can get you fined $20,000 and 10 years in jail. Just one marijuana joint constitutes possession. Trafficking in drugs can land you in jail for twenty to thirty years plus fifteen strokes of the cane. Just one blow from the cane will get your attention for a long, long time. Deal in fifteen grams of morphine or heroin and the penalty is death. This is almost a smoke-free society. No smoking is allowed in restaurants and some other public buildings. Smoking, eating, or drinking on public transportation, including elevators, will get you a fine of $500 to $1,000. Chewing gum is illegal. It'll cost you $50 to jaywalk and $150 to fail to flush the toilet. I assume the "toilet police" are plainclothes persons. Littering will also cost you a bundle. Need to spit? Choke on it, for it's illegal too. Of course, these are Singapore dollars, which are worth only two-thirds as much as American money. And women? Treat them with great respect. A pinch, pat, or even a bump is considered "outraging their modesty" and can result in imprisonment or a heavy fine.

Having been ashore daily, I have seen some of the minor rules breached. Some of the prettiest women I have seen have outraged their own modesty by the way they dress. I suspect that these people work the bars since streetwalking is also illegal. But courtesy seems to characterize these people. It receives constant low-key encouragement through signs and billboards. The same concern applies to motorists. Anyone cutting into line at the causeway going into Malaysia will be turned back. It's also a $500 fine for a motorist to attempt to leave Singapore with less then three-fourths of a tank of gas. The only flagrant discourtesy I have witnessed was that of a lady bus driver. A car turned a little too close in front of her. She then passed the car and slammed on the brakes. Nice ride for the passengers too.

Predictably, this is a very clean city, even with 2.7 million people packed into 238 square miles. The population comprised mainly of Chinese, Malays, Indians, and Eurasians have a history of racial harmony. The stunningly modern architecture of the downtown buildings adds to the clean appearance. But even with all the development, much more construction is underway. The first Malaysian words I learned were "bahaya jangan dekat" (danger keep out). Singapore, the busiest port in the world, gives the appearance of a prosperous city on the move. A ship comes or goes every ten minutes. You can buy anything here, and there is so much to see and do.

Tuesday evening I, along with a lot of Sailors, welcomed the opportunity just to get off the ship and run after a two-week and 5,000-mile confinement to the ship. Leaving the ship I ran/walked the four miles through near-by Sembawang Park, including a short stretch of beach. The vegetation here is lush and beautiful, being about 100

Singapore Park

miles north of the equator. It reminds me of Panama—bougainvillea, 25-foot plumeria trees in bloom, mangos—the usual beautiful tropical plants.

I used Wednesday to try to get a quick overview of the main areas of interest in the downtown sector. For six dollars I bought a ticket on a bus that looks like a trolley that makes a downtown circuit every hour. Passengers can get on and off at key spots. A map shows the key points. Getting a late morning start, I stopped first at TGIF where my bus ticket entitled me to a free smoothie. I added a salad and called it lunch—my last American lunch since arriving. The Botanical Gardens engaged my interest for the next few hours. It's partially landscaped to typical British perfection.

The rest is a rain forest undisturbed except for a few trails. Within the forest, birds shut out all human noise, making my solitary walk very peaceful. Within the landscaped area, an orchid bower bloomed in profuse colors. Another area was dedicated to roses, another to palm trees and so on. Adjacent to a small pool, hedges formed a large, workable clock. White swans graced a larger pond, which reflected towering cypress-like trees. A marble ball about three feet in diameter rotated slowly over a small fountain, being suspended only by the water pressure. A bird playing in the water hopped off a few paces to scold me as I moved in to take a picture. Japanese tourists taking pictures of each other filled the orchid grove. A small group of young girls asked me to take their picture. As I returned the camera, I bowed and said, "Arigato gozaimashita." They smiled their approval of my "thank you" in their language.

Being a fast walker, I covered the entire garden, but a nature lover could easily spend a day there. Construction is underway to significantly expand the garden's size.

Returning to the trolley I noticed points I wanted to return to, one being the Long Bar at the century-old Raffles Hotel, which was frequented by such writers as Rudyard Kipling, Joseph Conrad, Ernest Hemingway, and W. Sommerset Maughan. Although I don't care for alcohol, every visitor to Singapore goes to the Long Bar for a Singapore Sling. It's just a thing to do. The drink was originally a drink for ladies because it's pink. The recipe includes gin, cherry brandy, cointreau, benedictine and fruit juices. I'm not sure it has any hooch in it all, for I neither smelled, tasted, nor felt it. It was good, but as far as I could tell, it is just an expensive glass of fruit juices topped with a small chunk of pineapple and a cherry.

Completing the trolley's circuit I then alighted at Lau Pa Sat, a downtown market that dates back many years. But recently, it has had a multi-million dollar face-lift and is a delightful place to eat and browse for everything from clothing to trinkets. The inside food court partially surrounds a stage for live entertainment. It covers a full city block, and at night, one street is blocked off so that two-dozen food kiosks can augment the food selections inside.

After the first night, I was hooked. The cool insect-free night, the full moon, the music, the festive atmosphere, the exotic Chinese food (the likes of which I had never before tasted)—all these combined to return me for six consecutive nights to try a different food each time. Although I recognized only a few ingredients, all the food was delicious, was not particularly spicy, and sat well on the stomach. Whether Chinese or Muslim, the food is unique to Singapore. Except for barbecued meat, nothing is greasy. And desserts typically have only coconut milk or fruit juice as a sweetener. The low fat, low sugar diet makes it easy to understand why Asians are not an obese people. And you can get a main course with dessert and a sixteen-ounce nourishing drink for four dollars.

Singapore is so clean that food and drinks from just about any source can be safely eaten. On Saturday, I passed several sidewalk food vendors in China Town who were barbecuing pork slices for the Chinese lunar New Year. Two dollars got me a whole sack full of hot, delicious, lean meat.

On Thursday, I went to Johor, Malaysia—just across the causeway from Singapore. The petty officer on the Navy base that I consulted about the trip said that I would need a statement from the command of *Mobile Bay* stating that I am attached to the ship. I protested, saying that I had a passport. He said, "You don't have an option, sir." An hour later, I was on my way with the signed document, with instructions to the XO to notify the American Embassy if I were not back in 24 hours.

Entering Malaysia, I found out I was "special" because of the letter and had to fill out more than the usual form. And they still stamped my passport. Ah, bureaucracy! A pretty little Malaysian girl also entering the country took it upon herself to guide me through some of that. People frequently come to my aid in such situations, and I don't know why unless it's the dumb look on my face. Maybe there really are guardian angels.

Before striking out, I changed some U.S. dollars to Malaysian ringgits and bought a snack at a restaurant that opened onto the side-walk. I learned the hard way in Wolfe City, Texas, a long time ago to eat where and what the locals eat. Looking around to see what most of the natives were eating, I ordered the same thing. The cook took a piece of dough and twirled it like pizza until it was crepe thin. Then he put it on the table, smashed an egg on it, folded the sides of the dough over the egg and dropped it on the grill. The praltha dale was good served with hot tea with the milk and sugar already in it. Before leaving, I learned two very important expressions: terima kaseh (thank you), and tandas (toilet) or biler air (bathroom).

Leaving the restaurant, I made my way through narrow, back streets heavily traveled by motorists who apparently have little regard for pedestrians, the absence of signals making it difficult to cross streets. Emerging from this old section of town, I faced a wide boulevard paralleling the waterfront with a strip park between the road and the water. The Malaysians are proud of their flowers. Pick one and it will cost you $500, about $200 American. But it could be worse. The first sign to greet a newcomer over the causeway reads, "Trafficking in illegal drugs carries the death penalty." Asians know from a long history what opium can do to their society and just don't tolerate it any more. America should take note.

My twenty-mile hike through Johor took me by most of the inter-esting places to see. First, there was this sculpture of a pineapple in the waterside park. Three young girls in native dress were standing near. When I raised my camera, they began to move away. I smiled and motioned for them to stay in the picture, but they just giggled, turned, and walked away. Later, I saw them in town and again indi-cated that I would like to photograph them. Again, they just giggled and turned their backs. I didn't try to get any more close-ups of people in native dress although there were other good opportunities. Both a man and woman in native dress were along with me on a road near the zoo. The woman dutifully followed the man a few paces behind him.

I hadn't planned to go to the zoo, but since I had accidentally stumbled onto it, and it was free, I walked in. It was quite limited, not very well kept, and very smelly. I didn't stay long. The birds were the most interesting to me. Some of the big ones had huge beaks that look like they were made of driftwood.

Down the road a short distance from the zoo, the mournful, singsong call to prayer emanated from Mastid Sultan Abu Bakar, a beautiful white, multi-towered mosque completed in 1900 after eight years of construction. Religiously, Malaysians are a mixture of Muslim, Hindu, and Shinto. In addition to the mosque, there is a Hindu temple and a Chinese temple, all of which I photographed. Because of the Chinese celebration of the New Year, the temple swarmed with people vying for room to burn incense.

One of the town's most interesting buildings is Bangunan Sultan Ibrahim, the State Secretariat Building. A travel brochure indicated the visitors could enter the grand hall. At first, I was denied entrance. But when I showed the authorities the language in the brochure, they allowed me to proceed. I didn't photograph the hall for two reasons. First, it was being renovated and scaffolding covered some of the walls. Second, since I had to argue my way in, I didn't want to press my luck and have to argue my way out. At one end of the domed hall sat a squared throne about six feet by six feet high. I don't know what occasion it is used for.

By late afternoon, I noticed the beginning symptoms of heat exhaustion, having spent the whole sunny day in short sleeves and without a hat. I did remember to use my sun block after the damage was done. I found a cool spot to start putting cold juice into my body. Then I wandered through Plaza Pelangi, the town's large, air conditioned mall, until I cooled down some more.

I had saved the market for last, thinking that if I found something to buy, I wouldn't have to carry it so long. I showed my map to two young men to verify the location of the market, and from their knowing looks at each other, I knew I was in for a disappointment. There, the scent of Chinese incense gave way to the odors of fresh meat, fish, fruit, vegetables, and a dirty, wet floor. A quick walk-through sent me back to Singapore.

At the customs complex, a man in uniform told me I had to enter through another complex about a half a mile away. When I went there to board the bus, another uniformed man told me I had to go to the bus station to get a ticket instead of simply dropping coins in a meter as I did in Singapore. The bus station was as far away as Singapore! I opted to walk back, passing close by the first uniformed man. Where was the pretty little Malaysian girl when I really needed her? Clearing customs into Singapore, I then boarded a bus and asked the driver if it would take me to the naval base. She said yes, but it didn't. I ended up at the train station mid-way between the naval base and downtown Singapore. So I went back to Lau Pa Sat for Muslim food, limejuice, and a Chinese dessert.

After dinner, I went to Marina Bay across from Merlion Park where the Chinese New Year celebration was in full swing. There were many booths and a carnival complete with various rides. The previous night, I had been in the right place at the right time to see all the spectacular, lighted floats go by in a parade. Dragons and other creatures of Chinese legend stared wide-eyed and open-mouthed at the spectators.

Back on the ship, I sadly surveyed the sunburn and cooled down with a long cold shower followed by an application of hydrocortisone to my face. The treatment worked. The next day I bought a hat and used sun block.

While walking on the causeway, I was impressed with the volume of motorcycles I faced—one every two seconds. That is more than double the rate of all other vehicular traffic combined. Singapore strongly discourages car ownership with a stiff tariff. A car costing $25,000 in the U.S. will cost more than $200,000 here. In addition, only cars with special stickers can enter the restricted zone downtown. If caught by police or camera, the car owner gets a bill for $50.

Although my day in Johor was long and tiresome, I'm glad I went. If I ever get a chance to go back to Malaysia, I would like to have enough time to see other parts of it.

On Friday, I had planned to go to Batam Island, Indonesia, a thirteen-mile ferry ride in the opposite direction from Malaysia. The travel agent said that there was not much sight seeing, but excellent water sports. Had I been in company with other men or had a hotel room there, I would have gone, but I would have had to go back to the ship for my swim gear and figure out what to do with my valuables while I was parasailing or whatever. Just getting organized would have shot the day.

Consequently, I took the cable car from the World Trade Center to Sentosa Island, which could qualify as the "Pearl of any Ocean." Sentosa, located a mile south of the mainland of Singapore, is a blend of ultra development and untouched nature, of theme parks, amusements, museums, beaches, and nature trails. After visiting a museum, which depicted the history of Singapore and its occupation by and liberation from the Japanese in World War II, I descended the top of the hill through an immaculately groomed and terraced landscape of scented and spice plants. This included a small forest of plumeria trees in white and pink blossoms. Appropriate music complemented the scene with a speaker never more than ten feet away from a hearer.

Where the plants ended, water fountains took over and ran in a straight course for several hundred yards. Descending farther, I came upon a pristine beach washed by clear, clean water and lined with coconut palms and hedges of bougainvillea. I spent quite a while just walking in the sand. A sign on a little shelter said that two monkeys trained to harvest coconuts would put on an exhibition at 3:00 p.m. I hung around until 3:30 and later learned that the monkeys performed at another location. I'm sorry I didn't get to see them, but there is a worse fate than sitting under a palm tree on a tropical island in February just watching the waves lap the shore.

While sitting under the palm tree, I saw a young couple on bicycles ride up to the nearly deserted beach. To my surprise, he plunged into the ocean fully dressed. Then the girl followed in her dress. Later, dripping wet, they wanted me to take their pictures with their respective cameras. She was from France, he from Canada. They had met two days earlier.

I spent the whole day on Sentosa, taking in the various attractions such as the rain forest, dancing waters set to music, and a marine life exhibit called Colorama. Here, wild monkeys mingled with peafowl outside the exhibit. Fences contain neither, both being contained by their appetites.

On Saturday, I went to the Raffles Hotel Museum. Here, memorabilia was gathered from many visitors as well as items preserved by the hotel over the years. Although more than a century old, Raffles still is one of the best hotels in the world, costing a minimum of $400 per night for a room. Besides the aforementioned famous authors, Raffles always has been the haunt of the rich and famous. Pictures in the museum include the following: Charlie Chaplin, Claudette Colbert, a young Liz Taylor, a young Ava Gardner, a young Prince Edward of Wales, and President George H. W. Bush who stayed here in January 1992. But the most intriguing display was the lengthy quotations from books by Joseph Conrad, which were used as accurate captions for pictures of landscapes and seascapes. Some of the scenes had people in them. Somebody had to be very familiar with the works of Conrad and still spend an enormous amount of time to perform such a feat.

With camera in hand, I spent the rest of the day looking for "Kodak moments" mostly in China Town and Merlion Park. Merlion is a contraction of the words mermaid and lion. Legend says that the discoverer of Singapore saw a being that was half fish and half lion upon first arriving here.

Anyway, the mermaid with the lion's head is the official symbol of Singapore. Passing by some Chinese junks anchored just offshore

Merlion

from the park, I was accosted by a turbaned Indian who wanted to tell my fortune. Brushing him aside, I turned to face a snaggled-tooth Indian of ancient vintage selling postcards. I bought several. When I handed him the money, I spoke the only Indian word I know, "nangree" (thank you). His leathery old face lit up in a wide grin. And more than one Chinese has responded favorably to my "cis ceh" (thank you) and "hwan eng" (you're welcome). People all over the world appreciate courtesy. And nothing seems to be more appreciated than a sincere "thank you" in their native tongue.

I've been to about forty foreign countries, and I guess I never met a country I didn't like. But Singapore will rank right up there with the best of them.

Hong Kong, March 7, 1994

The ship left Singapore the morning of March 1 to rendezvous with the carrier USS *Independence* about forty miles from Phattaya, Thailand. The carrier crew had enjoyed liberty there while the *Mobile Bay* crew played in Singapore. Over the next few days, while in the Bay of Thailand, the command conducted small arms qualifications for a number of men on the fantail and held GQ drills. During this time we swung around Cambodia and passed within about forty miles of the coast of Viet Nam in the South China Sea. Although I had been told repeatedly that the seas would be rough once we rounded the Cambodia/Viet Nam peninsula, the seas were almost as calm as they had been for the earlier part of the cruise. Six-foot swells with scattered white caps gave the ship a slight pitch like a see saw motion. At amidships, the movement was barely noticeable. Still, some of the younger Sailors got seasick.

We arrived at the Hong Kong harbor shortly after 0600 under

A street in Hong Kong

leaden, overcast skies. Flanking the harbor, were fog-shrouded, coni-
cal hills and small islands that appeared to have been formed by a
giant ant colony. Standing on the main weather deck amidships, I
was not quite warm in my fur-lined jacket. What a change from
Singapore!

South China Sea, March 13, 1994

As usual, after working hard aboard ship, I played hard in port.
My idea of play is to see the country, meet many of the people, and
learn about their culture and history. Hong Kong took me by surprise.
It is a huge city with a skyline larger than that of Houston or Dallas.

The architecture of skyscrapers with
glass facades is even more bizarre
than Houston's. American architects
designed some of these buildings.

I spent most of my first two
days in port shopping for Christmas
presents and bought two tailor-made
shirts for me, my first ever. The price
was even less than many off-the-
counter shirts in the U. S. Jade, fake
jade, and poor quality jade is omnipresent. Having gone to an open-air,
two-block jade market in Kowloon
across the bay from Hong Kong, I
was overwhelmed by the quantity
and variety of merchandise available.
After surveying the entire area, I was
pondering my options when a blond-

Hong Kong office buildings

headed man sidled up beside me and said, "Are you having fun?"

I replied, "I have no idea how to proceed here." Ernest Wilhelm, born in Holland, now living in Vancouver, is in the business of buying and selling jade. While his Chinese wife was visiting relatives in China, he had time on his hands and took me under his wing for the rest of the day. What are the odds of meeting a jade merchant, and the only other Westerner, in a Chinese jade market? I still don't know much about jade, but I know more than I did before I met Ernest.

Before I left Texas, the one thing Nita requested from the Orient was a piece of jade. I bought an expensive piece of old jade that had been a part of the family jewels of some Chinese family. It seems that after the Communists came to power in China that many people were reduced to selling such valuable possessions just to survive.

Wednesday evening, I took a night tour of Hong Kong that started out by bus and ended up with a harbor cruise. In between, I went to the most opulent restaurant I have ever seen. It is one of three elegant restaurants floating side by side. Inside and out, brilliantly lighted red and gold walls sporting dragons and other designs typical of the Orient created a festive atmosphere. A large lazy Susan served multiple dishes of delicious Cantonese food. The fog and/or hazy clouds never lifted during our time in port, so the night obscured some of the scenery during the tour. Although most of the people in Hong Kong live in high-rise apartments, the super rich dwell in palatial homes along the mountainside. Hong Kong has more than 1,000 Rolls Royces. One was parked at the residence of a man who owns 130 merchant ships. A person in Hong Kong who hasn't quite made it financially is reduced to driving a Mercedes Benz.

From the side of a mountain, I did get a good view of a huge racetrack. Because some people compulsively gamble on the horses, suicide is common. Those who take their lives sometimes take their families with them.

Earlier in the day, I rode a double decked bus to Stanley, about a 30-minute ride one way. The trip afforded an excellent overview of the mountains, valleys, and pristine beaches of Hong Kong. Even in these rugged areas, high-rise apartments dominated the scene. One high-rise that had a huge hole in it intrigued me. About 15 floors up, apartments ceased for several floors. Because there were so many buildings close together here, a big hole had to be left in one of them to "let the dragons out of the mountain." This has something to do with the Chinese concept of "fung shui." They also have a number of traditions about the placement of doors and windows in a building.

On Thursday, I took a tour to Shenzhen, China. Crossing the border was as easy as crossing any other border—no guns, no intimidating soldiers or police, which are prevalent in some other parts of the world. First, we took in a market of fresh meats, fish, fruit, vegetables, and household items. Although the cutting tables would not conform to American standards, the freshness, variety, and quantity of the produce was typical of a Western market. Even though fresh, some of the meats would not appeal to most Americans—fish heads, chicken feet, hogs ears.

Next, I saw a small museum featuring miniatures of the terra cotta soldiers unearthed some years ago at Xian, China. A few life-sized men and horses were included in the display. Lunch in a hotel restaurant was a repeat of the evening before.

Shenzhen is one of a few special cities that China is developing with foreign joint ventures. Six McDonalds are located here. The city is on an incredible building boom. Fifteen years ago, the town had 30,000 people. Now it has in excess of three million. As in Hong Kong, high-rise buildings dominate the skyline and dozens more are under construction. A revolving restaurant sits atop a 53-story building. Even so, expansion of the city seems to be progressing in an orderly fashion. No factories are allowed in the central business district. In fact, small hills in the fringe area of the city are being leveled for additional factory construction. Good roads and freeways

Scenes along the Great Wall of China

Scenes along the Great Wall of China

already exist with more under construction. The same intense building is also going on in Zhongshan, across the border from Macao. If China ever does fully embrace free enterprise and democracy, look out, world! They have the manpower and resources to dominate.

But what fascinated me most about Shenzhen was the theme park called Splendid China. Theme parks normally hold little interest for me. However, this beautiful, impeccably landscaped park covered every major period of Chinese history with tens of thousands of miniature people, houses, and buildings—even the Great Wall of China. I easily could have spent the whole day there.

The next day, I took the jetfoil for the 40-mile ride to Macao, a Portuguese city whose population is about ninety-five percent Chinese. Here, it was necessary to go through customs and then again when I crossed into Zhong Shan, China. Only seven people were on this tour—a young couple from Australia, a British woman now living in Norway, her daughter who lives in Macao, and a British couple named David and Sheila Jarman. The Briton from Norway spent five years in the British Navy during World War II and meets every other year with other women who served in the Navy with her.

Forty years ago, Zhongshan was nothing but farms and fishing boats. The Chinese government designated it a special zone for development in 1980 and now, with a population of 400,000, it is booming just like Shenzhen. People with good jobs here earn between $150 and $300 per month. Others average about $75.

I visited a village where farmers live. The houses are primitive by American standards with kitchens comparable to those on the American frontier 200 years ago. Still, the farmers have others to work their farms. Viewed from the road, their houses looked like mere hovels. Nevertheless, the fields appeared to be well kept. They use what they refer to as a "hand tractor." Essentially, this is an oversized garden tractor, capable of pulling tools or a trailer.

Garden tractor

I also visited the home of Sun Yat-Sen, the Hawaiian-educated Chinese revolutionary who overthrew the Manchu Dynasty about 1911 and is revered in both Nationalist China and Communist China. A school dedicated to his memory is located near his home. However, his picture that used to adorn the front of the auditorium was set aside in preference to Mao Tse Dong.

Students in China are highly motivated to educational excellence. They must take a national examination in order to qualify for college. Those who pass the exam move on to good jobs. Those who don't must work at whatever they find available. This system creates enormous pressure on the students. Those who fail the exam lose face with their peers and family. Some can't handle it and commit suicide.

Outside of the family and friends, suicide probably is of little concern to people since China has well over a billion people. To control the population, boys cannot marry until they are 23, girls 20. They are allowed one child. Any subsequent pregnancies must be aborted. Parents of twins are considered very lucky because they get to keep both children.

My visit to China was quite enlightening. The people I met were gracious and friendly. But it should be remembered that I went to showcase cities, both of which are next to Hong Kong, which will be taken over by the Chinese in 1997. Macao will follow in 1999. I have met people who are very apprehensive about the future of Hong Kong. I guess that is understandable, but I tend to go with the people who back their faith with their money. In spite of the size of Hong Kong, construction is proceeding there at a rapid rate also. I can see how Hong Kong, Shenzhen, and Zhongshan could become one very powerful economic center. Whatever else might be said about the Chinese government, it is not run by fools, and I see no reason for them to do anything to impede the progress in Hong Kong—especially when they have poured such enormous resources into Shenzhen and Zhongshan.

However, one ominous tale came to me by way of a young tour guide. Some friends of hers had a relative with business in both Hong Kong and China. When he went to China, his family lost contact with him. Subsequently, the police in the town where he went notified the family that he was dead with instructions to come get the body. Meanwhile, his organs had been taken from his body and sold. When the family tried to move the China business to Hong Kong, the police told them that they must find someone in China to continue to operate their business, and that if they told the Hong Kong authorities what happened, they would send someone to Hong Kong to kill them. Even if the Chinese government were disposed to control that kind of mischief, they would be hard pressed to monitor all such police in China.

I finished the day by having coffee with David and Sheila at their hotel, and then we went to Harry Ramsden's, a famous British restaurant, for fish and chips. Nice couple. We traded addresses.

East China Sea, March 15, 1994

The South China Sea lived up to its billing compared to the rest of this cruise. For three days out of Hong Kong, high winds and six-foot swells kept the weather decks secured. The ship didn't rock all that much, but spray made the decks too slippery to be safe. Today, the seas are much calmer, but the temperature has dropped into the 40s.

The story in USA Today about the young American sentenced to caning for vandalism in Singapore caught the interest of a number of officers in the wardroom. Apparently, the story caught the attention of everybody in America from the President on down. The consensus here seems to be that America ought to just butt out of Singapore's legal affairs. As mentioned previously, Singapore is an extremely clean city. I never saw any graffiti anywhere, and I only saw one instance of it in Hong Kong. Singapore has a low crime rate simply because it doesn't tolerate crime. If the caning sentence is actually carried out, it isn't likely that the accused, or any one who knows him, will ever again mar any public places in Singapore.

Yokosuka, Japan, March 19, 1994

When the ship arrived in Yokosuka two days ago, relatives of the crew crowded the pier, festive with streamers, balloons, and "welcome home" signs. The ship had been gone for four months. One officer has a 13-month-old baby who didn't even recognize him, and in fact, withdrew from him. Sea duty is rough on many Navy families. If military cutbacks force the remaining ships to extend the length of their cruises, the problems associated with family separations will be exacerbated. In addition, ships will be operating with less in-port maintenance, causing more problems such as the one experienced by this ship between Bahrain and Singapore.

My Navy world gets smaller all the time. A new officer came on board in Hong Kong, introduced himself to me, and said he was on the USS *O'Brien* with me in 1990. In addition, the day we arrived, I went to a Laundromat about 200 yards from the ship. Finding the soap dispensers empty, I was about to leave when an enlisted man from the USS *Bunker Hill* offered me some of his soap. He said that he had seen me in Hong Kong but had just figured out who I am. He was one of my students on the USS *Gridley* when it was in dry dock in San Diego in 1990. Also, when I went to the Community Service Center on the Navy base to convert dollars to yen, pick up a base map, and get what information I could about available activities while I am in port, Chie Sekizawa, the Japanese girl behind the desk, immediately recognized me. She was the tour guide in 1990 who personally escorted me all over the huge park in Tokyo when all the Sailors on the bus took off in different directions. Later, she picked up my pictures from a local camera shop and sent them to me in Texas when the ship I was on (USS *Cushing*) left port a day early. But most surprising of all was my encounter with Torpedo-man First Class Dan Francis as I was leaving the family center. He was on the USS *Belknap* in Italy when I was there in 1989 and also 1993. He treated me to a Russian dinner at one of the local hotels. The food was outstanding and different from any I had ever eaten before. Then we spent two hours in the Blue Note, an upstairs coffee shop overlooking Yokosuka's main street, drinking cappuccino while we reminisced about mutual friends and funny incidents involving language problems.

Today, Dan and I took the train to a station near Anjin Koen. This is the mountaintop burial site of William Adams and his Japanese wife Miura. He was the Englishman who came here in about 1640 during the Shogun era, and was the central character in the book Shogun, which was made into a TV series in the late 1970s. The town of Anjin Zuka sits on the fief of land granted to Adams; the town of Miura sits on the fief of land granted to his wife. Yokosuka separates the two towns.

The view from the burial site affords a panoramic view of the naval base, some of Yokosuka, and cherry trees in bloom. Besides the cherry trees, a considerable amount of wild growth covers the mountainside. Dan said that poisonous snakes called mamushi and habu occupy some of the wild areas. Venom from the mamushi attacks the nervous system and kills in 20 minutes. Strangely, the Japanese have created a drink whereby a live mamushi is placed in a mixture of sake and honey and left for a year before serving as a drink. Since the poison is still in the snake, only a small quantity, depending upon a man's weight, can be consumed. The drink is a male aphrodisiac. Apparently, some men will do anything—even risk death—to try to enhance their sexual prowess.

Opting to walk back from the park, we paused long enough for some excellent cheesecake and hot chocolate. Later, we munched out on tako yaki (fried octopus), my first—and last. I gamely put away half of mine, much to Dan's admiration for trying. Then we returned to the Blue Note for a concoction that looks like coffee Jell-O overlaid with a small amount of cream. After liquid sweetener is added, the ingredients are stirred and then eaten with a spoon. It was rather tasty, but we still had cappuccino and spent another two hours swapping yarns.

On the surface, Dan seems like a benign person. But early on, he learned the necessity of perfecting violence for self-preservation. At age 15, he thought he was tough enough to take on his dad who was a Navy Seal. When the short fight ended in full view of cheering neighbors, Dan required hospitalization and wore one arm in a sling for a while. His contribution to the fight was to vomit on his father. While his mother and younger brother took him to the hospital, his dad went out for a beer. They have had a good father/son relationship ever since. He credits the Navy for keeping him out of trouble. Dan owns a house here and likely will stay here and seek civilian employment when he completes his naval service.

Yokosuka, Japan, March 29, 1994

Trying to teach PACE courses in a ship's homeport is not a good idea because some students just do not have the discipline to attend class when other activities beckon. But the students that are hanging in are good ones. My schedule has been changed from late night to four hours in the morning and will be changed again tomorrow to afternoon. Any change always creates an attendance problem. For the first ten days we were in port, the crew essentially was on vacation with just a minimum of personnel on board at any given time. Now they're back on a work schedule.

I have used my spare time to get reacquainted with Yokosuka. Much new construction—both on and off the naval base—has taken place since I was here four years ago. The Prince Hotel, which includes a ground floor shopping mall and theater for stage productions, is a pleasing addition to Yokosuka's skyline. Across the street from it, is the five-story Shoppers Plaza. When I went there a few days ago, three Japanese boys and a girl dressed in cowboy hats, boots, and jeans were giving a professional, English rendition of bluegrass music in the lobby.

I returned to Mikasa Park, the site of the *Mikasa* battleship now used as a museum.

Japanese Bluegrass musicians

This time, I went inside to study the exhibits. *Mikasa* was the flagship of Admiral Heihachiro Togo at the battle of Tsushima Straits at which time the Japanese destroyed the Russian fleet and brought an end to the Russo-Japanese war in 1905. Because of the invincibility of this British-made battleship, 35 of the 38 Russian ships were either sunk or captured. Since Japan suffered no losses, the victory is one of the most complete in the annals of sea warfare. The ship is a source of national pride for the Japanese.

Leaving the ship, I went once again through the rest of the park, which includes a giant man-made waterfall, which flows into a large shallow pool filled with fountains. I arrived at this site just as the music and dancing waters began their performance.

Last Saturday, I was invited for a two-hour visit into the home of Mr. and Mrs. Nubuyuki Shoji at Kita Kurihama, which is a short train ride from Yokosuka. At the train station, I must have been wearing my dumb look again. While I was studying the train schedule—written in Japanese, of course—a polite Japanese man asked if he could help me. Within a minute, I had my ticket, track number, time of departure, and the number of stops to my destination. I could have figured it all out eventually, but it was reassuring to have a native give me explicit directions.

I couldn't have been more impressed with the Shoji's gracious hospitality. Typically, their house was small but inviting. Western style décor graced the living room, but an adjoining room exposed a traditional washitsu with a tatami floor. Here, they kept a rather ornate Budha shrine as well as a simple Shinto shrine. Paneled paper shades covered the windows that looked out onto a small garden. Mr. Shoji is quite fluent in English, having traveled all over the world and having lived and worked in London for a number of years. He is the general manager of the Prince Hotel. Even though that position throws him into the company of top naval brass and other local bigwigs from time to time, he seems to be a quiet, unassuming man of quick wit and good humor. His wife speaks almost no English but is no less the charming for it. Unexpectedly, she presented me with a beautiful sugar bowl made of persimmon wood to give to my wife. The bowl is the color of persimmon, the lid and spoon, brown. After she served refreshments, judging by her smile, I evidently made her day by saying, "Gochiso sama deshita," a phrase I picked up from Dan Francis. He said it is about the highest compliment a hostess can receive.

Sunday afternoon, I went to Kamakura to revisit some of the shrines that I saw when I was last here. Emerging from the train station, I was greeted by two university girls who are members of The

Kanagawa Student Guide Federation, a group that gives free escorts to English-speaking people so that they can practice their English. Taeko Ohtsu and Masako Sekine proved to be highly intelligent as well as very polite and charming. They certainly know their history and culture of Kamakura, and their speed in assimilating new English words astonished me. When they found out that I was a teacher of English, they were especially pleased. With them as my guide, I went into the interior of one of the shrines for the first time and listened to them explain the meaning of the various acts and traditions that went on there. The most impressive shrine was in a small, dense bamboo forest where we quietly drank green tea and contemplated the small waterfall and the flowers emerging along the resultant stream. I doubt that I ever would have found this place without the guidance of Taeko and Masako.

At the Tsurugaoka Hachimangu shrine, the largest in Kamakura, the girls insisted that I shake a numbered stick out of a box, which would determine a scroll on which would be my fortune. The scroll told me (in Japanese) what I already know—I have good luck and can expect more of the same. I believe the girls told me that this shrine is in honor of Yoritomo Minamoto who founded the Kamakura shogunate that lasted from 1185 to 1333.

A walk lined on each side by cherry trees, starting in downtown Kamakura, and leading to this shrine is guarded by two large stone dogs called Komainu. One has his mouth open (ah); the other has his mouth closed (um). Just beyond the dogs are the first of two large, red tori.

We explored Kamakura shrines until we started to run out of daylight. Then we went to a Japanese restaurant where I treated the girls

Entrance to Kamakura shrines

to dinner and let them order for me. They made an excellent choice. Conversation over a leisurely dinner entailed more additions to their speech. I introduced them to prefixes, which quickly expanded their vocabulary by several dozen words. They were especially delighted to learn English idioms, something their formal education evidently does not include. Later, standing in the cold night air at the train station, the girls gave me their addresses, indicating their interest in Texas and "horses." As the train pulled away, I waved to the girls, and one of them blew me a kiss.

Today, Chie Sekizawa and her husband Kazuhiko (Kazu) took me to dinner after she got off work at the Community Service Center on the naval base. We drove to the Torigin, an upscale restaurant in Hayama, a short distance from Yokosuka. Again, I let the local folks choose my meal, which turned out to be quite good. Chie brought along some pictures of their wedding. She was strikingly beautiful in a white gown with a short train. Kazu is also a handsome young man. It must have been a spectacular wedding. They had two receptions at which they dressed in traditional Japanese wedding attire. I thought it was unusual for them to have three sets of wedding garments, but Chie said that they rented all of them to save money. And the picture of the combined families contained mostly men. When wedding invitations are sent to family members, only one member may attend, and it usually is a man.

As Kazu and Chie were dropping me off at the naval base gate, I said to Kazu who doesn't speak English, "Gochiso sama deshita" and his face brightened as much as Meiko Shoji's did. I now have six Japanese people with whom to correspond plus Dan Francis. If I ever get back to Yokosuka, I think my social life is assured.

Yokosuka, Japan, April 5, 1994

Students took their final exams yesterday, and I will leave Yokosuka early tomorrow. A prepaid ticket awaits me at Narita Airport for a direct flight to Dallas. It's been fun, but I'm ready to go. I had hoped to go to Tokyo with Dan Francis last Saturday, but he had to cancel, and I didn't want to go alone. The students who have hung in are the kind of people I would like to be a part of my future. Past experience tells me this is not likely. The captain and executive officer may be exceptions.

Captain Steven G. Smith is due for a transfer within a short time. He may become a one-star admiral in the Pentagon. Although not from Texas, he has a soft spot for Texas and was graduated from Texas University in Austin when Senator Kay Bailey Hutchinson was a cheerleader there.

CDR Philip H. Cullom, the executive officer, has an intriguing future. He just returned from an interview in Florida for a possible assignment in Washington. Twenty positions are going to be filled on the staffs of people in the Clinton Administration. He hopes to be assigned to either the State Department or the Treasury Department. Two or three years in such an assignment would greatly enhance his naval career. With all the cutbacks in the military, his dream of being a ship's captain could take far too long by the conventional career path. Phil has a master's degree from Harvard, and is one of the few really knowledgeable nuclear engineers in the country that could contribute some significant input toward national policy. Originally, three thousand people applied for the twenty positions. Applicants were eliminated through a series of cuts. Phil learned this morning that he is in the final group of thirty. So now he is going to Washington for a three-day interview. One way or the other he will be off the ship by June. Both Steve and Phil have expressed an interest in staying in touch with me.

(Note: Phil won the Washington assignment. Upon completing it, he became captain of the USS *Mitscher*, a guided missile destroyer. Nita and I attended his change of command ceremony in Norfolk, Virginia, in 1999. In 2003, he was assigned to the USS *Peleliu* as Sea Combat Commander, i.e. the Commodore for the squadron of frigates, destroyers, cruisers and amphibious ships (including the flag ship *Peleliu*, an amphibious assault ship) that comprised a first-ever deployment of an Expeditionary Strike Group (ESG). As of the publication date of this book, he is a two-star admiral and has recently relinquished command of a battle group aboard the USS *Dwight D. Eisenhower*.)

I was delighted to learn that Jim Embry, one of my students from Westbury Christian School where I formerly taught in Houston, is attached to the naval base at Yokosuka. He graduated in 1987. This

Capt. Cullom and author
(Photo courtesy photographer, USS Peleliu)

afternoon we spent a few hours together. After we enjoyed a long leisurely dinner, he drove me around parts of Yokosuka that I had not seen. Following boot camp, the Navy assigned him to a submarine. Even though Jim was already an accomplished guitarist, the Navy sent him to music school prior to his assignment to the Seventh Fleet Band. Consequently, he has spent most of his Navy career playing his guitar. Judging from some of his comments, as well as those of his supervisor and other band members that I have talked to, Jim's talent is making him quite famous throughout the Navy's music world all over the Far East. In the meantime, he is engaged to a Japanese girl who has traveled the world and has a degree from a West Coast university. Since they plan to marry in Houston in December, it appears that Jim is winding down his Navy career. I was really glad to run into him half way around the world, reminisce about old times, and share the latest word about our mutual friends. (Subsequently, Nita and I attended the wedding of Jim and his fiancé in Houston.)

Early tomorrow morning, I will take a bus to Narita Airport near Tokyo for a direct flight to Dallas. The last two months have been fun, but home beckons.

Epilogue

My assignment to the USS *Mobile Bay* concluded my association with the Navy's PACE program. Because a physical examination upon my returning home from the USS *Mobile Bay* revealed some cancer, I turned down additional requests to teach aboard ships in order to give my full attention to eliminating the cancer. Refusing conventional cancer treatments, I devoted myself to building up my immune system. Thankfully, in the following years, all subsequent tests have shown no evidence of cancer.

After teaching writing for so many years, I decided to write for pleasure and profit. When my first book *Nine Years in the Saddle* achieved some modest success, many people encouraged me to write about my experiences as a world traveler. It is my sincere hope that my adventures have enriched your own life in some way.

Glossary

AAV – Amphibious Assault Vehicle

BAC – Blood alcohol content

BIG EYES – Pedestal-Mounted high-powered binoculars

BOQ – Bachelor Officers Quarters

CAG – Commander Air Group. Commands an air wing aboard an aircraft carrier

COD – Carrier on Delivery. A small aircraft for ferrying personnel and supplies to and from a carrier

EVOLUTION – Any military operation

PHIBRON – Abbreviation for Amphibious Squadron, which usually consists of three amphibious ships

FLANK SPEED – Faster than full speed, a ship's maximum speed

FLIGHT QUARTERS – A readiness condition whereby a deck crew prepares to launch or receive an aircraft

FO'C'SLE – What navy people the ship's forecastle

FORECASTLE – The section of the upper deck of a ship located at the bow

GPS – Global Positioning Satellite

GQ – General quarters, battle ready

HEAD – Shipboard restroom

HMMB – High-Mobility Multi-Purpose Wheeled Vehicle

LARC – Lighter, Amphibious Re-supply, Cargo – an aluminum-hulled amphibious cargo vehicle

LAV – Light Armored Vehicle

LCAC – Landing Craft Air Cushion, a craft capable of floating over water or land

LCM – Landing Craft Mechanized

LCU – Landing Craft Utility

LCVP – Landing Craft Vehicle Personnel

LPD – Landing Pad Dock

LST – Landing Ship Tank, a large amphibious vessel

MAC – Military Airlift Command

MIKE – See LCM

MILITARY TIME – The clock is divided into 24-hour segments instead of two 12-hour segments. For example, 4 p.m. is 1600 hours military time

MRE – Meal Ready-to-Eat

1MC – Public address system

OVERHEAD – The ceiling of a ship's compartment

P.A.C.E. – Program for Afloat College Education

P.O.D. – Plan of the Day

RHIB – Rigid-Hulled Inflatable Boat

SEA AND ANCHOR DETAIL – An operation to enable a ship to get underway

SMOKER – A boxing event

STOL – Short Takeoff and Landing aircraft

TRANSLANT – Crossing the Atlantic Ocean

UNREP – Underway replenishment

VERTREP – A replenishment of supplies from a supply ship via helicopter

VTOL – Vertical Takeoff and Landing aircraft

WESTPAC – A deployment into the Western Pacific Ocean

XO – Executive Officer

Zodiacs – Inflatable boats